# BEHOLD THE MAN

Deacon Harold Burke-Sivers

# BEHOLD THE MAN

## A Catholic Vision of Male Spirituality

IGNATIUS PRESS    SAN FRANCISCO

Imprimatur: Archbishop Alexander K. Sample
Archdiocese of Portland in Oregon
June 8, 2015

Front cover photo by Claire E. Sivers
Back cover photo by Joe Usher

Cover design by
www.AmpersandMiami.com

© 2015 by Ignatius Press, San Francisco
All rights reserved
ISBN 978-1-58617-887-1
Library of Congress Control Number 2014959900
Printed in the United States of America ∞

*To the Benedictine monks of Newark Abbey*

# CONTENTS

# ACKNOWLEDGMENTS

I would like to thank those men who have been incredible influences in my life growing-up, most especially Dr. Allan H. ("Doc") Toub and Mr. Michael DiPiano, Sr. ("Mr. D").

I would like to acknowledge those men who are like brothers to me, and whose love, guidance, and counsel over the years have both inspired and challenged me to be the man God created me to be: Craig Allen, Walter Wiggins, Patrick Atagi, Jim Moore, Fr. Mitch Pacwa, S.J., Fr. Larry Richards, Fr. Nicolaus Marandu, ALCP, Fr. Brian Mullady, O.P., Fr. John Almsberry, Mark Andreas, Todd Cooper, Dr. John Goldrick, J.D., Carl E. Olson, Jay Wonacott, Patrick Madrid, Hector Molina, Jesse Romero, and Noah Lett.

I would also like to thank a few of the shepherds whose leadership and example have given me the courage to speak the truth in love: Cardinal Raymond L. Burke, Archbishop Alexander K. Sample, Archbishop Salvatore Cordileone, Bishop Thomas Olmsted, Bishop Donald Hying, and Bishop Michael Warfel.

I would like to give special recognition and thanks to Monsignor John Cihak, S.T.D. Monsignor Cihak's treatment of the subject of fatherhood as it relates to the priesthood is unparalleled. Consequently, rather than my trying to construct my own thesis around this topic as a non-priest, Monsignor Cihak has given his kind and generous permission to republish his article, "The Priest as Man, Husband, and Father" in its entirety in this book.

Finally, I would like to thank my incredibly loving and supportive wife—my battle partner, Colleen—for her unwavering belief in me even during those times when I didn't believe in myself. I love you with all my heart!

# ABBREVIATIONS

CCC    *Catechism of the Catholic Church*

CL    John Paul II, Post-Synodal Apostolic Exhortation *Christifideles Laici* (The Lay Members of Christ's Faithful People), December 30, 1988

DCE    Benedict XVI, Encyclical Letter *Deus Caritas Est* (God Is Love), December 25, 2005

DV    Vatican Council II, Dogmatic Constitution on Divine Revelation, *Dei Verbum*, November 18, 1965

FC    John Paul II, Apostolic Exhortation *Familiaris Consortio*, On the Role of the Christian Family in the Modern World, November 22, 1981

GS    Vatican Council II, Pastoral Constitution on the Church in the Modern World, *Gaudium et Spes*, December 7, 1965

LE    John Paul II, Encyclical Letter *Laborem Exercens* (On Human Work), September 14, 1981

LG    Vatican Council II, Dogmatic Constitution on the Church, *Lumen Gentium*, November 21, 1964

MD    John Paul II, Apostolic Letter *Mulieris Dignitatem*, On the Dignity and Vocation of Women, August 15, 1988

RC    John Paul II, Apostolic Exhortation *Redemptoris Custos* (Guardian of the Redeemer), August 15, 1989

RP    John Paul II, Post-Synodal Apostolic Exhortation *Reconciliatio et Paenitentia* (Reconciliation and Penance), December 2, 1984

VS    John Paul II, Encyclical Letter *Veritatis Splendor* (The Splendor of Truth), August 6, 1993

# FOREWORD

In a popular essay written by Dr. Peter Kreeft entitled "The Winning Strategy",[1] the well-known Catholic author makes the point that our civilization is in crisis. We are living through what Saint John Paul II called the "culture of death".[2] In other words, we are at war. Dr. Kreeft also boldly and unequivocally points out who the enemy is. We are in a spiritual warfare and the enemies we face are two. The first is no less than Satan himself and his demons, the fallen angels. The second is sin—our own sin.

Dr. Kreeft goes on to point out that the one and only weapon that will defeat our enemies and cause us to prevail in this spiritual battle is holiness. It will take saints. What will truly change the world and the culture for the better are people who are willing to pay the price of giving everything to the Lord. We need saints who will sacrifice it all. Such people, sadly, seem to be in short supply these days. Perhaps that has always been the case.

Just three weeks before I received word from the Papal Nuncio that I had been named a bishop, I was on my annual retreat. I had just finished making my confession, and the priest was about to give me absolution. Then out of the blue he gave me a final piece of spiritual direction. The confessor, to whom I was known, said, "The Lord does not want just part of you. He wants it all. He wants you to give him everything, holding nothing back."

I guess my confession had given the priest a pretty clear picture of the lukewarmness that had crept into my life. I have always considered that piece of spiritual advice as being very providential, given

---

[1] See Dr. Peter Kreeft, "The Winning Strategy", *The Integrated Catholic Life: Helping You to Integrate Faith, Family and Work*, March 22, 2013, http://www.integratedcatholiclife.org /2013/03/kreeft-the-winning-strategy-3/.

[2] See John Paul II, Encyclical *Evangelium Vitae* (The Gospel of Life), March 25, 1995, http:// w2.vatican.va/content/john-paul-ii/en/encyclicals/documents/hf_jp-ii_enc_25031995 _evangelium-vitae.html.

the news I was about to receive. We are being asked to give our lives completely to the Lord, no matter what our state in life.

The Spanish priest and author Father Francisco Fernández Carvajal wrote a book about the spiritual malady from which many of us suffer. He titled it *Lukewarmness: The Devil in Disguise*.[3] It is the subtitle that has always intrigued me. The Evil One has his own strategy. He does not reveal himself to us directly and overtly. He is far too clever for that. He comes subtly into our lives, playing on our weaknesses and sinful inclinations, and convinces us to settle for the status quo. We convince ourselves that our spiritual lives and the living of our faith are "good enough".

It is this spiritual sickness that Deacon Harold Burke-Sivers takes head-on in this latest contribution to the area of Catholic male spirituality. This is no time for spiritual lukewarmness among Catholic men. It is the time for saints, men who are willing to step up and actively engage in the spiritual warfare that threatens our families, our Church, our society, and even our own salvation. It is the time for men who are willing to sacrifice all, holding nothing back.

Deacon Burke-Sivers engages in a very deep and thorough examination of the state of affairs present in the contemporary culture. But his analysis, reflections, and remedies are in some ways timeless. This is no superficial study of what is needed in today's world from Catholic men. It is actually a wonderful catechesis on the Catholic spiritual life, rooted in Sacred Scripture, Sacred Tradition, and the sacramental life of the Church.

It is my humble observation that in recent times men have been somewhat marginalized in modern Catholic life. It seems we have placed such low expectations on what is needed from them. This, combined with cultural factors that have also minimized and distorted the true and proper place for men in the family, Church, and society, has left many men wondering how to navigate life in the contemporary world. The opening words of Deacon Burke-Sivers' book say it all: "The Catholic man is an endangered species."

Strong Catholic men—fathers, husbands, brothers, sons, uncles, priests—are needed today. This takes nothing away from the vitally

---

[3] Francis Carvajal, *Lukewarmness: The Devil in Disguise* (Princeton, N.J.: Scepter Publishers, 1997).

important role for women in our lives, much less posing a threat to their unique place. Rather, strong Catholic men will learn to love as Christ loves, laying down their lives in service to those around them, especially the women in their lives.

One of the aspects of Deacon Burke-Sivers' treatment of this important topic that I especially appreciate is the broad appeal that he makes to all men. He speaks not just of the role of husbands and fathers in their own families, but also integrates into his reflections the role of spiritual espousal and fatherhood that priests (and even bishops!) embrace through their lives of consecration. The same is true for those embracing the evangelical counsels as consecrated religious, and even single men living a life of dedication to Christ in the world. There is something here for all of us, and I must say that I am particularly challenged (and encouraged) by Deacon Burke-Sivers' analysis, even as his own archbishop!

This is an extremely well researched and documented study of Catholic male spirituality for our own day. The footnotes themselves are a rich treasure of teaching and information. Don't miss them! Deacon Burke-Sivers' writing here is also deeply rooted in the papal Magisterium, especially that of Saint John Paul II, whom many consider the "pope of the family". Saint John Paul's teaching about the theology of the body plays a prominent role in this marvelous study of male spirituality and exhortation to moral virtue.

Deacon Burke-Sivers also holds nothing back in sharing his own personal story and the sometimes imperfect experiences of his own life and struggles. He clearly understands the struggle men face today, and he is not afraid to talk bluntly and clearly about it. I think many will especially appreciate the honesty.

As you pick up this volume, be prepared for a very sobering analysis of what ails modern culture, both inside and outside the Church. Be prepared to see yourself and your own struggles reflected in these pages. But also see a hopeful picture of what could be if men put on the armor of faith, hope, and charity in a meaningful and serious way.

As you begin this book, stop and truly say a prayer to the Holy Spirit to open your mind and heart to what God wants to say to you. Ask the Lord to help you understand and to be ready to make the changes he asks of you. Everything in your life may depend on it.

The Lord and his Church need saints. I hope you, the reader, will be one of them.

May our Blessed Mother enfold you in her mantle of love and protection, holding you and all who are dear to you close to her Immaculate Heart!

Archbishop Alexander K. Sample

# INTRODUCTION

Christ, the final Adam, by the revelation of the mystery of the Father
and His love, fully reveals man to himself and makes his supreme
calling clear.

— *Gaudium et Spes*, no. 22

The Catholic man is an endangered species. Unlike other such species who can trace their path toward extinction back to an extrinsic
cause, Catholic men are destroying themselves by their own free-
willed choice. We choose pornography and masturbation over the
one-flesh union of the conjugal act in marriage or the intimacy of
celibate life. We choose abortion and contraception over serving,
protecting, and defending a woman's dignity and building a culture
of life. We choose spiritual sloth and laziness over witnessing to the
truth of our faith with passion and conviction. We've become timid.
We've stopped leading. We no longer desire holiness. We've compromised our values and abdicated our responsibility. Catholic men
were created for greatness but instead choose to be purveyors of
immorality and mediocrity.

How did we get here? In a nutshell, by abdicating our responsibility to live as godly men we have allowed ourselves to become
effeminized by the culture and have turned our backs on the authentic moral teachings of the Church, especially in the area of human
sexuality. The root causes can be traced back to a plethora of events,
including the advent of birth control and dissention against Pope
Paul VI's encyclical letter *Humanae Vitae*, in the late 1960s; the rise
of the feminist movement and the so-called sexual revolution; the
approval of no-fault divorce; the legalization of abortion; the "spirit
of Vatican II" mentality, which led to liturgical experimentation,
uninspired and banal church architecture, watered-down catechesis
and music, a pedestrian translation of the Mass, and the popularity

I

of inclusive language—all of which contributed to the loss of a sense of the sacred in the 1970s and early 1980s;[1] the precipitous decline of a truly Catholic identity among many Catholic colleges and universities (particularly those run by religious orders); the meteoric rise and popularity of pornography and the proliferation of video games with the introduction of computers and the Internet in the late 1980s through the 1990s; and, in recent decades, the sexual abuse scandals among clergy, the acceptance of the homosexual lifestyle, the redefinition of marriage, and the rise of neo-atheism, which have all played a role in the reformation of our conscience away from God and the objective truths of the Catholic faith (what Pope Emeritus Benedict XVI called the "dictatorship of relativism"), leading to the demise of authentic Catholic manhood.

The entertainment industry inundates society with prosaic images, half-truths, and transient moral values that often depict male characters as laughable buffoons, sex-starved womanizers, and money-loving jocks. The following exchange between a man and his girlfriend from an episode entitled "Just a Whore" on the CBS television show *Two and a Half Men*[2] illustrates this point:

*Scene.* A man believes his girlfriend is cheating on him. He and his male friend arrive at a home to confront her.

*Girlfriend.* "This isn't what you think.... It's time for me to tell you the truth."

*Boyfriend's friend.* "Don't believe her. She's a cheating, drunk whore."

*Girlfriend.* "Remember you told me your fantasy was to see me with another woman?"

*Boyfriend.* "Yeah."

*Girlfriend.* "I've arranged for your dream to come true."... [*Call girl enters.*]

*Boyfriend.* "You did?... Wait a minute. Is this for real?"

---

[1] I am not implying that the Church sanctioned these aberrations. I am simply documenting what actually occurred during the post-Vatican II era that I believe contributed—along with the other factors mentioned—to the demise of the Catholic man.

[2] "Just a Whore", *Two and a Half Men*, CBS.com, accessed November 10, 2013, www.cbs.com/shows/two_and_a_half_men/video.

*Girlfriend.* "Happy birthday, baby!"...

*Boyfriend's friend.* "Wow, a threesome. That's quite a gift."...

[*Girlfriend goes into the bedroom with the call girl.*]

*Boyfriend.* "Isn't this great! She's not a cheating whore. She's just a whore!"

These portrayals are symptoms of a much larger disease: the influence of secularization, radical individualism, and moral relativism that slowly erode the hearts, souls, and spiritual lives of Catholic men. The implications for the Church and family life are serious and significant. Catholic clinical counselor Dave McClow notes that

the Church is losing men! The typical Sunday Mass has about 60% women and 40% men. Many men see going to Church as women's work. There are 76% of baptized Catholics who don't attend Mass regularly. But if fathers thought that going to Church was important and went, their children and wives would follow. Fathers have a profound effect on the next generation according to a census study from Switzerland. If mom and dad attend regularly, 34% of their kids will attend regularly. If mom goes regularly and dad goes irregularly or not at all, that drops to 2% or 3% of their kids who will attend regularly. If dad goes regularly and mom irregularly or not at all, the percentage jumps to 38% or 44%! This alone should give us pause to look at how to engage men for the New Evangelization![3]

Robbie Low further adds:

A mother's role will always remain primary in terms of intimacy, care, and nurture.... No father can replace that relationship. But it is equally true that when a child begins to move into that period of differentiation from home and engagement with the world "out

---

[3] Dave McClow, "Toward a Theology of Authentic Masculinity", Patheos (blog), December 4, 2013, http://www.patheos.com/blogs/faithonthecouch/2013/12/toward-a-theology-of-authentic-masculinity. The study cited in the article was authored by Werner Haug and Phillipe Warner, "The Demographic Characteristics of the Linguistic and Religious Groups in Switzerland", in Werner Haug et al., *The Demographic Characteristics of National Minorities in Certain European States, Population Studies No. 31,* volume 2, Federal Statistical Office, Neuchatel (Strasbourg: Council of Europe Directorate General III, Social Cohesion, 2000).

there," he (and she) looks increasingly to the father for his role model. Where the father is indifferent, inadequate, or just plain absent, that task of differentiation and engagement is much harder. When children see that church is a "women and children" thing, they will respond accordingly—by not going to church, or going much less.[4]

Many of these misconceptions are fueled by a culture that has turned men into caricatures, extolling the vice of egocentrism and portraying men as individuals that should not be taken seriously. A society steeped in political correctness and indifferentism says to men, "As long as you are a 'good person', you don't need anyone to tell you what to do or how to live." A society mired in a distorted sense of true freedom sees the "self" as the center of the universe and the supreme arbiter of truth (i.e., "I am an end in myself"). These approaches perceive Catholicism as heteronomous—as an external imposition of intrinsically hostile, archaic rules and regulations upon society's enlightened view of freedom devoid of absolute truth. As a result, the moral lives and consciences of men are being shaped and influenced not by a vibrant faith but by the dictates of secular culture leading many men to believe, "I am truly free and authentically a man when I accumulate as much money, power, and sex necessary to make me happy and fulfilled." In short, men have bought into the lie of the culture, and, in a fleeting attempt at some semblance of spirituality framed within this narcissistic context, incoherent stereotypes of male spirituality have prevailed. We begin to think and act like the culture instead of putting on the mind of Christ as the apostle Paul exhorts:

> Now we have received not the spirit of the world, but the Spirit which is from God, that we might understand the gifts bestowed on us by God. And we impart this in words not taught by human wisdom but taught by the Spirit, interpreting spiritual truths to those who possess the Spirit. The unspiritual man does not receive the gifts of the Spirit of God, for they are folly to him, and he is not able to understand them because they are spiritually discerned. The spiritual man judges all things, but is himself to be judged by no one. "For who

---

[4] Robbie Low, "The Truth about Men and Church", Touchstone 16, no. 5 (June 2003), http://www.touchstonemag.com/archives/article.php?id=16-05-024-v#ixzz2E0cciQGr.

has known the mind of the Lord so as to instruct him?" But we have the mind of Christ.[5]

When men allow the culture to shape their consciences in accord with its false truths, the results within the family and society are devastating. There is, as mentioned above, the redefinition of marriage that undermines the covenant relationship—the life-giving love between one man and one woman, and any children that may come from that union—that serves as the cell and foundation for culture and society. In the business world a growing ambivalence toward socioeconomic equality puts profits ahead of persons, resulting in widespread corruption and greed in the workplace. The divorce rate among Catholics is almost equal to the divorce rate of secular society.

A culture rooted in subjective truth says that love does not mean commitment, self-gift, and sacrifice. Instead, love means whatever you decide it to mean. Nowhere is this more evident than in the classic cultural affirmation "If it feels good, do it." Marching to the anthem of relativism, men "play the field", fornicating frequently with multiple partners and engaging in extramarital affairs, sometimes resulting in the birth of children that these men, for the most part, have no interest in raising or financially supporting. There exists an entire generation of fathers who have physically, emotionally, or spiritually abandoned their wives and children. Thus, in the absence of fathers to lead, support, and nurture their families, women have compensated either by assuming masculine roles within the family or by constructing innovative support networks for themselves and their children. This changing dynamic has brought us to a critical juncture as men: we are at the genesis of a systemic and fundamental shift in family life where in the near future, if we continue to live as men of the culture, fathers in the family may be considered optional and, in many cases, unnecessary. Again, the implications are significant:

> We are ministering in a society that is increasingly unfaithful in spiritual and physical relationships. There is a huge number of single-parent families and a complexity of step-relationships or, worse,

---

[5] 1 Cor 2:12–16 (Revised Standard Version, Second Catholic Edition); with the exception of the Psalms, all Scripture passages will be taken from this source, unless otherwise indicated.

itinerant male figures in the household, whose primary interest can almost never be someone else's child. We are ministering in churches that accepted fatherlessness as a norm, and even an ideal. Emasculated Liturgy, gender-free Bibles, and a fatherless flock are increasingly on offer. In response, these churches' decline has, unsurprisingly, accelerated. To minister to a fatherless society, these churches, in their unwisdom, have produced their own single-parent family parish model in the woman priest.... The constant pressure for "flexibility," "sensitivity," "inclusivity," and "collaborative ministry" is telling. There is nothing wrong with these concepts in themselves, but as they are taught and insisted upon, they bear no relation to what a man (the un-neutered man) understands them to mean.

Men are perfectly capable of being all these things without being wet, spineless, feeble-minded, or compromised, which is how these terms translate in the teaching. They will not produce men of faith or fathers of the faith communities. They will certainly not produce icons of Christ and charismatic apostles. They are very successful at producing malleable creatures of the institution, unburdened by authenticity or conviction and incapable of leading and challenging. Curiously enough, this new feminized man does not seem to be quite as attractive to the feminists as they had led us to believe. He does not seem to hold the attention of children (much less boys who might want to follow him into the priesthood). But a priest who is comfortable with his masculinity and maturing in his fatherhood (domestic and/or pastoral) will be a natural magnet in a confused and disordered society and Church.[6]

In addition to the breakdown of the nuclear family, an underperforming educational system, whose contemporary pedagogical methods are often geared toward meeting State or government academic benchmarks and standards—without considering the fact that boys and girls learn differently—has also contributed to the downfall of Catholic men who attend such institutions. As a result, "boys consistently receive lower grades than girls [and] score lower than girls on both direct and indirect measures of writing skills. Boys outnumber girls in remedial English and math classes. Nearly two boys are held back in grade for each girl held back. Boys receive 70% of the D's and F's on report cards. 77% of children expelled from public elementary and secondary schools are boys [and] 76.4% of children

---

[6] Low, "Truth about Men and Church".

diagnosed with emotional disturbance are boys."[7] Even after taking
into account disparate factors in cultural and societal expectations, as
well as psychological, cognitive, and sexual development between
boys and girls, gender gaps in learning remain prevalent in many traditional school settings.

> By almost every benchmark, boys across the nation and in every
> demographic group are falling behind. In elementary school, boys are
> two times more likely than girls to be diagnosed with learning disabil-
> ities and twice as likely to be placed in special-education classes. High-
> school boys are losing ground to girls on standardized writing tests.
> The number of boys who said they didn't like school rose 71 percent
> between 1980 and 2001, according to a University of Michigan study.
> Nowhere is the shift more evident than on college campuses. Thirty
> years ago men represented 58 percent of the undergraduate student
> body. Now they're a minority at 44 percent. This widening achieve-
> ment gap ... has profound implications for the economy, society,
> families and democracy.[8]

Self-described "notorious Amazon feminist" Camille Paglia, com-
menting on how the educational system has failed boys, notes that

> what you're seeing is how a civilization commits suicide.... Primary-
> school education is a crock, basically. It's oppressive to anyone with
> physical energy, especially guys.... They're making a toxic environ-
> ment for boys. Primary education does everything in its power to
> turn boys into neuters.... This PC gender politics thing—the way
> gender is being taught in the universities—in a very anti-male way,
> it's all about neutralization of maleness.... Masculinity is just becom-
> ing something that is imitated from the movies. There's nothing left.
> There's no room for anything manly right now.[9]

[7] "Boys in Crisis", YouTube video, 4:40, posted by Mobilis Mobili Education Blog, April 28, 2010, https://www.youtube.com/watch?v=nMLaXr1sFZc. The video is also available on the Gurian Institute's website at http://gurianinstitute.com/professional-development/helping-boys-thrive/.

[8] Peg Tyre, "Education: Boys Falling Behind Girls in Many Areas", Newsweek online, January 29, 2006, http://www.newsweek.com/education-boys-falling-behind-girls-many-areas-108593.

[9] Bari Weiss, "Camille Paglia: A Feminist Defense of Masculine Virtues", Wall Street Journal online, December 28, 2013, http://online.wsj.com/news/articles/SB10001424052702303997604579240022857012920.

Furthermore, relationships abound in which immediate self-gratification takes precedence over chastity, where the inherent dignity of the woman is all but eliminated, and what self-respect remains is exploited for the superficial pleasure of men. Prostitution and pornography—rampant examples of this cultural and spiritual plague where women are viewed as nothing more than material possessions and objects to be discarded when no longer useful or holding men's attention and interest—are multibillion dollar industries. Domestic abuse and other forms of senseless violence against women have reached epidemic proportions. Left unchecked, this self-aggrandized way of thinking has led to a collapse of truth, integrity, and the destruction of our own spiritual heritage as men.

A spirituality that truly embraces what it means to be a man of God is the weapon of choice against the ever-encroaching culture of death. Agreeing that this is the case is one thing, but how men actually attain a spirituality that embraces the authentic gift of masculinity is something else.

The Catholic contribution to male spirituality was relatively sparse until the 1990s, when, largely sparked by the success of the Protestant Promise Keepers movement, interest in strengthening the faith of men and helping them to deepen their relationship with God through conversion and reconciliation—while increasing their knowledge of the Catholic faith through apologetics and catechesis—began to rise.[10] Today, the resurgent Catholic men's movement has yielded

---

[10] Some early examples include Clayton C. Barbeau, *The Head of the Family* (Collegeville, Minn.: Liturgical Press, 1970); Martin W. Pable, O.F.M.Cap., *A Man and His God* (Notre Dame: Ave Maria Press, 1988); John Carmody, *Toward a Male Spirituality* (Mystic, Conn.: Twenty-Third Publications, 1989). More contemporary examples include Stephen Wood, *Christian Fatherhood: The Eight Commitments of St. Joseph's Covenant Keepers*, rev. ed. (Greenville, S.C.: Family Life Center Publications, 1997); Tim Gray and Curtis Martin, *Boys to Men: The Transforming Power of Virtue* (Steubenville, Ohio: Emmaus Road Publishing, 2001); Rick Sarkisian, *Not Your Average Joe: The Real St. Joseph and the Tools for Real Manhood in the Home, the Church and the World* (Fresno, Calif.: LifeWork Press, 2004); Jason Evert, *Pure Manhood* (San Diego: Catholic Answers, 2007); Curtis Martin, *Made for More* (Denver: Epic Publishing, 2008); Fr. Larry Richards, *Be a Man! Becoming the Man God Created You to Be* (San Francisco: Ignatius Press, 2009); Brian Caulfield, ed., *Man to Man, Dad to Dad: Catholic Faith and Fatherhood* (Boston: Pauline Books and Media, 2013); David N. Calvillo, *Real Men Pray the Rosary: A Practical Guide to a Powerful Prayer* (Notre Dame: Ave Maria Press, 2013); Clayton C. Barbeau, *The Father of the Family: A Christian Perspective* (Manchester: Sophia Institute Press, 2013); Jared Zimmerer, ed., *Man Up! Becoming the New Catholic Renaissance Man* (Waterford, Mich.: Bezalel Books, 2014); and Joe McClane, *Muscle Memory: Beating the Porn Temptation* (Lulu.com, April 23, 2014), Kindle e-book.

a steadily growing number of conferences, study programs, prayer groups, and several male-oriented Catholic television series.[11] Much of the Catholic literature has focused on fatherhood, but recent works have broadened the spectrum, embracing a more holistic approach to male spirituality.[12]

Despite these positive developments, outmoded stereotypes of male spirituality still linger, leaving many men with the impression that developing a spiritually rich interior life is primarily a feminine trait. For some Catholic men, male spirituality evokes images of an encounter group where men sit in circles and "get in touch" with their feminine side.[13] For others, male spirituality is a pseudo-spiritual

[11] Some examples include the National Fellowship of Catholic Men (www.nfcmusa.org), Fathers for Good (www.fathersforgood.org), the King's Men (www.thekingsmen.org), That Man is You (www.paradisusdei.org), and the following three series on the Eternal Word Television Network: *Behold the Man: Spirituality for Men*; *Crossing the Goal*; and *Priests and Deacons: Ministers of Mercy*.

[12] See works by Jason Evert, Curtis Martin, Fr. Larry Richards, David N. Calvillo, and Jared Zimmerer in footnote no. 10 above. Interestingly, the Church's Magisterium has not produced a developed theology of male spirituality, with only a few documents that speak directly to a Catholic man's spiritual life. These include the following papal documents and Vatican II documents, which can be found by navigating the Vatican's official website at http://w2.vatican.va/content/vatican/en.html: Leo XIII, Encyclical *Quamquam Pluries*, April 15, 1889 (the encyclical is on Saint Joseph); Vatican Council II, Pastoral Constitution on the Church in the Modern World, *Gaudium et Spes*, December 7, 1965; Vatican Council II, Decree on the Apostolate of the Laity, *Apostolicam Actuositatem*, November 18, 1965; John Paul II, Apostolic Exhortation *Familiaris Consortio*, On the Role of the Christian Family in the Modern World, November 22, 1981; John Paul II, Post-Synodal Apostolic Exhortation *Christifideles Laici* (The Lay Members of Christ's Faithful People), December 30, 1988; John Paul II, Apostolic Letter *Mulieris Dignitatem*, On the Dignity and Vocation of Women, August 15, 1988; John Paul II, Apostolic Exhortation *Redemptoris Custos* (Guardian of the Redeemer), August 15, 1989; and John Paul II, *Letter to Families*, February 2, 1994. See also the following official Church document: United States Conference of Catholic Bishops, *Hearing Christ's Call: A Resource for the Formation and Spirituality of Catholic Men* (Washington, D.C: USCCB, 2002).

[13] The approach of the Franciscan priest Richard Rohr and his definition of male spirituality provides an excellent example: "What is [male spirituality]? Quite simply it is the other side of the feminine energy. It is the other pole, the contrary, the balance.... As a celibate male religious I can make little sense of my state, unless I find some way to awaken and love my own inner feminine soul. Without it, I am merely a self-centered bachelor, a would-be creator, a dried-up root. A man without his feminine soul is easily described. His personality will move toward the outer superficial world and his head will be his control tower. He will build, explain, use, fix, manipulate, legislate, order and play with whatever he bothers to touch, but will not really touch it at all. For he does not know the inside of things" (Richard Rohr, O.F.M., "Praying–Spirituality for Everyday Living", *National Catholic Reporter*, September–October 1988, http://www.stjamesstratford.com/files/Men's%20ministry%20documents/Masculine%20Spirituality[1].pdf).

experience where Jungian archetypes of the "mature masculine" and
elements of New Age spirituality converge.[14] Many would conjec-
ture that male spirituality simply means being a "good man" (student,
priest, husband, or father) and going to Mass on Sundays. All of these
perceptions are either inaccurate or overly simplistic. What is needed
is a fuller expression of the spiritual man that transcends (though not
excludes) social science and establishes a more intrinsic connection
between theology and male spirituality.

What, then, is Catholic male spirituality? It is a man's response
to God's invitation to life-giving communion through an ever-
deepening revelation and discovery of Him via a life of sacrifice and
service that imitates Christ crucified, meditates on God's Word
and responds to that Word in faith, and, through the Holy Spirit
and in the sacraments, makes him truly a son of God and part of the
Mystical Body of Christ. An authentic male spirituality is first and
foremost an encounter, that is, an encounter with the Living God
in the person of Jesus Christ, who is the quintessential example of
what it means to be a man. Catholic male spirituality is truly genuine
when it is "a spirituality centered in Jesus Christ and through him
to the Trinity".[15] Saint Paul confirms the nature of male spirituality
when he says to the Corinthians, "[W]e preach Christ crucified ...
[f]or I decided to know nothing among you except Jesus Christ and
him crucified."[16] To be authentically spiritual means that we must
enter into the life of Christ and transform our hearts, minds, and wills
to that of the Lord's.[17] Since it is only through Christ that we can
receive salvation,[18] a truly genuine Catholic spirituality for men must
be Christ-centered at its very core, faithful to the deposit of faith, and
obedient to the Church's Magisterium.

Men's spirituality is "a participation in the mystery of Christ
through the interior life of grace".[19] "Mystery" here means a relationship of loving communion between God and man that is so

---

[14] See, for example, Robert Moore and Douglass Gillette, *King, Warrior, Magician, Lover:
Rediscovering the Archetypes of the Mature Masculine* (San Francisco: HarperCollins, 1991).

[15] Jordan Aumann, O.P., *Spiritual Theology*, 7th ed. (London: Sheed and Ward, 1993), 17.

[16] 1 Cor 1:23; 2:2.

[17] "For I have come down from heaven, not to do my own will, but the will of him who
sent me" (Jn 6:38).

[18] "Jesus said to him, 'I am the way, and the truth, and the life; no one comes to the Father,
but by me'" (Jn 14:6).

[19] Aumann, *Spiritual Theology*, 18.

rich and profound, that no temporal explanation could sufficiently articulate its fullness. This relationship, in which men seek perfect union with the Father's will in the image of the crucified Christ, is the goal, purpose, and objective of male spirituality. It "defines the nature of the supernatural life"[20] and draws us into the heart of Christian faith.

A Christ-centered male spirituality fosters and nurtures growth in holiness, while strengthening and sustaining men in the constant struggle to live their faith every day. It encourages men to become defenders of a culture of life; inspires men to become faithful witnesses who are committed and dedicated to the Catholic faith in a society that needs strong, masculine role models, and to become loving servants of their wives and families, and—as priests and religious— loving servants of the Church; and develops an understanding and appreciation of the human body as the temple of the Holy Spirit.[21] Jesus became incarnate in the womb of the Virgin Mary to lead us into deeper relationship with God the Father. Thus, by weaving the fabric of our spiritual lives into the garment of Christ's death and Resurrection, men are capable of becoming clothed in Christ, of truly sharing and partaking in God's own Trinitarian life.

Catholic male spirituality also has an ecclesial component that is expressed in a most personal and special way by our participation in the liturgy and sacraments, through which we can receive God's grace and where "our most personal, most interiorized relationship with God Himself in His transcendent reality is fully recognized and formally cultivated".[22] The Catholic heart of men's spirituality is centered in Christ crucified and receives strength and life from the sacraments, most especially the Eucharist.

The Eucharist is the experience of God's presence, power, and purpose par excellence where Christ gives us, not only His divine grace, but the gift of His very self. The Eucharist is a "sacrament of love, a sign of unity, a bond of charity",[23] in which we remember

---

[20] Ibid., 22.

[21] See 1 Cor 6:19–20.

[22] Louis Bouyer, *Introduction to Spirituality*, trans. Mary Perkins Ryan (Belgium: Desclee, 1961), 5.

[23] Vatican Council II, Constitution on the Sacred Liturgy, *Sacrosanctum Concilium*, December 4, 1963, no. 47, in Walter M. Abbott, S.J., ed., *The Documents of Vatican II* (New York: Corpus Books, 1966). All references to the documents of the Second Vatican Council will be taken from this source.

the salvific action of Christ's death and Resurrection, and "unite ourselves to Christ, who makes us sharers in his Body and Blood to form
a single body".[24] This is possible because Christ is *truly, really, and
substantially*" present.[25] The Eucharist is not a symbol or representation of Christ but the reality of the Living God with whom we are in
loving relationship. The Eucharist is at the center of a man's faith and
spirituality precisely because it is Christ Himself, the visible, tangible,
and sacramental reality of communion with God. The Eucharistic
sacrifice leads to an expanded spiritual life in which this powerful
encounter with God's grace increases men's charitable desires and
actions, leading to deeper union with Christ and fraternal solidarity
with one another.

The Eucharist, therefore, flows from the Cross and is the place
where men receive the strength, power, and grace to seek the Lord
in faith, hope, and love, and "is for the soul the most certain means
of remaining united to Jesus".[26] It is a deepening of the relationship
that began in Baptism[27] and realizes a level of intimacy that is inherently supernatural and mysterious, yet inexhaustive. By receiving the
Body and Blood of Christ in the Eucharist, we literally become one
with God in a way that is purposeful and real; we become more of
who we already are in Christ Jesus, "who maintains and increases the
Divine life in us".[28]

Living an authentic male spirituality means that we must learn to
listen to God's Word as He reveals Himself to us in Sacred Scripture
and the sacramental life of the Church, and discern how to respond
to that Word in faith through the Holy Spirit. It means embracing
the Cross in our own lives and meditating on what it means to make
a complete gift of ourselves in loving sacrifice and service, since it

---

[24] *Catechism of the Catholic Church*, 2nd ed. (Washington, D.C.: Libreria Editrice Vaticana—
United States Conference of Catholic Bishops, 2000), no. 1331 (hereafter cited as *CCC*).

[25] Council of Trent (1551): DS 1651, quoted in *CCC* 1374; emphasis appears in the
*Catechism*.

[26] Abbot Columba Marmion, O.S.B., *Christ, the Life of the Soul: Spiritual Conferences*, 11 ed.,
translated by a nun of Tyburn Convent (London: Sands, 1925), 261.

[27] "The followers of Christ ... are justified in the Lord Jesus, and through baptism sought
in faith they truly become sons of God and sharers in the divine nature. In this way they are
really made holy" (Vatican Council II, Dogmatic Constitution on the Church, *Lumen Gentium*, November 21, 1964, no. 40; hereafter cited as *LG*).

[28] Marmion, *Christ, the Life of the Soul*, 263.

is in giving ourselves away in love that we truly find ourselves in Christ. Unlike the spirituality of the culture, an authentic Catholic male spirituality will inspire men to live their faith with joy, enthusiasm, and in loving fidelity to God's holy will. By doing so, men will become freer to love and more open to receive the gift of grace in response to the Lord's call to "be perfect, as your heavenly Father is perfect."[29]

The temptations and challenges faced by men today, resulting from the gross misinterpretation of the relationship between truth and freedom, are rooted in the inability to make ourselves vulnerable. The culture has convinced men that it is a sign of weakness to open ourselves fully and share our hearts and souls with others. Our role model, however, is not the culture but the Lord Jesus Christ,[30] and it would be an egregious affront to our identity in Christ to dismiss this invitation to deeper relationship and intimacy with him. It is Christ's vulnerability on the Cross in the work of our salvation—in giving his life for his Bride in the ultimate act of self-gift—that is the source and summit of male spirituality. We are truly fulfilled as men when we make a firm commitment to live Christ's Paschal Mystery.

As people of the Cross, Catholics do not soon forget that there is no Resurrection without Crucifixion. Spiritual men must learn to take hold of the Cross in their lives—to open themselves to the love, the peace, and the real joy that flows from the Sacred Heart of Jesus, and to live this reality every day of their lives. The Cross is the hermeneutic of male spirituality. It is only when we begin to understand the gift of vulnerability lived from the Cross that we will know what it means to be a man of God.

If men willingly and lovingly cooperate with what God wants to do in us, then His grace will truly heal, elevate, and perfect our human nature. Every phase of our lives as men of faith will be deepened and strengthened by a previous experience of God's grace. When we make a serious effort to live as men of God and make frequent

[29] Mt 5:48. See also *LG* 40.
[30] For example, consider what Jesus said to Saint Paul, and Saint Paul's response: "'My grace is sufficient for you, for my power is made perfect in weakness.' I will all the more gladly boast of my weaknesses, that the power of Christ may rest upon me. For the sake of Christ, then, I am content with weaknesses, insults, hardships, persecutions, and calamities; for when I am weak, then I am strong" (2 Cor 12:9–10).

reception of the sacraments of Reconciliation and the Eucharist—and time before our Lord in Adoration—an important part of our lives, God's grace will imbue men with the courage to live as the person He created us to be: made in His image and likeness.

*Chapter One*

# Biblical Manhood

Since Holy Scripture must be read and interpreted in the sacred
spirit in which it was written, no less serious attention must be given
to the content and unity of the whole of Scripture if the meaning of
the sacred texts is to be correctly worked out.

—*Dei Verbum*, no. 12

There is no doubt that by prayerfully reading the Bible, men can have
a deeply meaningful and profound encounter with God the Father.
Men can personally experience Christ, the Word who became flesh,
through a fuller and deeper understanding of how to read the Bible
as a Catholic man, come to acknowledge that this is important, and
realize that he can use the Bible for moral and ethical guidance. Being
open to the Holy Spirit, the Catholic man will take his Bible off the
shelf and start reading it every day, begin to see himself and his life in
the pages of Scripture, and then use this knowledge to grow spiritually as a man of God.

The "divinely revealed realities which are contained and presented
in sacred Scripture have been committed to writing under the inspiration of the Holy Spirit".[1] God is the author of Scripture because
the Holy Spirit is its inspiration and guide; it is God telling His story.
He uses human authors as instruments to communicate the truth of
divine revelation, that is, how God reveals Himself in salvation history for the purpose of inviting us into intimate, personal, loving, and
life-giving communion with Him.

In Sacred Scripture, God the Father speaks to us, and "since
God speaks in Sacred Scripture through men in human fashion, the

---

[1] Vatican Council II, Dogmatic Constitution on Divine Revelation, *Dei Verbum*, November 18, 1965, no. 11 (hereafter cited as *DV*).

interpreter of Sacred Scripture, in order to see clearly what God wanted to communicate to us, should carefully investigate what meaning the sacred writers really intended, and what God wanted to manifest by means of their words."[2] True human authors make full use of their power and faculties to formulate and articulate thought into writing. When we examine the human contribution to Scripture, we see a variety of audiences, literary forms, and editorial license. The literary style that is employed affects the way we understand the truth that God is revealing to us. For example, Psalm 111:10 says, "To fear the Lord is the first stage of wisdom; all who do so prove themselves wise."[3] Examining this verse out of context, the reader assumes that he needs to be afraid of God in order to show he has wisdom. This interpretation would contradict the God of love[4] who created us in His image and likeness.[5] The word for "fear" (*yare* in Hebrew) also means "honor, reverence and respect". This is the proper context for understanding why we must "fear" God. This is the attitude that a loyal son shows to his father, and the God of the universe is truly our Father in heaven.

"In order to discover the *sacred authors' intention*, the reader must take into account the conditions of their time and culture, the literary genres in use at that time, and the modes of feeling, speaking and narrating then current."[6] This is an important point. The reason why some passages in the Bible (especially in the Old Testament) appear confusing is that we are trying to read it with a twenty-first century mindset without recognizing how someone within the time period would have understood what was being said.

Let us imagine, for example, that we are in the year 2101. A group of archeologists are digging at a recently discovered twentieth-century actor's theatre in San Francisco that was destroyed by an earthquake in 1989. Buried in the rubble, they find a videocassette recorder (VCR) tape. The very excited scientists carefully excavate the tape and bring it to a nearby museum that has a working

---

[2] *DV* 12.

[3] *The Abbey Psalter* (New York: Missionary Society of Saint Paul the Apostle, 1981). All Psalm passages will be taken from this source.

[4] See 1 Jn 4:15–16.

[5] See Gen 1:27.

[6] *CCC* 110 (emphasis in original).

VCR player. After painstakingly repairing and restoring as much of the tape as they could, the archeologists load the VCR tape into the machine and push "play". The tape is grainy and somewhat choppy, but they are able to decipher some of the content. It reveals a conversation between two actors. One of the actors is heard saying to the other, "Get out there and break a leg!" The scientists are horrified. One of them writes an article about the VCR artifact stating that the tape clearly reveals that twentieth-century men were barbarians.

The above example illustrates the importance of literary form, genre, syntax, and so on, when attempting to read and understand Sacred Scripture. Like the archeologists who viewed the VCR tape with a twenty-second-century mindset, thereby not appreciating the fact that the twentieth-century colloquial expression "break a leg" actually means "good luck", those who read Scripture without understanding the proper literary and historical context (which leads to the deeper, spiritual meaning) will not understand and, consequently, misinterpret what they are reading.[7] This is why the Catholic Church has a "both-and" approach to understanding and interpreting the Bible, known as the four "senses" of Scripture.

The first is the literal (also called the literal-historical) sense. "The *literal sense* is the meaning conveyed by the words of Scripture and discovered by exegesis, following the rules of sound interpretation."[8] This does not mean necessarily we are to read every verse in the Bible and interpret it literally. Rather, we are to use sound interpretive methods to determine what the human author intended to teach and have his audience understand. The literal sense is about getting inside of the author's mind in such a way that we really understand what

---

[7] "Those who search out the intention of the sacred writers must, among other things, have regard for 'literary forms.' For truth is proposed and expressed in a variety of ways, depending on whether the text is history of one kind or another, or whether its form is that of prophecy, poetry, or some other type of speech. The interpreter must investigate what meaning the sacred writer intended to express and actually expressed in particular circumstances as he used contemporary literary forms in accordance with the situation of his own time and culture. For the correct understanding of what the sacred author wanted to assert, due attention must be paid to the customary and characteristic styles of perceiving, speaking, and narrating which prevailed at the time of the sacred writer, and to the customs men normally employed at that period in their everyday dealings with one another" (*DV* 12).

[8] *CCC* 116 (emphasis in original).

he is getting at. This is the typical method employed by and used in biblical commentaries on Scripture.

The next three senses are grouped together and are known as the spiritual senses of Scripture. Fuller and deeper than the literal, the spiritual senses are where we seek to discover what the Divine Author is intending to say through the Bible. They are called the allegorical, tropological, and anagogical senses.[9]

The allegorical sense allows us to acquire a more profound understanding of biblical events by recognizing their significance in light of Jesus Christ. The crossing of the Red Sea in Exodus 14, for example, where the Israelites escaped from slavery in Egypt, is seen allegorically as a precursor to Baptism where, by His death and Resurrection, Jesus frees us from slavery to sin and death.

The tropological or moral sense points out how we ought to live and act justly. The Ten Commandments in the Old Testament (see Ex 20 and Deut 5) and the Beatitudes in the New Testament (see Mt 5) would be examples of the moral sense of Scripture.

In the anagogical sense, we view realities and events in the Bible in terms of their eternal significance, leading us toward our true homeland, the heavenly Jerusalem. These passages in Scripture foreshadow what heaven is like. Jesus, for example, compares our experience in heaven to a wedding feast (see Mt 22 and Rev 19).

Knowing the senses of Scripture and why they are important is critical to a proper Catholic understanding of the Bible. The fourfold interpretative senses are fluid and dynamic since the full meaning of Scripture is itself inexhaustible. The better we know Scripture, the more we can see ourselves on every page. God's story is also our story. "God, who spoke in the past, continues to converse with the Spouse of his beloved Son. And the Holy Spirit, through whom the living voice of the Gospel rings out in the Church—and through her in the world—leads believers to the full truth, and makes the Word of Christ dwell in them in all its richness."[10] The eternal and perfect God—the Trinity—exists in a perfect and eternal relationship of love and creates humanity for the purpose of bringing individuals into that vibrant relationship. God made us so that we might participate in His

---

[9] See *CCC* 117.
[10] *CCC* 79.

life. The ultimate goal of understanding God's revelation in Scripture goes hand in hand with the ultimate goal of exegesis: personal transformation and intimate union with our Lord Jesus Christ.

The question now becomes, how do I see myself as a man of God in the Bible? Using the sense of Scripture outlined above, we will examine the biblical foundations and principles of authentic Catholic male spirituality rooted in the Book of Genesis (chapter 2) and in the Letter of Saint Paul to the Ephesians (chapter 5).

The first man of the Bible—literally—is Adam. In Genesis 2:15 we read, "The LORD God took the man and put him in the garden of Eden to till it and keep it." The word for "man" (*adam* in Hebrew) is derived from the Hebrew word for "dust" or "soil" (*adamah*), and, although depicted as male, he embodies the fullness of humanity. The word for "till" (*abad* in Hebrew) means a work in the form of service. The word for "keep" (*shamar* in Hebrew) means to guard, protect, and defend. Adam, then, is not simply a gardener but a steward who receives from God his mission and calling as a man: to serve, protect, and defend everything that the Lord has entrusted to him.

God then gives man his only commandment: "You may freely eat of every tree of the garden; but of the tree of the knowledge of good and evil you shall not eat, for in the day that you eat of it you shall die."[11] What is so special about the tree, and why is it in the garden? First, we see that God created man with freedom and self-determination rooted in both a healthy respect for his limits before God and a humble appreciation of the infinite chasm between God's authority (represented by the tree) and his own (to "till" and "keep"). Man's existence is a gift from God, and to use his freedom to contravene God's holy will would do violence to that gift and result in "death" (*mavet* in Hebrew), in cutting himself off from the life of God.

Second, we see that God's command is specific to "the tree of the knowledge of good and evil". The word for "knowledge" used here (*yada* in Hebrew) refers to knowledge that is gained by personal experience, that is, you come to "know" something through your experience of it. If you tell a child, for example, not to touch the hot stove, the child may use his free will and make a choice to touch

---

[11] Gen 2:16–17.

the stove anyway. They now "know" what "hot" means! The same is true in the Garden of Eden. The tree itself is not evil since everything that God creates is good. God's warning to man expressed His desire that man use his free will to remain in loving and life-giving communion with Him. He did not want man to use his free will to experience or "know" separation from His divine life—namely, sin and death—symbolized in the eating of the fruit from the tree.

"Then the LORD God said, 'It is not good that the man should be alone; I will make him a helper fit for him.'"[12] Why is the man's solitary existence not a good thing? In his original solitude,[13] man realizes that he is superior to all of God's creatures, that he is self-aware (he can know himself) and he can know God. Man is also made in the image and likeness of God (see Gen 1:27), who exists as one God in a communion—a Family—of three Persons: Father, Son, and Holy Spirit. Man, therefore, is created to exist within a family, in a communion of persons who are three but, at the same time, are one: fathers, mothers, and children.[14] Man makes no sense by himself, and so God creates a "helpmate" fit for him.

The Hebrew word for "helpmate" is *ezer kenegdo*. The root of the word *ezer* means "power" and "strength". Combined with *kenegdo* ("opposite to" or "corresponding to"), the phrase was often used to denote one who stands opposite or parallel to the other who surrounds, protects, aids, helps, and supports, especially in battle. Woman

---

[12] Gen 2:18.

[13] "Original solitude" is a term used by Pope John Paul II in a series of 129 lectures given during his Wednesday audiences between September 1979 and November 1984 known as the Theology of the Body. In these series of talks, the Holy Father describes the original sense of man's aloneness rooted in ontological truths that differentiate him from the rest of creation. In his original solitude, man is called to name the animals and thusly becomes aware of his superiority to all other creatures. Man deepens his self-awareness by looking around and discovering that he has the gift of interiority and subjectivity that other creatures do not possess, and that his self-knowledge grows with his knowledge of the world. Man also recognizes that he is not part of the unconscious and programmed flow of nature. Man stands alone: self-conscious, self-determinate, and acutely aware of his individuality; that his personhood is expressed through his body. Man, through his own humanity, through what he is, is constituted at the same time in a unique, exclusive, and unrepeatable relationship with God Himself: he alone is made in God's image and likeness. The pope sees the human body as the revealing point of the person as a whole—the body mediates and expresses the person. God has engaged man personally in a covenantal relationship and made him a partner in the absolute (cf. CCC 357).

[14] The spiritual equivalent would be bridegroom (the priest), bride (the Church), and children (humanity).

is not created to be a maid or a servant to her husband—to make the meals, do the laundry, and clean the house. God created a woman in the same original solitude as the man (she is also superior to all of God's creatures, is self-aware, and can know God), but she possesses her own unique and special gifts from God that complete and perfect the gifts of the man. They are to battle sin and death—together.

"So the Lord God caused a deep sleep to fall upon the man, and while he slept took one of his ribs and closed up its place with flesh; and the rib which the Lord God had taken from the man he made into a woman and brought her to the man."[15] When God created woman, He did not start over with another lump of clay (see Gen 2:7). Rather, He takes a rib from the side of man to create the woman. Why a rib? If God used a bone from the lower extremities, she would be less than him. If God used a bone from the upper part of the body, she would be greater than him. The Lord uses a rib from the man's side, to show that she is equal to him, equal in dignity before God right from the beginning. Equal but not the same.

This is an extremely important point. We live in a culture today that insists "equality" and "sameness" are identical, expressing itself in the sentiment "In order to be equal you have to be the same." This fails the litmus test since there exists within the complementarity of men and women a fundamental and intrinsic unity. In other words, men and women are equal in dignity but are different physically, emotionally, and spiritually. The gifts from God that are unique and special to men complement and perfect the unique and special gifts of women. To be created and loved by God is not enough; what matters to us beyond existence is to be loved by another person.[16]

---

[15] Gen 2:21–22.

[16] Woman is made from the rib of man, which refers to the homogeneity of both: there is equality not superiority. Woman can help man bridge his solitude precisely because she too is constituted in that same solitude in regard to the world; she bridges the solitude by sharing with him the very features that create the solitude. Communion requires two distinctly self-aware, self-determining persons who join together. Oneness without distinction is a lower form of unity, while unity in distinction is the highest form of unity, precisely because oneness in distinction images the relationship of the Trinitarian God within Himself. The interchange of knowledge and love between the Father, Son, and Holy Spirit is a more profound and deeper unity than being indistinguishably one because it is a unity of love and life. It is *in relationship* that one comes to a deeper knowledge and awareness of oneself, which leads to deeper communion with the other. Real communion requires a personal presence to self that can bridge to another person. Communion of persons can be formed only on the basis of the double solitude of the man and the woman.

The overflow of God's infinite love is continued and perfected by the creative power of human love between a man and a woman in the covenant relationship of marriage, and between Christ and His Church in the covenant relationship of celibacy.

"Then the man said, 'This at last is bone of my bones and flesh of my flesh; she shall be called Woman, because she was taken out of Man.' "[17] Here, the man acknowledges the splendor and magnificence of his wife. How so? Semitic languages like Hebrew and Aramaic do not have superlatives, that is, they do not have words that express an idea or concept to the highest degree, words like "greatest", "best", and "most". Superlative ideas are typically expressed in two ways in those languages. They would either repeat something three times[18] or they would use a prepositional phrase.[19] Consequently, when the man says his wife is "bone of my bones and flesh of my flesh", he is saying that she is "the greatest of my bone and the greatest of my flesh. She is the greatest part of who I am. She is my equal." By calling her woman (*ishshah* in Hebrew), the man (*ish* in Hebrew)[20] recognizes (with enthusiasm!) that woman has the same being, nature, and dignity as himself, that she has a distinctive character within her nature that is uniquely feminine and perfectly complements his, and that she, like himself, is created in the image and likeness of God and is equally endowed with self-knowledge and free will ("she was taken out of Man"):

[17] Gen 2:23.

[18] For example, by repeating "holy" three times in the following two Scripture passages, the biblical authors show that the highest glory and honor belong to God alone: "And one called to another and said: 'Holy, holy, holy is the LORD of hosts; the whole earth is full of his glory' " (Is 6:3). "And the four living creatures, each of them with six wings, are full of eyes all round and within, and day and night they never cease to sing, 'Holy, holy, holy, is the Lord God Almighty, who was and is and is to come!' " (Rev 4:8).

[19] For example, in Revelation 19:16 we read, "On his robe and on his thigh he has a name inscribed, King of kings and Lord of lords", and in 1 Timothy 6:15, "[T]his will be made manifest at the proper time by the blessed and only Sovereign, the King of kings and Lord of lords". By utilizing a preposition, both authors show that Jesus Christ is the greatest of all kings and the Lord of all lords.

[20] "From the very beginning therefore, humanity is described as articulated in the male (*ish*)–female (*ishah*) relationship. This is the humanity, sexually differentiated, which is explicitly declared 'the image of God' " (Congregation for the Doctrine of the Faith, *Letter to the Bishops of the Catholic Church on the Collaboration of Men and Women in the Church and in the World*, May 31, 2004, no. 5, http://www.vatican.va/roman_curia/congregations/cfaith/documents/rc_con_cfaith_doc_20040731_collaboration_en.html).

The man, who is still referred to with the generic expression *Adam*, experienced a loneliness which the presence of the animals is not able to overcome. He needs a helpmate who will be his partner. The term here does not refer to an inferior, but to a vital helper. This is so that Adam's life does not sink into a sterile and, in the end, baneful encounter with himself. It is necessary that he enter into relationship with another being on his own level. Only the woman, created from the same "flesh" and cloaked in the same mystery, can give a future to the life of the man. It is therefore above all on the ontological level that this takes place, in the sense that God's creation of woman characterizes humanity as a relational reality. In this encounter, the man speaks words for the first time, expressive of his wonderment: "This at last is bone of my bones and flesh of my flesh" (Genesis 2:23).[21]

Pope Benedict XVI expresses this idea beautifully in *Deus Caritas Est*:

The first novelty of biblical faith consists ... in its image of God. The second, essentially connected to this, is found in the image of man. The biblical account of creation speaks of the solitude of Adam, the first man, and God's decision to give him a helper. Of all other creatures, not one is capable of being the helper that man needs, even though he has assigned a name to all the wild beasts and birds and thus made them fully a part of his life. So God forms woman from the rib of man. Now Adam finds the helper that he needed: "This at last is bone of my bones and flesh of my flesh" (Genesis 2:23).... The idea is certainly present that man is somehow incomplete, driven by nature to seek in another the part that can make him whole, the idea that only in communion with the opposite sex can he become "complete."[22]

"Therefore a man leaves his father and his mother and clings to his wife, and they become one flesh."[23] The verse indicates that a man's relationship with his wife (and vice versa) supersedes all previous relationships, including that of parents, and that the conjugal union of a man and a woman occurs within the covenant relationship of

---

[21] Ibid., no. 6.

[22] Benedict XVI, Encyclical Letter *Deus Caritas Est* (God Is Love), December 25, 2005, no. 11 (hereafter cited as *DCE*).

[23] Gen 2:24.

marriage. This is particularly important today where marriage is being redefined as a contractual relationship between people who love each other. Thus, it is important to understand the difference between a contract and a covenant.

All throughout the Bible, when God wants to establish a relationship with His people, he establishes a covenant not a contract. A contract is an exchange of goods: "This is yours and this is mine." It is an agreement between two parties that can be dissolved if one party is dissatisfied. A covenant is an exchange of *persons*: "I am yours and you are mine." In a covenant, you make a complete gift of yourself to someone, and that someone makes a complete gift of himself back to you in an outpouring of life-giving love—in love that is free, faithful, total, and fruitful—that endures for the entire life of the spouses in marriage[24] and eternally in the relationship between Christ and the Church.[25] It is a love that gives everything and holds nothing back. This is the love of Christ on the Cross, a love that lasts forever.

In making a gift of yourself to the other in covenant relationship, the two become one flesh, not one person. In other words, you do not lose anything of the individual person God created you to be. You don't lose yourself—you find yourself. In the mutual subjection of covenant intimacy expressed in sacramental marriage or lived out in celibacy, you actually become *more* of the person who God created, gifted, and called you to be, not less.[26]

---

[24] "The sacrament of Matrimony can be regarded in two ways: first in the making and then in its permanent state. For it is a sacrament like to that of the Eucharist, which not only while it is being conferred, but also while it remains, is a sacrament; for as long as the married parties are alive, so long is their union a sacrament of Christ and his Church" (Fr. Peter J. Elliott, *What God Has Joined: The Sacramentality of Marriage* [New York: Alba House, 1990], 112, citing Pius XI, *Casti Connubii*, December 31, 1930, no. 110, citing Saint Robert Bellarmine, *De controversiis*, Tom. III, *op. cit.*, cap. vi, p. 628).

[25] "The Church, equipped with the gifts of her Founder and faithfully guarding His precepts of charity, humility and self-sacrifice, receives the mission to proclaim and to establish among all peoples the kingdom of Christ and of God. She becomes on earth the initial budding forth of that kingdom. While she slowly grows, the Church strains toward the consummation of the kingdom and, with all her strength, hopes and desires to be united in glory with her King" (*LG* 5).

[26] "God did not create man as a solitary. For from the beginning 'male and female he created them' (Genesis 1:27). Their companionship produces the primary form of interpersonal communion. For by his innermost nature man is a social being, and unless he relates himself to others he can neither live nor develop his potential" (Vatican Council II, Pastoral Constitution on the Church in the Modern World, *Gaudium et Spes*, December 7, 1965, no. 12; hereafter cited as *GS*).

Covenant relationship is a relationship of sacrifice centered in love of God and love of our brothers and sisters made in God's image and likeness.[27] Covenant love is not the arrogant self-love of the culture that places the individual at the center of all meaning and existence, and where truth can be changed to fit one's personal beliefs, situation, and circumstances. Covenant relationship desires Jesus Christ—"the way, and the truth, and the life"[28]—above all else, by seeking what is true, good, and beautiful in others.

"And the man and his wife were both naked, and were not ashamed."[29] In their original nakedness,[30] they are not ashamed of their bodies because they are looking at each other through God's eyes; what they see is what God sees. "In this way, the human body, marked with the sign of masculinity or femininity, 'includes right from the beginning the nuptial attribute, that is, the capacity of expressing love, that love in which the person becomes a gift

---

[27] "In the language of the Bible, to be born in someone's 'image and likeness,' means to be that person's child. The expression 'image and likeness' expresses the Father-son relationship of God and His people (see Genesis 5:1–3; Luke 3:38). From the very beginning, then, we see that God intended people to be His children, His divine offspring" (Saint Paul Center for Biblical Theology, "Lesson Two: From Sabbath to Flood", accessed January 12, 2015, http://www.salvationhistory.com/studies/lesson/covenant_from_sabbath_to_flood#TheChild Like). For an excellent overview of covenant theology, see Scott Hahn, *A Father Who Keeps His Promises: God's Covenant Love in Scripture* (Cincinnati: St. Anthony Messenger Press, 1998).

[28] Jn 14:16.

[29] Gen 2:25.

[30] "Original nakedness" is another term used by Pope John Paul II. It refers to the "nuptial" meaning of the body and points to God's divine revelation in Genesis as the starting point for understanding the nuptial event. The nuptial meaning of the body occurs within the context of weddedness rooted in covenant relationship and the communion of persons. This archetype in Genesis (that of earthly marriage) can be expressed in other ways in the life of the Church, for example, in the celibate state. God's burst of creative giving, springing from love, has been passed on to man so that he too experiences the yearning for self-gift: a pure and naked communion of mutual self-giving in which the body expresses the gift of the inner man. In his state of original nakedness man is aware of the procreative capacity of his body and his sexuality, which he controls and masters, free from the coercion of the bodily impulse. For a man to behave compulsively destroys his ability to give himself as a gift to the other, for example, in an act of contraception. What kind of knowledge does man and woman experience in each other in the sexual act? (1) Carnal knowledge in which a body knows another body intimately, and through sexual intimacy personal knowledge is gained, that is, there is an experiencing of the person that the body expresses. (2) Joyful fulfillment that stems from mutual giving. Man and woman know this sexual relationship is a gift. (3) A third comes into the world in their image. As a direct and tangible result of the conjugal expression of one-flesh communion, children remind us that another image of God has entered the world.

and—by means of this gift—fulfils the meaning of his being and his existence.'"[31]

This is God's plan for man, yet here we are, mired in sin. What happened?

In Genesis 3, Satan arrives on the scene and begins his attack on the family—which is still his number one target today—seeking to destroy covenant relationship with God. He enacts his plan by pursuing the woman first. Why her?

"God is love".[32] Thus, His very essence, nature, and being is love itself. All creation, then, is an overflow, an outpouring of God's immense and limitless love. What uniquely distinguishes men and women from the rest of creation is that God made us in His image and likeness: "'Let us make man in our image, after our likeness; and let them have dominion over the fish of the sea, and over the birds of the air, and over the cattle, and over all the earth, and over every creeping thing that creeps upon the earth.' So God created man in his own image, in the image of God he created him; male and female he created them".[33] How do men and women "image" God? How do they see themselves as participating in God's life and "likeness", while maintaining their distinctive yet complementary masculine and feminine character?

In this regard, Pope John Paul II observed:

The first account of man's creation, which ... is of a theological nature, conceals within itself a powerful metaphysical content. Let it not be forgotten that this text of Genesis has become the source of the most profound inspirations for thinkers who have sought to understand "being" and "existence." Notwithstanding certain detailed and plastic expressions of the passage, man is defined there, first of all, in the dimensions of being and of existence ("*esse*"). He is defined in a way that is more metaphysical than physical.[34]

---

[31] Congregation for the Doctrine of the Faith, *Letter to the Bishops*, no. 6. The document continues, "On the basis of the principle of mutually being 'for' the other in interpersonal 'communion', there develops in humanity itself, in accordance with God's will, the integration of what is 'masculine' and what is 'feminine.' ... Here we find the heart of God's original plan and the deepest truth about man and woman, as willed and created by Him. Although God's original plan for man and woman will later be upset and darkened by sin, it can never be abrogated."

[32] 1 Jn 4:16.

[33] Gen 1:26–27

[34] Pope John Paul II, *Original Unity of Man and Woman: Catechesis on the Book of Genesis* (Boston: Daughters of St. Paul, 1981), 24.

Men, in their way of imaging God, analogously point to God's "outer life", to His "otherness" and transcendence, "to all the works by which God reveals Himself and communicates His life".[35] The word for "image" in Hebrew is the masculine noun *tselem*, which means a shadow that is the outline or representation of the original. When there is light, our physical bodies cast a shadow that is an outline of our bodies and moves as we move. God is pure Spirit, and His light casts the shadow of His love on our souls. Thus, we become temples of the Holy Spirit, who represent the love of God in our actions. Catholic men are called to carry out God's original plan given to Adam in the Garden of Eden: to serve, protect, and defend all that God has entrusted to his care. Adam failed by his disobedience, and Christ, the new Adam, has fulfilled the Father's plan for salvation by the obedience of faith through His Passion, death, and Resurrection: "If Christ has not been raised, your faith is futile and you are still in your sins. Then those also who have fallen asleep in Christ have perished. If for this life only we have hoped in Christ, we are of all men most to be pitied. But in fact Christ has been raised from the dead, the first fruits of those who have fallen asleep. For as by a man came death, by a man has come also the resurrection of the dead. For as in Adam all die, so also in Christ shall all be made alive."[36] Men are made to exercise leadership and authority in the image of God as fathers, and for service and sacrifice in the image of the crucified Christ, our brother.

Women, on the other hand, in the likeness of God, analogously point to God's "inner life", His heart and "withinness" where God, in the mystery of His inmost life, exists in an eternal interrelationship of loving and life-giving communion. The word for "likeness" in Hebrew is the feminine noun *demuth*, which means "similar". Being similar in this context does not mean physical similarity. Since God is pure Spirit, we bear a *spiritual* similarity to God, who has filled us with the breath of His divine life. Thus, being in God's "likeness" analogously points to the relationship of a child who shares a similar nature with his mother. In Isaiah, God's love for us is expressed in the love and compassion of a mother for her child: "Can a woman forget her sucking child, that she should have no

[35] CCC 236.
[36] I Cor 15:17–22.

compassion on the son of her womb? Even these may forget, yet I will not forget you."[37]

"In God's eternal plan, woman is the one in whom the order of love in the created world of persons takes first root. The order of love belongs to the intimate life of God himself, the life of the Trinity. In the intimate life of God, the Holy Spirit is the personal hypostasis of love. Through the Spirit, Uncreated Gift, love becomes a gift for created persons."[38] In other words, in God's mind from all eternity, when He decided to create beings made in His image and likeness, and imbue them with life-giving love, it is within a woman's being—within her heart and soul—where His love first establishes a foundation and home. Women are the very heart of God's love and have a special relationship with the Holy Spirit that men will never fully understand or appreciate. By their very nature, all women are mothers (either physical or spiritual) because they share an intimacy with the Holy Spirit as life-bearers and life-givers. In this sense, women are the quintessential examples of what it means to be fully human and the teachers of love to all humanity. "*The dignity of woman is measured by the order of love*, which is essentially the order of justice and charity."[39] By targeting the woman, Satan is trying to destroy the family by separating the loving and life-giving dimensions of covenant relationship that flow from the heart of God Himself.

Prior to the Fall, the consciences of the man and his wife were directed toward their Ultimate End: the Beatific Vision, life forever in heaven with God. Satan, through his lies and deceptions, forms the consciences of our first parents away from God and toward themselves. Sadly, he has been using the same technique over and over again, century after century and millennium after millennium, that continues to destroy the hearts, minds, and lives of those who seek life-giving communion with God.

Exactly how does he do it? Let's say your favorite football team only has one play in their playbook. Just one play. How many games would they win? The answer, of course, is none because every time they touch the ball the other team knows what play they are going to

---

[37] Is 49:15.

[38] John Paul II, Apostolic Letter *Mulieris Dignitatem*, On the Dignity and Vocation of Women, August 15, 1988, no. 29 (hereafter cited as *MD*).

[39] Ibid. (emphasis in original).

run. There is no way your team can win. It is the same with Satan. He only has one play in his playbook, but we keep losing! Here is how it works.

Satan's first words to the woman are in the form of a question: "Did God say, 'You shall not eat of any tree of the garden'?".[40] The purpose of this question is to plant the seeds of confusion and doubt in her mind—doubt about what God said and who God is in her life—in order to form her conscience away from God by questioning the Lord's authority over her life. Her answer reveals that she is, in fact, confused: "We may eat of the fruit of the trees of the garden; but God said, 'You shall not eat of the fruit of the tree which is in the midst of the garden, neither shall you touch it, lest you die'".[41] If we look back at Genesis 2:16–17, God commands not to eat the fruit of the tree, but He never says anything about *touching* it. In her confusion, the woman puts words into God's mouth that He did not say. Satan then capitalizes on the last part of her answer regarding the consequence for choosing self over God—death: "You will not die. For God knows that when you eat of it your eyes will be opened, and you will be like God, knowing good and evil".[42] Satan lies to her about the meaning of death and tempts her with the proposition that she does not need God at all—that by eating the tree's fruit she can become her own god, "knowing good and evil". Satan's premise is entirely false because God cannot "know" (experience) evil, since He is complete and perfect Good. Hence, there is no possibility of man becoming "like God" in the way Satan has proposed. Through his temptation the devil twists, confuses, and distorts the truth of God's command so that the man and his wife freely close their hearts to God's will, leading them not to the intimate embrace of the Beatific Vision but to the "knowledge" of separation from God's life in the throes of Original Sin.

"So when the woman saw that the tree was good for food, and that it was a delight to the eyes, and that the tree was to be desired to make one wise, she took of its fruit and ate; and she also gave some to her husband, and he ate."[43] One of the reasons Satan chose the

---

[40] Gen 3:1.
[41] Gen 3:2–3.
[42] Gen 3:4–5.
[43] Gen 3:6.

"tree of the knowledge of good and evil" to entice the woman into sin was because "it was a delight to the eyes". The tree was pleasurable to behold, and God gives man things that are pleasurable for our enjoyment and benefit. The experience of pleasure on earth is a means to an end; it anticipates the joy of eternal covenant love in heaven as it raises our hearts and minds to God, our Ultimate End. Satan, the author of subjective truth, takes pleasure out of its proper context of orientation toward the Ultimate End and elevates it as an end in itself. The result: pleasure becomes our god. Satan understands that covenant love means sacrifice, and that men, in aspiring to live holy lives day after day, "realize how difficult it is to achieve total abandonment to God's will, which comes only at the cost of a profound and painful purgation of self-love".[44] It is exactly during times of temptation that Satan seduces men with egotistic pleasures that undermine and stifle the work of grace.

The woman's husband is finally mentioned in Genesis 3:6, although he has been there the entire time. Though the woman succumbed to Satan's mendacity, the man is no less culpable than his wife. There is no indication that he attempts to remind the woman of what the Lord had said, nor does he intervene in any way. Incredibly, while Satan is tempting his wife, the man says and does nothing. He takes no action to protect and defend the heart of love. Instead, his response to sin is weak and pathetic: "She also gave some to her husband, and he ate." His silence is deafening and confirms his complicity in disobeying God's commandment.

What makes matters worse is that today, as Satan proceeds to devastate the heart of love over and over again, many men not only continue to stand by and do nothing but also actively contribute to and encourage Satan's path of destruction. Satan, who appeared as a serpent in the garden and who comes to us now under the appearance of moral relativism, laughs in our faces as he shapes our hearts with his lies. Once again, the response to sin is weak and pathetic: men spend billions of dollars on pornography and prostitutes. We dull our senses with drugs and alcohol. We actively practice and promote contraception. We procure abortions and engage in sexual acts outside of the marriage covenant. We perpetrate acts of

---

[44] Jordan Aumann, O.P., *Spiritual Theology*, 7th ed. (London: Sheed and Ward, 1993), 40.

domestic violence and abuse. Our complacency has led to the separation of love and life, and introduced a culture of chaos, emptiness, and death.

The verse does not imply that the woman tempted her husband into sinning, as is sometimes thought, but that he was a willing participant with his wife in introducing sin into the world. He was supposed to protect and defend her, but he did not, and we are still living with the consequences of that decision today, as evidenced in the aftermath of the Fall:

> Then the eyes of both were opened, and they knew that they were naked; and they sewed fig leaves together and made themselves aprons. And they heard the sound of the LORD God walking in the garden in the cool of the day, and the man and his wife hid themselves from the presence of the LORD God among the trees of the garden. But the LORD God called to the man, and said to him, "Where are you?" And he said, "I heard the sound of you in the garden, and I was afraid, because I was naked; and I hid myself." He said, "Who told you that you were naked? Have you eaten of the tree of which I commanded you not to eat?" The man said, "The woman whom you gave to be with me, she gave me fruit of the tree, and I ate." Then the LORD God said to the woman, "What is this that you have done?" The woman said, "The serpent beguiled me, and I ate."[45]

The man no longer sees his wife the way God sees her. She has been reduced to an object for pleasure and gratification. He is ashamed as he looks upon her with a love tainted by concupiscence and carnal

---

[45] Gen 3:7–13. In the *Theology of the Body*, Pope John Paul uses the term "original innocence" that describes the state of man prior to the Fall and which also encompasses original nakedness ("the man and his wife were both naked, and were not ashamed" [Gen 2:25]). "Naked" and "not ashamed" describes the state of their consciences and their mutual experience of the body, of the masculinity and femininity of the other, as revealed in the nakedness of the body. This innocent awareness of "otherness" deteriorates after the Original Sin. The realization of their nakedness is a radical paradigm shift that is not only physical but fundamentally alters the meaning of the body. Prior to sin, the husband sees in his wife someone whom he can give himself to totally and completely, and who reciprocates the gift of herself in return in a mutual exchange of love and life. After the Fall, the potential arises for "taking" from the other, of exploitation and self-gratification. The sexual union has become tainted by lust, so the value of the deeper, inner person is eclipsed.

desires (eros devoid of agape).[46] She is ashamed as he looks at her body and not her soul. Hence, they both hide themselves from the presence of God. Sadly, many women today are no longer ashamed of a man's lustful gaze but have, in fact, accepted and embraced it. It has become culturally acceptable for women to encourage their own exploitation either for economic benefit (prostitution and pornography) or simply to be noticed by men (minishorts and thong bikinis).

The man admits that he was afraid and hides himself. Fear is the reason why so many men do not accept or practice the Catholic faith. Fear has made it easier for men to accept the lies of the culture rather than embrace the fullness of truth found in the Catholic faith. Fear makes men spiritually and intellectually lethargic; we have become satiated by the banquet of indifferentism and drunk on the wine of mediocrity. Fear makes us hide from God behind the veneer of being a "good person" in order to justify our sinful behavior. We make excuses why we cannot find time to strengthen and deepen our faith life. Uniting ourselves to Christ in the Holy Sacrifice of the Mass is not a priority. Fear prevents men from becoming priests in both the hierarchical and domestic churches, and, instead, we worry about being politically correct and put our trust in worldly ideals and possessions. We eschew Eucharistic Adoration, the Rosary, and other devotional practices that cause us to be still and know God, admonishing them as "boring" and "old-fashioned" as the din of the world deafens the voice of God in our hearts. Fear makes us spiritual geldings.

The father-son paradigm is ageless. It is older than human history. The "rays of fatherhood" contained in this formulation belong to the Trinitarian Mystery of God Himself, which shines forth from Him, illuminating man and his history. This notwithstanding, as we know from

---

[46] "The more the two, in their different aspects, find a proper unity in the one reality of love, the more the true nature of love in general is realized. Even if *eros* [physical, sensual love] is at first mainly covetous and ascending, a fascination for the great promise of happiness, in drawing near to the other, it is less and less concerned with itself, increasingly seeks the happiness of the other, is concerned more and more with the beloved, bestows itself and wants to 'be there for' the other. The element of *agape* thus enters into this love, for otherwise *eros* is impoverished and even loses its own nature" (*DCE* 7). The highest form of love is agape, a love that seeks the good of the other. Eros becomes directionless and self-centered (temporal) without being rooted and fulfilled in a love that looks outside of the self (transcendent). Eros finds its purpose and truest meaning (i.e., "it makes sense") only when united to agape.

Revelation, in human history the "rays of fatherhood" meet a first resistance in the obscure but real fact of original sin. This is truly the key for interpreting reality. Original sin is not only the violation of a positive command of God but also, and above all, a violation of the will of God as expressed in that command. Original sin attempts, then, to abolish fatherhood, destroying its rays which permeate the created world, placing in doubt the truth about God who is Love and leaving man only with a sense of the master-slave relationship.[47]

From His cherubim in heaven, God looks down to earth and upon the insanity unleashed by the dictatorship of relativism, upon His sons—the Catholic men of the world who are Christ's foot soldiers in the Church militant—and asks, "Where are you? Where are the men that My Son died for?"

When God asks the man directly for an explanation of why he failed to keep the commandment about the tree, he cannot find the moral fortitude to "man-up" and accept responsibility for failing to serve, protect, and defend. In his cowardice, he assigns blame to his wife. Following the example of her husband, the woman assigns blame to Satan. Instead of making a gift of themselves to each other in truth and freedom, now—as slaves to sin—they shift personal culpability for their offenses against God to one another. "Although he was made by God in a state of holiness, from the very dawn of history man abused his liberty, at the urging of personified Evil. Man set himself against God and sought to find fulfillment apart from God. Although he knew God, he did not glorify Him as God, but his senseless mind was darkened and he served the creature rather than the Creator."[48]

How do we get ourselves back on track as faithful and steadfast men of God? In Ephesians 5:21–33, Saint Paul juxtaposes the relationship between a husband and wife in the marriage covenant with the relationship between Christ and the Church. These verses lay the foundation for an authentic male spirituality ensconced in the image of the crucified Christ.

Saint Paul frames this particular set of verses around the theme of equality between a husband and his wife. Ephesians 5:21 emphasizes

---

[47] Pope John Paul II, *Crossing the Threshold of Hope* (New York: Alfred A. Knopf, 1994), PDF e-book, 117.

[48] GS 13.

mutual subjection ("Be subject to one another out of reverence for Christ"), while Ephesians 5:31 quotes directly from Genesis 2:24, emphasizing the one-flesh union in marriage ("For this reason a man shall leave his father and mother and be joined to his wife, and the two shall become one flesh"). With these bookends firmly established, Saint Paul explores the nature of covenant relationship in Christ through the lens of sacramental marriage.

Ephesians 5:22–24 says, "Wives, be subject to your husbands, as to the Lord. For the husband is the head of the wife as Christ is the head of the Church, his body, and is himself its Savior. As the Church is subject to Christ, so let wives also be subject in everything to their husbands." These verses can be grossly misinterpreted without understanding the literal sense of Scripture.

In Genesis 3:16, God says to the woman, "I will greatly multiply your pain in childbearing; in pain you shall bring forth children, yet your desire shall be for your husband, and he shall rule over you." The Hebrew phrase "and he shall rule over you" is *v'hu yimshol bach*. There are two words for "rule" in Hebrew: *melech* and *moshel* (also transliterated as *mashal*). *Melech* means a king who rules in a democracy, but a *moshel* is a dictator who rules by force, which serves as the root for *yimshol* ("rule over"). One of the temporal (earthly) punishments for sin after the Fall is the husband ruling over his wife like a tyrant (*yimshol*), and not devoutly serving she who was born from his side as his equal. The husband as "boss" is not part of God's plan for covenant relationship but the result of Original Sin.

With this idea firmly in mind, we turn back to Ephesians. In Ephesians 5, the word for "subject to" in Greek is *hupotasso*, a military term for arranging troop divisions under the command and mission of a leader. So wives are to place themselves under their husband's mission just as the Church places herself under the mission of Christ, her spouse. What is the husband's mission? "Husbands, love your wives, as Christ loved the Church and gave himself up for her".[49] A husband's mission is to imitate the crucified Christ, to give his life and die every day to himself through acts of sacrificial love and service so that he can live for his wife and children, just as Christ the Bridegroom gave His life for His Bride, the Church.

---

[49] Eph 5:25.

Every man is called to be the chief servant of his family, whether he serves as a husband and father in the domestic church (the church of the home), as a parish priest in persona Christi (in the person of Christ) for the Church on earth, or as a young man who serves as an example of sanctity and virtue within society as he discerns God's will for his life, "that he might sanctify her, having cleansed her by the washing of water with the word, that he might present the Church to himself in splendor, without spot or wrinkle or any such thing, that she might be holy and without blemish".[50] Our Lord Himself teaches us by his example: "For the Son of man also came not to be served but to serve, and to give his life as a ransom for many",[51] and, "He who is greatest among you shall be your servant; whoever exalts himself will be humbled, and whoever humbles himself will be exalted."[52] Our spirituality as men must flow from the Sacred Heart of Jesus and His call to live the Gospel with both fervor and humility. Humility does not mean thinking less of ourselves; it means thinking of ourselves less. Humility means making our relationship with Jesus the single most important relationship in our lives.

Saint Paul boldly proclaims that he and the other apostles preach "Christ crucified"[53] and that "I decided to know nothing among you except Jesus Christ and him crucified."[54] As men, when we look at Christ on the Cross what do we see? Do we see ourselves? The Cross is a mirror into the souls of men, but we have become so immersed in those things that prevent us from making our relationship with Christ our highest and most important priority that we have stopped looking at the Cross because it's either too painful or we simply feel nothing at all. We have become the living dead. We live our lives in silent fear, ashamed and afraid to make ourselves vulnerable—afraid to give ourselves totally and completely to our wives and children, and to our Church and culture.

If we are to be true men of God, we must willingly and lovingly lay down our lives in service to our brides, bearing witness to the awesome power and testimony of the crucified Christ. We must have the courage to say with Saint Paul, "I have been crucified

---

[50] Eph 5:26–27.
[51] Mk 10:45. See also Mt 20:28.
[52] Mt 23:11–12. See also Mk 9:35.
[53] 1 Cor 1:23.
[54] 1 Cor 2:2.

with Christ; it is no longer I who live, but Christ who lives in me; and the life I now live in the flesh I live by faith in the Son of God, who loved me and gave himself for me."[55] When men pick up their Crosses and follow Christ, they unite their sufferings to His Passion, receive everlasting life from His death, and draw their strength from his weakness. "My grace is sufficient for you, for my power is made perfect in weakness", the Lord said to Saint Paul, prompting Saint Paul to say, "I will all the more gladly boast of my weaknesses, that the power of Christ may rest upon me. For the sake of Christ, then, I am content with weaknesses, insults, hardships, persecutions, and calamities; for when I am weak, then I am strong."[56]

Being vulnerable means not being afraid to be countercultural—to embrace the fullness of truth and become servants of all that is good and beautiful. Being vulnerable means recognizing that the Sacrament of Reconciliation allows men to open our hearts and trust the Lord completely, not being afraid to say, "Lord, I love you, but I am human and, in my weakness, I've made a mistake", and then receive God's mercy and forgiveness. Being vulnerable means emptying ourselves before the Eucharistic Christ in complete surrender to the will of God so that the Lord can fill us with His life. Being vulnerable means exposing the deepest parts of who we are before our "brides": our spouses and the Church. We cannot continue to be afraid to express fully who we are in Christ, and until male spirituality moves beyond the confines of the cultural status quo—until we acknowledge and appreciate what it means to be a gift to others—we will consistently face obstacles and uncertainty within our families, parishes, and communities.

[55] Gal 2:20.
[56] 2 Cor 12:9–10.

*Chapter Two*

# Covenant Relationship

God is love, and in himself he lives a mystery of personal loving communion. Creating the human race in His own image and keeping it in being, God inscribed in the humanity of man and woman the vocation, and thus the capacity and responsibility, of love and communion. Love is therefore the fundamental and innate vocation of every human being.

—John Paul II, *Familiaris Consortio*, no. 11

"God is love" is the most basic and fundamental reality of all creation and existence. This perfect truth is the fabric that binds the entire universe together, and it is God's love that gives all things life, meaning, and purpose. "God is love" flows so easily from our lips that we often fail to appreciate fully the power behind these three simple words. Yet, there is nothing more important, more relevant, and more central to who we are as men than to be in God's mercy and love.

Love is not a self-determined concept. It is not a theory or ideology defined by secular culture and the political establishment. Love, at its core, is Being Himself. To love as God loves means that we must love the Lord with all of our heart, soul, mind, and strength: it is the total giving of ourselves to God and to others for God. It is the complete outpouring of our spirit in loving sacrifice for our families and parishioners, as well as for the elderly, the stranger, the poor, and the unborn. To love God means that we must use the unique gifts and talents bestowed upon each one of us to live the Gospel with our whole being; it is giving everything we are back to God just as Jesus did on the Cross, with our last ounce of strength and our last breath of life.

We experience the depth of God's love and life in us by receiving Him in the Most Blessed Sacrament of the Eucharist. There is no greater way to remain in His love than to join our bodies with His so that we may have life and our joy may be complete.[1] In the Eucharist, we unite ourselves to Christ, whose gift of "love and obedience to the point of giving his life is ... 'a sacrifice that the Father accepted, giving, in return for this total self-giving by His Son, ... new immortal life in the resurrection.' "[2] In offering His sacrifice for the Church, Christ has also made His own the spiritual sacrifices of each one of us, who offer our manhood in union with Christ's salvific act of love on the Cross.[3]

Covenant love is free, faithful, total, and fruitful. Loving as God loves means that our love must be a free choice of the will; we must use our personal freedom to choose to love God before and above all else. God's love means that the dignity and value of every person must be preserved, keeping in mind that all of God's children are made in His image and likeness. God's love means that our love must be a self-gift: we must surrender ourselves in love for the sake of others and so enter more deeply into the life of Christ. God's love means that our love must be permanent, because God will not accept anything less than our total, complete, and lifelong commitment to serving Him. God's love means that our love must be life-giving—that every act of love must necessarily be an intimate partnership of love and life—for our God is not a God of sterility and death: He is the Lord and Giver of life.

Due to our sinfulness, however, love's true meaning is often distorted and reduced to inane platitudes and clichés that permeate much of society ("love means never having to say you're sorry", for example). The culture presents men with various alternatives to loving as God loves, preferring acts of "use" that exploit love as a commodity (love as self-centered) while impugning the fullness of love, which always seeks the good of another (love as other-centered). In the culture's disintegrated vision, where God's life-giving dimension is intentionally separated from its foundation in love, contraception,

[1] Cf. Jn 15:9–13.

[2] John Paul II, Encyclical Letter *Ecclesia de Eucharistia*, On the Eucharist in Its Relationship to the Church, April 17, 2003, no. 13.

[3] Cf. Ibid.

homosexuality, and pornography become "loving" acts. In reality these acts undermine the intimacy of a truly loving relationship with God by rejecting the inherent openness to life-giving love that models God's own Trinitarian life.

Love, when experienced solely on a physical, "feeling" level, creates a spiritual void that can only be filled by following in the footsteps of Jesus. Christ on the Cross is the embodiment of love's response to God's will in our lives: "[L]ove one another as I have loved you."[4] By loving as God loves, we learn to speak the language of communion that reveals our inner life with God and the innate dignity of our humanity by which we come to some knowledge of God Himself. Jesus teaches the richness and beauty of this reality in the Gospels: "As the Father has loved me, so have I loved you; abide in my love. . . . I have called you friends, for all that I have heard from my Father I have made known to you."[5]

The actual grace that allows us to develop and mature as spiritual men—to be true disciples of Jesus Christ—is a free gift from God. God's love works in and through the Holy Spirit, who teaches us the meaning of His love and empowers us to live in His name—in short, to become holy. Holiness is "cultivated by all who are moved by the Spirit of God, and who obey the voice of the Father, worshipping [Him] in spirit and in truth".[6] An authentic male spirituality necessarily fosters and nurtures growth in holiness when we remove everything that separates us from the Father's love, abandon ourselves to God's divine providence, prayerfully discern God's will for us through a life of devotion and sacrifice, and draw deeply from the wellspring of graces given to us in the sacraments. Holiness is our acceptance of God's invitation to intimate, personal, loving, and life-giving communion with Him in the heart of the Trinity.

Yet, in response to the call to holiness, Christ commands us to do the seemingly impossible: to "be perfect, as your heavenly Father is perfect".[7] How can we do this? God's word in Sacred Scripture provides the answer.

[4] Jn 15:12.
[5] Jn 15:9, 15.
[6] LG 41.
[7] Mt 5:48.

In the Book of Daniel, the sun and the moon, the rain and wind, mountains and hills, seas and rivers, plants and trees, reptiles and mammals—all of creation gives praise to the Lord.[8] In praising the Creator for its existence, each substance in the created order also blesses God by being what God created and intended that substance to be from the beginning. A rock, for example, blesses and praises the Lord by being true to its nature: by being a rock and not a tree. The wind does the same by being the wind and not the ocean. By existing in accord with its nature, each unique substance within creation responds to a distinctive call to perfection. But what about us? Who are we called to be? To answer this, we look once again to Sacred Scripture, specifically, to the creation narrative in the first chapter of the Book of Genesis.

In the first creation account, "God said, 'Let us make man in our image, after our likeness.'... So God created man in his own image, in the image of God he created him; male and female he created them. And God blessed them, and God said to them, 'Be fruitful and multiply, and fill the earth and subdue it'".[9] There are four significant components contained in this passage that, collectively, provide both the interpretive key allowing us to correctly understand the meaning of the text, and the proper context for recognizing the foundational elements contained therein. These include divine revelation, the love of God, the marriage covenant, and God's expectation of man.

*Divine Revelation.* Divine revelation originates in the action of God: God speaks first, and it is the inherent disposition of humanity to listen with the ear of our hearts. In speaking to mankind God unveils His relational nature for the purpose of inviting us into relationship. This happens first in His creation, then moves from what is manifested in creation to what is evidenced in the people of Israel, and finally to Jesus Christ, the definitive fulfillment of God's self-disclosure. Through His Son man beholds the face of God and touches His inner life, achieving a level of intimacy never before possible on earth. In Jesus the fullness of God resides, and in proclaiming the kingdom realized and present in Himself, He breathes new life into our souls,

---

[8] See Dan 3:35–66.

[9] Gen 1:26–28; also Gen 5:1–2: "When God created man, he made him in the likeness of God. Male and female he created them, and he blessed them and named them Man when they were created."

awakens our desire for conversion and reconciliation, and leads us into the loving arms of our Father in heaven.[10]

In Genesis 1:26, divine revelation begins when God reveals Himself through His Word ("God said"). This spoken Word of God is the second Person of the Trinity, who in the fullness of time became the Word-made-flesh, Jesus Christ: the final, complete, and absolute triumph of a relational God. The beauty of this resplendent truth sets the tone for John's Gospel: "In the beginning was the Word, and the Word was with God, and the Word was God."[11] In speaking through His Word, God reveals Himself and invites us to share in His life. Our response to God's invitation must be that of the prophet Samuel: "Speak, [LORD,] for you servant hears."[12]

*The Love of God.* Genesis 1:27 also says, "God created man in his own image, in the image of God he created him; male and female he created them." There are two key points that must be considered: first, that God made "man", and, second, that He made man "in his image and likeness".

It is important to point out that the verse in chapter 1 of the Book of Genesis does *not* say, "Let us make *a* man." On the surface, this seemingly minor omission of the definite article "a" appears trivial, but it is, in reality, crucial if we are to properly understand the text. If the text read, "Let us make a man", one would interpret "man" to mean one human male. But in stating, "Let us make man", the text clearly applies the word "man" in the broadest sense: to both men and women equally ("male and female he created them"). This definition, however, transcends the obvious distinction of gender and speaks to a much deeper reality and truth. In its fullest sense, "man" denotes a "personal being" imbued with God's life-giving love and oriented toward intimate friendship and communion with Him. As such, man possesses freedom rooted in the knowledge of God and expressed through the obedience of faith.[13] The concept of man as a "personal being" is equally situated in the distinct yet complementary gifts of "male and female".

---

[10] Cf. Mk 1:15.

[11] Jn 1:1.

[12] 1 Sam 3:10.

[13] The "obedience of faith" means more than submissive or deferential compliance to authority; it is a spirit of faith in which the People of God, with complete humility and magnanimity, obey, revere, and continually strive to discern and fulfill the will of God.

Men and women are different! We are different physically, psychologically, emotionally, and spiritually, but we live in a society that lies to us, saying, "In order to be equal, you have to be the same." This cultural affirmation denies the fact that, from the beginning, men and women are completely equal in God's eyes. Since both are made in the image and likeness of God, neither is denied the particular attributes inherent in their "maleness" and "femaleness"; hence, there is a fundamental unity within the complementarity of their being. As we have seen, it is precisely in this "one-flesh" union (see Gen 2:24) that men and women, each in a unique and special way, enter into communion with the Father, Son, and Holy Spirit.

It is also important to recognize that God made man "in his own image". The one God exists in an eternal, loving relationship of Trinitarian communion; He is Three yet One. Man's unity, perfectly expressed in the covenant relationship between man and woman (and in the covenant relationship between Christ and His Church), reflects his extraordinary state in the created order—that of differentiated human persons, who by nature possess equal dignity and the ability for interpersonal communion. This communion of body and spirit requires man and woman, as two unique and distinct persons (both endowed with the gifts of self-will and self-determination), to become a single sign of God's love and life; they are two, yet one. In this way man, in his distinctiveness as male and female, emulates the distinctive community of Persons in the One God.

*The Marriage Covenant* ("He blessed them"). Not long ago, a television show aired that depicted a "drive-thru wedding". A couple literally pulled up to a service window and were handed a menu. They ordered a wedding, and it was performed in the drive-thru while the couple sat in their car. After paying the appropriate fees, they drove away with a marriage certificate and a complimentary bottle of champagne. This scenario shows how pathetic and trivial marriage has become in our society.

We live in a culture that embraces the thirty-second sound bite as if it were divine revelation and rarely accepts the obligations and responsibilities of faith, lived in the light of truth, goodness, and beauty with all that Jesus demands and expects of us. If God's love is to have any effect in us at all, we must not be afraid to pick up our

Crosses and follow Christ in love: in love that is generous and selfless. Christ reveals the Father's love to us, so that we can become living examples of Christ to others.

A friend once asked me, "What are the most important priorities in your life?" I answered, "My relationship with God, my family, and everything else." He seemed surprised and said, "I thought for sure you'd say that your family came first", to which I said in reply, "If I don't put God first in my life, then I'm no good to my wife and children." In this exchange of life and love, spouses share all that they are and all that they will become. Husbands and wives promise to nurture and support each other so that they will always grow deeper in their love for God and one other. When a man and a woman give themselves to each other totally and completely, their union bears witness to God's plan for marriage: a sacramental covenant of loving and life-giving communion.

The Sacrament of Marriage is so central to God's love for us that He Himself chose to be born and grow up in a family, entering into human history with a mother and foster father. In a culture where prestige means everything, our Father in heaven shows us in the simple lives of a housewife and carpenter the divine connection between the human family and the family of God in the Trinity.

When I held my oldest daughter, Claire, in my arms for the first time on the day she was born, and when I realized that this new life was totally dependent upon my wife and me for her happiness and well-being, for her very life—a life that I helped to create—I was overwhelmed with a feeling of unconditional and abiding love. For the first time in my life, I had just an inkling, a glimpse, of what God's love must be like, and that God loves me infinitely more than I could ever love my own child. Covenant relationship "calls for nothing less than total self-donation.... Such a love is a summons to martyrdom. This invitation requires suffering and self-denial.... It demands nothing less than a constant dying to self."[14] Covenant relationship seeks the splendor of absolute truth in love.[15]

[14] Scott Hahn, *A Father Who Keeps His Promises: God's Covenant Love in Scripture* (Ann Arbor, Mich.: Servant Publications, 1998), 18.

[15] This is expressed in Psalm 119:137–38, 144: "LORD, you are just indeed; your decrees are right. You have imposed your will with justice and with absolute truth.... The justice of your will is eternal: if you teach me, I shall live."

Covenant relationship, of course, extends to all men, including those in the priesthood and in perpetual vows through a religious community, and those called to live as single, celibate men. The language of the marriage covenant can be applied in these cases as well, where the "bride/wife" is the Church and the "bridegroom/husband" is Christ. As such, these men truly represent Christ in unique and definitive ways. Priests, through the grace and indelible character of sacramental ordination, stand in the person of Christ as sacred ministers of the transcendent (heavenly) order. Religious men embody Christ through their sacred vows and perpetual consecration to the Father. Single, celibate men manifest Christ in the exercise of their baptismal call to holiness as priests, prophets, and kings in the temporal (earthly) order. As a consequence of covenant relationship, each particular vocation also gives life to God's children: priests through the administration of sacraments (most especially the Eucharist and Reconciliation); religious through a life of prayer, asceticism, and works of charity; and single men in their contributions made through the lay apostolate ordered to the common good and the well-being of all mankind.

The God of glory who created us and shares His life with us continually seeks us out in order to establish an everlasting bond of unconditional love. Although there is never a moment in our lives when God does not reach out to touch us with His loving embrace, we are often so caught up in the affairs of our busy lives that we hardly even notice or have time for God at all. But it is during the times that we least expect—when Dad has a sudden heart attack, when a family member is diagnosed with cancer, when you lose your job and have no idea how to support your family—it is during these cold, dark, and fearful periods of our lives that we turn to Jesus Christ, who leads us through the valley of tears, who guides us in the way of peace, and who has been patiently waiting for us our entire lives to answer His call to covenant love.

*God's Expectation of Man* ("Be fruitful and multiply, and fill the earth and subdue it"). We live in a world that increasingly rejects life: life on a material level, and life on the deeper and more profound spiritual level. It should come as no surprise, then, that we are increasingly conflicted about life. When we close ourselves to the Holy Spirit, then all of life—both in our perception and our experience of it—becomes distorted. We cannot, in a sense, live life as it is meant to be lived, as it truly exists, if we are not open to participating in the life of the Spirit.

Left to ourselves, untutored by God, unhealed by grace, untransformed by love, we would become increasingly singular, individual beings. Individualism, however, is not the primary vocation of man; he is not a being unto himself. Ultimately, men are not called to remain within themselves but to grow in unity and communion with one another. This dynamic of relational interdependence, of man existing in and needing community, is rooted in the life of God, who by nature exists as a Family.

The third Person of the Trinity, God the Holy Spirit, is the Lord and Giver of life. This truth expresses the dual dimension of God's immanent character and bears witness to the very essence of God's divine nature—love and life in communion—that dwells within man, who is made in His image and likeness. The apostle John captures this insight beautifully: God is love, and he who lives in love, lives in God, and God lives in him.[16]

The love-enabling dimension includes conjugal love, which is the unique love that a man and a woman share between each other in a marriage covenant. This unity within the complementarity of their being speaks to the capacity of the body to reveal the person and recognizes the first act of conjugal love as "self-gift": the mutually consenting, self-sacrificing exchange of intimate communion between spouses, where each spouse makes a complete gift of himself to the other. Conjugal love is an animating and vivifying love that enlivens covenantal marriage. In turn, the marriage covenant protects the fecundity of the conjugal love that enlivens it.

There is also a life-giving dimension of covenant love that is inextricably woven into the fabric of conjugal love: the procreation and education of children. Through marriage, the Lord calls spouses and enables them to be co-creators with Him, as well as educators and nurturers of new human lives. God desires husbands and

---

[16] See 1 Jn 4:16. Also, "God pours out His love into our hearts through the Holy Spirit, who has been given to us. Thus the first and most necessary gift is that charity by which we love God above all things and our neighbor because of God. If that love ... is to grow and bring forth fruit in the soul, each one of the faithful must willingly hear the Word of God and with the help of His grace act to fulfill His will" (LG 42).

wives to be fruitful and multiply, not only in numbers, but also in faith and sanctity, bringing up Christian children in the love and service of God.

Raising children is what makes marriage distinct from any other kind of human relationship or institution. People who are friends tend to be united by a common cause or interest, and, within this context, men and women often have close, even lifelong friendships filled with companionship and mutual assistance. But unlike a close friendship, marriage is a covenant having as its primary ends *both* unitive (loving) *and* procreative (life-giving) dimensions. Marriage is a mutual commitment to build a community of faith and love into which new human life can be welcomed, educated, and cherished. Therefore, marriage must, by definition, be open to new life, and spouses must be willing to devote themselves generously to their children and care for them selflessly. In this way, husbands and wives in marriage subordinate themselves to an extrinsic good, to a good that is beyond themselves, in imitation of the Lord Jesus Christ: "Greater love has no man than this, than a man lay down his life for his friends."[17]

Moreover, children, in a very real way, contribute substantially to the spiritual welfare of their parents. Parents dedicate years of their lives and expend tremendous amounts of time, energy, happiness, and heartache for their children. The practice of this kind of self-sacrificing, self-giving, persevering love can sanctify the souls of mothers and fathers in the course of raising their children. Children, as the principal fruit and expression of conjugal love, are nourished in faith and love by their parents' care for them, while parents grow in faith and love in filling the hearts of their children. Thus, marriage paves the road to holiness precisely because moms and dads, with the help of God, give life and love to their children who, in turn, as the greatest gift of marital life, not only bring parents deep emotional joys and sorrows but also give husbands and wives a path to heaven that goes through their own hearts.

God also charged man with the responsibility of exercising "dominion over the fish of the sea and over the birds of the air and every other living thing that moves upon the earth."[18] Being made

---

[17] Jn 15:13.
[18] Gen 1:28; cf. Gen 9:3 and Wis 9:2–3.

in God's image and likeness, man shares in the Father's love and life personally, both in His body and in His industry. King David, in contemplating the profound mystery of man's participation in the life of God, marveled at the grandeur of Yahweh's divine providence: "What is man that you should keep him in mind; mortal man that you care for him? Yet, you have made him little less than a god; with glory and honor you crowned him, gave him power over the works of your hand, put all things under his feet."[19] Thus, in acknowledging his role as caretaker and steward over God's creation, man discovers both integrity and nobility in the work entrusted to him, through which he gives praise and glory to God.

A cursory glance at the reality of human existence both around us and within us, however, clearly reveals that we still have much to achieve. In spite of the spectacular strides in science and technology— and the still untapped potential of innovations yet to come—we find that man has failed to uphold God's command to "rule the world in holiness and righteousness".[20] In 1964, the Reverend Dr. Martin Luther King Jr. noted that "there is a sort of spiritual poverty which stands in glaring contrast to our scientific and technological abundance. The richer we have become materially, the poorer we have become morally and spiritually."[21] The Church echoes this sentiment in our own day: "The problem is not simply economic and technological; it is moral and spiritual."[22] We have learned to process complex data at billions of computations per second and have developed intricate surgical methods and procedures that have prolonged and enhanced our lives, but somehow we still cannot manage to live in peace with each other and in harmony with our world.

So how do we restore balance and unity both in our world and in ourselves? By truly living the greatest commandment: "You shall love the Lord your God with all your heart, and with all your soul,

---

[19] Ps 8:4–6.

[20] Wis 9:3.

[21] Martin Luther King Jr., "The Quest for Peace and Justice" (Nobel lecture, University of Oslo, Oslo, Norway, December 11, 1964).

[22] John Paul II and Patriarch Bartholomew I of Constantinople, Declaration on Environment Signed by Pope and Patriarch Bartholomew of Constantinople, "We Are Still Betraying the Mandate God Has Given Us", June 10, 2002, available on Zenit.org, June 11, 2002, http://www.zenit.org/en/articles/declaration-on-environment-signed-by-pope-and-patriarch -of-constantinople.

and with all your mind. This is the great and first commandment. And a second is like it, You shall love your neighbor as yourself."[23] Every aspect of our approach to social and environmental responsibility must be in accord with the dignity of the person and a genuine sense of fellowship and solidarity with all men. In this way, the communitarian nature of man, through the free-willed gift of himself in love, extends beyond the boundaries of his family to all of humanity. This is the harmony sought by Christ as He prayed to his Father "that they may be one even as we are one ... that the love with which you have loved me may be in them, and I in them."[24] This unity in Christ demands a reorientation of man's moral compass toward its true heading: toward the East, to Christ. He is the New Dawn from heaven that gives light to those who dwell in darkness and the shadow of death, and who guides our feet into the way of peace and, through His Church, into the way of truth.[25]

Man's radical conversion in Christ and his adoption of a truly Christian ethos is just the first step to building a better world. Man must now take the richness, beauty, and truth of Catholic moral and social teaching and apply it to all aspects and areas of human development. "A new approach and a new culture are needed, based on the centrality of the human person within creation and inspired by environmentally ethical behavior stemming from our triple relationship to God, to self, and to creation. Such an ethics fosters interdependence and stresses the principles of universal solidarity, social justice and responsibility in order to promote a true culture of life."[26]

Not only does humanity benefit from God's generous distribution of particular talents and abilities among men; God is also able to use human history, even the everyday course of events, to bring about His divine plan. In the Incarnation, where the Eternal Word became enfleshed in the womb of the Virgin Mary, God the Father says something wonderful about all of us made in His image and

---

[23] Mt 22:37–39. Cf. Deut 6:5 and Lev 19:18.

[24] Jn 17:22, 26. The Second Vatican Council, reflecting on this very point, notes that when Jesus "prayed to the Father ... He implied a certain likeness between the union of the divine Persons, and in the union of God's sons in truth and charity. This likeness reveals that man, who is the only creature on earth which God willed for itself, cannot fully find himself except through a sincere gift of himself" (GS 24).

[25] Cf. Lk 1:78–79.

[26] John Paul II and Patriarch Bartholomew I, "We Are Still Betraying the Mandate".

likeness: that we are called to draw deeply from the Fountain of Life, that we possess the spark of the divine within us, and that we have the freedom to abandon ourselves in His love. Mary shows us firsthand through her incredible witness and example of obedience in faith how to live in the presence of God.[27]

Despite our sins, the God of love, in His infinite mercy, does not leave us without hope. He intervenes in human history, setting into motion a plan for man's redemption: since it was through the heart of love that sin entered into the world, it will be through the heart of love that God effects salvation for the world. The covenant of love and life lost through the no of the "mother of all living" (Gen 3:20) will be restored in Christ through the yes of the Mother of the Redeemer. This is why men, if we are to overcome our slavery to sin and truly serve the heart of love, must foster a deeper affection for and devotion to the Blessed Virgin Mary. Eve offered us fruit born from the tree that lead to death; the New Eve brings forth the fruit of her womb, who gives us everlasting life.

After the Fall in chapter 3 of the Book of Genesis, God says to Satan, "I will put enmity between you and the woman, and between your seed and her seed; he shall bruise your head, and you shall bruise his heel."[28] This verse is critical to our understanding of the role the Blessed Mother would play in the fullness of time.

> Since the "seed" of the woman must be Jesus Christ, the seed of victory who will triumph over the seed of sin, therefore the woman must ultimately refer to Mary, the Mother of Jesus Christ.... This is a

---

[27] "Mary figured profoundly in the history of salvation and in a certain way unites and mirrors within herself the central truths of the faith. Hence when she is being preached and venerated, she summons the faithful to her Son and His sacrifice, and to love for the Father" (LG 65).

[28] Gen 3:15. This passage is often referred to as the protoevangelium (the first Gospel). Mariologist Mark Miravalle, S.T.D., makes the following observation regarding "he shall bruise your head": "There has been some modern biblical discussion over whether the pronoun referring to the person who crushes the head of the serpent should be 'he' or 'she'.... Since some male Hebrew pronouns from the Old Testament can be also understood in the feminine sense, the female translation of 'she' remains a legitimate translation. Nonetheless, some recent translators have changed the traditional translation of 'she' to 'he.' Regardless of the gender of the pronoun, what is clear in the text is that the Woman is integrally involved with the seed of victory, Jesus Christ" (Mark Miravalle, Introduction to Mary: The Heart of Marian Doctrine and Devotion, 3rd ed. [Santa Barbara, Calif.: Queenship Publishing, 2006], 24–25).

great prophetic verse which foretells a victory over sin in the future, a victory only possible through Jesus Christ, and hence the woman who is to be future mother of this victorious seed must refer to Mary.[29]

Enmity was also established between the woman and Satan ("he shall bruise your head, and you shall bruise his heel"). But how can we be certain that the "woman" spoken of here in Genesis is the Blessed Virgin Mary and not Eve?

Note that in the narrative of Genesis 3:15, God is addressing the snake alone, yet the snake's punishment involves both he and the "woman" who, at first glance, appears to be Eve. Eve receives her consequence for sin in Genesis 3:16, but Satan is not mentioned. Yet the snake's rebuke involves both he *and* the "woman". If Satan's reproof includes both parties, it makes sense that God would admonish them together.

The problem is resolved when you realize that God is speaking to Satan alone precisely because the woman in Genesis 3:15 is *not* Eve. The "woman" referenced here is the same woman who will be with our Lord at the wedding feast of Cana ("O woman, what have you to do with me?"[30]). It is the same woman who our Lord, from the Cross, entrusted to the apostle John's care ("When Jesus saw his mother, and the disciple whom he loved standing near, he said to his mother, 'Woman, behold, your son!' "[31]). It is the same woman who is "clothed with the sun, with the moon under her feet, and on her head a crown of twelve stars".[32] The Lord speaks only to the snake because of the three figures in the Garden; only Satan will be present when Genesis 3:15 is fulfilled.

Additionally, the verse prophesies complete and perfect opposition between the seed of the woman and the seed of Satan. However, in the conjugal union, it is the man who provides the seed, not the woman. The woman of Genesis 3:15, therefore, could not be Eve, because her offspring were conceived with her husband's seed: "Now Adam knew Eve his wife, and she conceived and bore Cain.... And again, she bore his brother Abel.... And Adam knew his wife again,

[29] Miravalle, *Introduction to Mary*, 24.
[30] Jn 2:4.
[31] Jn 19:26.
[32] Rev 12:1.

and she bore a son and called his name Seth".[33] At the Incarnation, Mary did not receive a "seed" but was overshadowed by the Holy Spirit and was filled with the Word of God.[34] The physical body of Jesus was conceived in Mary's womb, and the Word became flesh through her "seed", assuming a human nature.

Jesus, as the Son of God, possesses a perfect divine nature from all eternity. Jesus, as the Son of Mary, received his perfect human nature from her; she gave flesh to the Word of God. Mary could not pass on to Jesus what she herself did not possess, which means that Mary must possess a human nature that is in perfect enmity—that is, in total, complete, and perfect opposition—to sin. In other words, Mary is created in the same state of original grace and justice that Eve had when God created her, but, unlike Eve, Mary freely chose to follow God's will perfectly.

The Gospel of Luke also testifies to Mary's sinless nature. At the Annunciation, the angel Gabriel says to the Virgin, "Hail, full of grace, the Lord is with you!"[35]

> In the angelic greeting, Mary's name is nowhere used. Rather, the title "full of grace" is used as a substitute for Mary's name by the angelic messenger of God. These words refer to a fullness of grace, a plenitude of grace that is part of Mary's very nature. So much is Mary's very being full of grace that this title serves to identify Mary in place of her own name, which, biblically, always expresses the person. It is also true that no person with a fallen nature could possess a fullness of grace, a perfection of grace appropriate only for the woman who was to give God the Son an identical, immaculate human nature. Mary was conceived in the plan of God to be the woman who would give her own immaculate nature to God when God became man. Certainly we can see the appropriateness of God receiving a human nature from a human mother, and receiving an immaculate nature from a truly immaculate mother.[36]

---

[33] Gen 4:1–2, 25.

[34] "And the angel said to her, 'The Holy Spirit will come upon you, and the power of the Most High will overshadow you; therefore the child to be born will be called holy, the Son of God'" (Lk 1:35).

[35] Lk 1:28.

[36] Miravalle, *Introduction to Mary*, 65–66.

All of this comes together in Luke's Gospel, where Mary is shown to be the quintessential heart of love. Mary and Joseph bring Jesus to the temple, where "Simeon blessed them and said to Mary his mother, 'Behold, this child is set for the fall and rising of many in Israel, and for a sign that is spoken against (and a sword will pierce through your own soul also), *that thoughts out of many hearts may be revealed.'* "[37] Simeon prophesies that Mary's soul will be pierced through and her heart torn open by the pain of watching her only Son suffer and die.

In accepting God's will in faith and love, Mary allowed herself to become vulnerable before the Lord, and this vulnerability opened her heart to accept the pain of suffering. In this way, the woman Mary—the immaculate heart of love through whom God pours His love into the hearts of men—allows us to unite our souls with hers through the suffering we endure.

Mary's cooperation with the Holy Spirit can only be truly realized in a loving relationship of communion, to which God calls man through suffering. Mary's example of perfect fidelity shows us that this cooperation happens by grace, which is a free gift of God, and the only thing that we contribute is our free-willed fiat (our yes) in submission to God's holy will. The work of salvation belongs to God, but, nevertheless, man has a role through his cooperation.[38] By making ourselves vulnerable before the heart of love, through the pierced soul of the Virgin Mary, we can truly unite our hearts to the heart of Christ and make more fully ours what He has accomplished on the Cross: personal and life-giving union with the Father.

Jesus teaches us that when you love someone with all your heart, with the depth of your soul, and with all your being—when you love someone with a love that is selfless and pure—then you are willing to sacrifice everything for the sake of the other. This is what the Father has done for us in the Incarnation: God has given us the gift of Himself in and through His Word, Jesus Christ, so that we may have life in Him.

Mary says yes to becoming the Mother of God. This affirmation of God's will not only shows complete trust in God but "is from the very beginning a complete openness to the person of Christ, to

---

[37] Lk 2:34–35 (emphasis added).
[38] Cf. Col 1:24 and Phil 1:29–30.

his whole work, to his whole mission. The words, 'Behold, I am the handmaid of the Lord' testify to Mary's openness of spirit: she perfectly unites in herself the love proper to virginity [which is the complete giving of oneself, body and soul, to God] and the love characteristic of motherhood [which is the complete giving of oneself, body and soul, to the raising of children]."[39] The Blessed Mother "served on earth as the loving mother of the divine Redeemer ... and the Lord's humble handmaid. She conceived, brought forth, and nourished Christ. She presented Him to the Father in the temple, and was united with Him in suffering as He died on the cross. In an utterly singular way she cooperated by her obedience, faith, hope, and burning charity in the Savior's work of restoring supernatural life to souls."[40]

Like any child, Jesus had some of the physical features, characteristics, and mannerisms of His mother. People probably said, "He has Mary's eyes", or, "He has His mother's smile." What do people say about us as Catholic men? We are called to imitate Christ and to become living witnesses of our faith every day. Can people see the face of Jesus in us? Can people say to us, "You have the heart of Jesus", or, "I can see the light of Christ burning within you"? Our Baptism and Confirmation leaves the permanent mark of God imprinted on our souls, and like Mary, who bore God in her womb, we bear God within us each time we receive the Blessed Sacrament of the Eucharist. How do we give birth to God's love and truth through this great gift of His love? How well do we bear the labor pains of ridicule from a society that mocks us because of our Catholic faith? How do we give life and meaning to our faith amid a culture of sin and death? Mary shows us the way. The Blessed Mother not only gave birth to God in her body, but she also gave birth to the Word by her example of quiet prayerfulness, deep humility, patient obedience, unwavering trust, and enduring love. We can and *must* make Mary's virtues our own if we are to become the men God created us to be.

Mary is the monstrance—she is the first vessel that held, within the tabernacle of her womb, the Body, Blood, Soul, and Divinity of Jesus Christ. She is the new ark of the covenant. In the Old

---

[39] John Paul II, Encyclical Letter *Redemptoris Mater*, Mother of the Redeemer, March 25, 1987, Vatican translation (Boston: Pauline Books and Media, 1987), no. 39.

[40] LG 61.

Testament, the ark of the covenant built by the Israelites (see Ex 25:8–22) contained the Ten Commandments (see Ex 25:16, 21–22), the manna from heaven (see Ex 16:32–33), and the staff of Aaron, high priest and shepherd of the people (see Num 17:9–10).[41] In the New Testament, Mary—the new ark of the covenant built by God Himself—contained within the tabernacle of her womb the Word-made-flesh (see Jn 1:14), the Bread that came down from heaven (see Jn 6:35–59), and the Good Shepherd, who is both priest and victim (see Jn 10:11–16).

The home of Mary and Joseph was the first Adoration chapel. Mary's visit to her kinswoman Elizabeth was the first Eucharistic procession. "And when Elizabeth heard the greeting of Mary, the child leaped in her womb; and Elizabeth was filled with the Holy Spirit and she exclaimed with a loud cry, 'Blessed are you among women, and blessed is the fruit of your womb! And why is this granted me, that the mother of my Lord should come to me? For behold, when the voice of your greeting came to my ears, the child in my womb leaped for joy.' "[42] When the Blessed Mother arrives, John the Baptist recognizes the presence of God in the womb of Mary and begins to adore. In fact, Elizabeth confirms that her son began leaping for joy after hearing Mary's greeting, meaning that John the Baptist recognized the presence of the Lord in the voice of the Mother of God. Mary is truly the living monstrance of God. Imagine what this world would be like if every man who looked at a woman saw what Saint Joseph saw.

Mary gave the God of the Universe a human face; she gave flesh to the Father's Word. Through the Blessed Mother, "the Holy Trinity is glorified and adored; the Cross is called precious and is venerated throughout the world; the heavens exult; the angels and archangels [rejoice]; demons are put to flight; the devil, that tempter, is thrust down from heaven; the fallen race of man is taken up on high; all creatures possessed by the madness of idolatry have attained

---

[41] Also, Hebrews 9:3–4 in the New Testament reads, "Behind the second curtain stood a tent called the Holy of Holies, having the golden altar of incense and the ark of the covenant covered on all sides with gold, which contained a golden urn holding the manna, and Aaron's rod that budded, and the tables of the covenant".

[42] Lk 1:41–44. The word for "leapt" is *skírtáo* in Greek and *dalag* in Hebrew. The word is often used to describe movement similar to a deer or goat. See Is 35:6 and 2 Sam 22:30.

knowledge of truth; believers receive holy baptism; the oil of gladness is poured out; the Church is established throughout the world; pagans are brought to repentance."[43]

God has shown both the depth of his love and His abiding respect for the dignity of our human nature by becoming man. Through Mary, God wants us to know that He understands what it is like to live in the depths of poverty—that He understands what it is like to experience great sadness and humiliation, unbelievable pain and suffering, and even the darkness of death itself. God wants us to know that we are not alone, and by becoming enfleshed in the womb of Mary, He shows us a human being like ourselves who humbles herself in love before God and opens her heart to His holy will, devoting herself completely to discipleship in Christ. Therefore, we too, by her perfect example of what it means to be fully human, can share in the divine life of the Trinity and participate in God's saving plan for the destiny of all mankind. Mary shows us that we all must become receptive wombs for God's Word—so that, filled with the Holy Spirit by our Baptism and Confirmation, and nurtured by the Eucharist, we give life to Christ by bearing witness to God's love and truth in the world through our Catholic faith. "Therefore, she is also hailed as a pre-eminent ... member of the Church, and as the Church's model and most excellent example of faith and charity."[44]

---

[43] Cyril of Alexandria, "Homily Delivered at the Council of Ephesus", Dedication of Saint Mary Major, August 5, *Liturgy of the Hours*, vol. 4 (New York: Catholic Book Publishing, 1975), 1272.
[44] LG 53.

# Chapter Three

# Sin and Forgiveness

To acknowledge one's sin, indeed ... to recognize oneself as being a sinner, capable of sin and inclined to commit sin, is the essential first step in returning to God.

—John Paul II, *Reconciliatio et Paenitentia*, no. 13

Not long ago, in our church parking lot, someone broke into our car during Mass. Since then, I often wonder what my reaction would be if I ever came face-to-face with the individual who committed this crime against my family. What would I say to the person who frightened my children, who demolished my family's sense of well-being and security, and who made me feel helpless? I know what I would want to do, but as a man of faith, the more important and significant question is, what does Christ call me to do?

What happened to me, however, pales in comparison to those who have been mentally, emotionally, or physically traumatized. What do you say to the father who abandoned you and your family? What do you say to the person who got you hooked on drugs, alcohol, or porn? What do you say to the person who molested you as a child? What do you say to the drunk driver who killed your spouse? The anger and hatred we feel burns like a fire in our hearts, and we want, more than anything, for the person who hurt us and our families to suffer greatly, even to the point of death.

Yet, in the midst of unimaginable anguish and pain, our Lord calls us to do the seemingly impossible: He tells us that we must forgive. Our Lord gives us no other options and makes no exceptions. It is no mistake that Jesus' most powerful and important parables concern forgiveness. Christ is the Word-made-flesh who dwelt among us, and He saw firsthand how evil and corrupt our human nature can be. Nevertheless, He who can read the hearts of all loves each one of us totally, completely, and unconditionally. He sees our flaws and weaknesses, and through the Sacrament of Reconciliation He forgives, renews, and restores our relationship with him.

We may say to ourselves, "Jesus is God and we are not, so it is much easier for Him to forgive." Yes, Jesus is truly God, but He is also fully man; He worked with human hands and loved with a human heart. He not only taught about forgiveness—He was a living witness and the embodiment of forgiveness itself.

While Jesus hung on the Cross dying, as those who condemned Him to death mocked Him, Jesus prayed to His heavenly Father to "forgive them; for they know not what they do."[1] While enduring agonizing torture and in the midst of excruciating suffering, our Lord pours Himself out in complete and perfect love. Jesus calls us to love as He loves, for it is in the crucified Christ that the true meaning of forgiveness and freedom are revealed. Jesus lives this fully in the total gift of Himself and invites us to share in His life. We are called to live in Christ: to follow Him, to carry the Cross, to pour ourselves out, to sacrifice ourselves in love, and to forgive—for it is in giving ourselves away that we truly find our freedom in God.

Forgiveness was so essential to the purpose and mission of Christ that when the apostles asked Jesus how to pray He gave them the Our Father, in which we ask God to "forgive us our trespasses, as we forgive those who trespass against us."[2] Christ wanted to make a very strong and direct link between God's forgiving us and our forgiving others. Jesus knows the human heart, and when our hearts are angry and bitter, when we harbor deep resentment—even though it may be justified—there is a part of us that is imprisoned by hate, a hate that can diminish or even block being open to forgiveness from others and receiving forgiveness from God.

God the Father's "outpouring of mercy cannot penetrate our hearts as long as we have not forgiven those who have trespassed against us. Love, like the Body of Christ, is indivisible; we cannot love the God we cannot see if we do not love the brother or sister we do see. In refusing to forgive our brothers and sisters, our hearts are closed and

---

[1] Lk 23:34.
[2] Mt 6:12; cf. Mt 6:9–16 and Lk 11:2–4.

this hardness makes us impervious to the Father's merciful love."[3]
"Forgive us our trespasses, as we forgive those who trespass against
us" means "help me, Lord, to forgive others so that I may receive the
forgiveness that You offer me."

Once we begin to live our lives in communion with God and
His holy will, in a spirit of reconciliation and forgiveness, Catholic
men will become witnesses of light, truth, and love's triumph over
sin to a self-centered, confused, and angry world. Jesus says that we
must forgive from the heart because He knows that in order for us
to have eternal life with God, we must participate intimately and
personally—from the depths of our hearts—"in the holiness and the
mercy and the love of our God".[4]

We cannot turn off our feelings or simply forget when someone
hurts us deeply, but the heart that offers itself to the Holy Spirit turns
injury into compassion and transforms the hurt into a prayer for those
who harmed us.[5] This is why Jesus gave the apostles the power to
forgive sins in His name. In the Sacrament of Reconciliation, our
hearts are opened to His grace. We ask God for forgiveness so that,
with clean hearts and steadfast spirits, we can be free to engage in the
difficult task of forgiving others—difficult, but not impossible, for
"with God all things are possible."[6]

Developing an authentic male spirituality allows us to get our spiritual houses in order so that we are well equipped to face the challenges and struggles of the Cross in our everyday lives. But when it
comes to the reality of our weakness and sinfulness—of those actions
that separate us from the love of Christ—it is sometimes easier for us
men to live our lives the way we want instead of completely trusting
in the providence and mercy of God, who calls us to face our fears so
that we can be free to love with our whole being.

Our Lord Himself fully understood this and knew that before He
could begin His public ministry—before He could begin preaching
the Gospel of salvation—He must first go into the desert and face
Satan. We too must go into the desert of our lives and come face-
to-face with our own human frailty. Try as we might to love God

---

[3] *CCC* 2840.
[4] Cf. *CCC* 2842.
[5] Cf. *CCC* 2843.
[6] Mt 19:26.

perfectly at every moment of our lives, the pleasure of sin is sometimes too strong, and we embrace those desires and values that contradict the Gospel: we indulge in acts of self-gratification, we worship at the altar of professional sports, or we make other excuses for not attending Mass every Sunday. We overeat, we drink too much, we mentally and physically abuse those we love, we kill unborn children, we do not stay faithful to our marriage or ordination vows, we steal from our employer, we stop praying, we lie to get out of difficult or embarrassing situations, we talk about people behind their backs, we worry about how much others have instead of counting our own blessings.

The desert can be a dry and lonely place, but our Lord Jesus Christ is the oasis in our spiritual desert. When Jesus emerges from His battle with Satan, He brings a message of hope: "[R]epent, and believe in the gospel [Good News]."[7] Jesus is alive and He enters our desert of sin and fills it with the life-giving waters of forgiveness, mercy, and love, but He does so only when we truly seek and desire to be filled with the Holy Spirit. Jesus gives us the gift of the Sacrament of Reconciliation that restores our broken relationship with God, heals our troubled conscience, and assists us in our struggle against sin.

The story is told of a young man—a faithful Catholic—who, during his lunch hour, decided to go to Confession and attend Mass at a local parish. As the young man was making his way back to his car after Mass, he was tragically struck and killed by a passing motorist. The driver, a fallen-away Catholic who embraced the values of the secular culture and who stopped going to Mass, was also killed in the accident. As both men stood before the seat of judgment, the driver who struck the young man asked Jesus, "Lord, out of all the sins I have ever committed in my life, which one was the worst?" Jesus then unfolded before his eyes all of the mortal sins committed after his last Confession that had taken place many years before. The young man, who had just gone to Confession and Mass, asked the same question: "Lord, out of all the sins I have ever committed in my life, which one was the worst?" Jesus looked at him with a smile and said, "I don't remember."

Jesus tells us that the kingdom of God is at hand, and the sacrament of forgiveness is a sure sign of that kingdom. Reconciliation is

7 Mk 1:15.

designed for spiritual healing and for the renewal of our relationship with Christ. In the case of mortal or serious sin, it restores sanctifying grace, which is the grace we received at our Baptism that "perfects the soul itself to enable it to live with God [and] act by his love."[8] In this beautiful sacrament of God's love and mercy, our sins are forgiven; the slate is washed clean.

Moreover, the *eternal punishment of sin*, that is, sin that makes us incapable of eternal life, is also remitted along with, in part, the *temporal punishment of sin*, which results from the unhealthy attachment to those things that separate us from God.[9] The sacrament also gives us supernatural power to help us avoid sin and occasions of sin in the future.

The Lord Jesus tells us that many are called but the chosen are few.[10] His invitation to share in God's own life is open to all, but even those who accept this invitation will be turned away if they choose to live according to the dictates of the culture and are not prepared to do battle for Christ. Jesus asks us to pick up our Cross and follow Him to eternal life—to turn away from the world's ways and keep our eyes fixed on Him. The gift of the sacraments, given to us by Christ, nourishes and strengthens us on our earthly journey toward everlasting life.

In the Eucharist, which is closely connected to the Sacrament of Reconciliation, Christ has given us the new and everlasting covenant: the self-emptying gift of His eternal love for us. The Eucharist exists to configure us more perfectly to Christ, where He invites us into personal, life-giving communion, and where His love transforms us from the inside out. The sacrifice of the Mass communicates and expresses truth, bears tangible witness to the active presence of Christ in the world, and makes concrete the reality of God's grace. Sin diminishes the effects of the Eucharist within us, and it is through sin that the Eucharistic Christ ceases to be the heart and center of our lives.

Our Holy Father of fond memory, Saint John Paul II, explored the reasons for man's sinfulness by pointing out his failure to recognize

---

[8] *CCC* 2000.
[9] Cf. *CCC* 1472.
[10] See Mt 22:14.

and acknowledge his sinful state.[11] In order for conversion and reconciliation to begin (which is critical in our growth as spiritual men!), this acknowledgment must be made. We must recognize that we are so ensconced in the "horizontal dimension of work and social life"[12] that we often neglect or forget the "vertical dimension", that is, man's life in and with God. The consequence of serious sin is devastating: our deliberate separation from God inevitably leads to separation from the rest of humanity and from all of creation.

Sin has both personal and social dimensions. Sin is personal because it is an individual abuse of freedom: the use of free will to intentionally alienate ourselves from God leads directly to sin. The willful act of sin, which can be influenced by both external and internal factors, "weakens man's will and clouds his intellect",[13] and impairs man's reason and judgment, damaging the relationship with himself and with God in the process. Sin is social in that the individual's sin has an effect on society and the whole human family. Social sin affects not only familial relationships but interpersonal and social relationships as well. This sin manifests itself through violations of basic human rights and privileges, and in the loss of dignity, honor, and freedom in all aspects of human life. From this perspective, we see that "the real responsibility lies with individuals",[14] and so all reconciliation, penance, and conversion must start with each man acknowledging his own sinfulness and turning back to God.

"Sin is before all else an offense against God, a rupture of communion with him [and] with the Church."[15] Sin "sets itself against God's love for us and turns our hearts away from it".[16] Simply stated, sin is choosing self-love and self-gratification over love of God.

---

[11] In John Paul II's 1984 Apostolic Exhortation *Reconciliatio et Paenitentia*, he invites all peoples to listen and respond to the message of the Lord Jesus Christ: "Repent and believe in the Gospel" (Mk 1:15). Throughout this document, the pontiff states that reconciliation and penance are essential elements in man's search to understand himself, his neighbors, and his world. This pursuit leads man to further introspection, to a deeper examination of conscience, and ultimately to the root cause of disunity and divisiveness in creation: sin.

[12] John Paul II, Post-Synodal Apostolic Exhortation *Reconciliatio et Paenitentia* (Reconciliation and Penance), December 2, 1984, no. 13 (hereafter cited as *RP*).

[13] *RP* 16.

[14] Ibid.

[15] *CCC* 1440.

[16] *CCC* 1850.

Scripture lists many types of sins,[17] and the Church evaluates these sins "according to their gravity".[18] The two levels of sin, mortal and venial, define the levels of separateness from God. This distinction is rooted in biblical principles:

> If any one sees his brother committing what is not a deadly [mortal] sin, he will ask, and God will give him life for those whose sin is not deadly. There is sin which is deadly; I do not say that one is to pray for that. All wrongdoing is sin, but there is sin which is not deadly.[19]

Mortal sin is "the act by which man freely and consciously rejects God [and] his law" and lives his life in a way that is "contrary to the Divine will".[20] This type of sin "destroys charity in the heart of man by grave violation of God's law"[21] and, in doing so, destroys our relationship with God, with each other, and with all of creation. "For a sin to be *mortal*, three conditions must together be met: 'Mortal sin is sin whose object is grave matter and which is also committed with full knowledge and deliberate consent.'"[22]

The tenets of subjective truth and moral relativism attempt to rationalize sinful behavior, positing that committing a mortal sin does *not* destroy my relationship with God, since I can rightly follow my conscience regarding the moral law. This kind of thinking (1) contravenes the natural moral law,[23] (2) negates the necessity of a well-formed and enlightened conscience, and (3) leads men to believe that they are the arbiters of truth for themselves.[24] It is this kind of

---

[17] See, for example, Gal 5:19–21.

[18] CCC 1854.

[19] 1 Jn 5:16–17.

[20] RP 17. See also CCC 1855–61.

[21] CCC 1855.

[22] CCC 1857.

[23] See Rom 1:19–20; 2:14–16. Natural law is rooted in the first principles of morality that can be known by practical reason. The core principal that serves as the heart of the natural law is to "do good and avoid evil". Synderesis is habitual knowledge of the natural law, that is, the first general principles of morality (do good and avoid evil). Conscience is taking synderesis and applying it to the specific case; it is the specific application of the general principles of natural law. See CCC 1776–802.

[24] Pope John Paul II is careful to make the distinction between mortal sin and (1) an individual's free determination that orients that individual toward or away from God in the "fundamental option", and (2) those acts that are always intrinsically and objectively evil. The idea of the fundamental option is that each person makes a basic choice whether or not to

thinking that leads a man to believe that after committing a mortal sin he can still receive the Eucharist without having first received the Sacrament of Reconciliation. The criterion for mortal sin becomes whatever he decides it to be. This is not only erroneous but also places a man's soul in eternal danger:

> Whoever, therefore, eats the bread or drinks the cup of the Lord in an unworthy manner will be guilty of profaning the body and blood of the Lord. Let a man examine himself, and so eat of the bread and drink of the cup. For any one who eats and drinks without discerning the body eats and drinks judgment upon himself. That is why many of you are weak and ill, and some have died.[25]

---

love God and to accept His truth. This fundamental orientation toward God is lived out each day of our lives by the individual choices we make to do good. These particular choices are a response to the God of love, who has approached us intimately and personally in Jesus Christ. Through the gift of sanctifying grace, the virtue of divine charity bears us directly toward God, allowing us to love Him and others with divine love. As such, our primary and original love of God is not an explicit, peripheral, and categorical love that manifests itself in outward acts, but rather a noncategorical, transcendental, and athematic love of Him that resides at the very core of our being. It is in this transcendent and dynamic orientation toward God that we grow and develop into authentic persons, that is, we become truly free. However, personal freedom—tainted by concupiscence—also provides man the opportunity to refuse God's grace and thus destroy the fundamental option toward God. The moderate branch of this theory states that there is a distinction, not a separation, between the transcendental and categorical levels of the self, and it is always through concrete acts that one manifests the inner, deeper core. Thus, one can engage in a categorical act that does not reflect the transcendental level of the self and does not change our fundamental option toward God (venial sin). Likewise, one can engage in an act that is, by its nature, mortally sinful and incompatible with our final end, thereby destroying our fundamental option toward God (mortal sin). The radical branch of this theory posits that as long as a categorical act is done in such a way that one does not detest or hate God, then, even though one is knowingly and freely committing a grave act of sin, one's fundamental option remains focused on God. Hence, a wedge is driven between the categorical and transcendental levels of the self, separating them in such a way that external, categorical acts are no longer determinative of the fundamental choice at the core of the being. It denies the fact that the categorical evidences the transcendental and the transcendental expresses itself through the categorical. Thus, for an action to be a mortal sin, it must be an expression of an explicit formal break with God, not reflected on the categorical level, but through our basic freedom of self-determination. Moreover, in this theory, "good" and "evil" acts are eliminated in favor of "right" and "wrong" choices. As such, mortal sin in the radical fundamental option theory becomes a "generic intention"; as long as an individual is sincere, he cannot, through his individual choices, change his fundamental orientation toward God. For more on this topic, see John Paul II, Encyclical Letter *Veritatis Splendor* (The Splendor of Truth), August 6, 1993 (hereafter cited as *VS*).

[25] 1 Cor 11:27–30. See also Lev 22:3.

The act of receiving the Eucharist in a state of mortal sin is so serious, that it led Pope John Paul II to reaffirm the constant teaching of the Church: "I therefore desire to reaffirm that in the Church there remains in force, now and in the future, the rule by which the Council of Trent gave concrete expression to the Apostle Paul's stern warning when it affirmed that, in order to receive the Eucharist in a worthy manner, one must first confess one's sins, when one is aware of mortal sin."[26]

Venial sin is less egregious and "does not deprive the sinner of sanctifying grace, friendship with God, charity and therefore eternal happiness, whereas just such a deprivation is precisely the consequence of mortal sin".[27] "One commits a *venial sin* when, in a less serious matter, he does not observe the standard prescribed by the moral law, or when he disobeys the moral law in a grave matter, but without full knowledge or without complete consent."[28]

In the conscience of man is rooted a "sense of sin" that, along with the moral conscience, has become "seriously clouded"[29] in the modern world. Thus, "when the conscience is weakened, the sense of God is also obscured, and as a result ... the sense of sin is lost."[30] Several key factors have contributed to inadequate and faulty conscience formation in men, including secularism, atheism, the errors made in evaluating the findings of science, poor catechesis, moral and historical relativism, and "when [the sense of sin] is wrongly identified with a morbid feeling of guilt or with the mere transgression of legal norms and precepts".[31]

This is the bottom line: men have lost their sense of sin. We have allowed secular culture to form our consciences and fill us with a false freedom that says, "As long as I am a good person, I don't need anyone to tell me what to do and how to live." In order to restore a proper sense of sin and begin the process of reconciliation and

---

[26]John Paul II, "Address to the Members of the Sacred Apostolic Penitentiary and the Penitentiaries of the Patriarchal Basilicas of Rome", January 20, 1981, in *AAS* 73 (1981), 203. Cf. Ecumenical Council of Trent, Sess. XIII, *Decretum de ss. Eucharistia*, chapter 7 and canon 11: DS 1647, 1661.

[27]*RP* 17. See also *CCC* 1855, 1862–63.

[28]*CCC* 1862.

[29]*RP* 18.

[30]Ibid.

[31]Ibid.

penance, we must be reminded "of the unchangeable principles of reason and faith" that the Church professes in her teaching and by her example, in catechesis, biblical theology, openness to the Magisterium, and through a "more careful practice of the sacrament of penance".[32] The Sacrament of Reconciliation strengthens us and helps us to realize our duty and obligation toward ongoing conversion. Every day we must convert again and again, and return to Christ anew. We must carefully examine our consciences and practice contrition daily, making ourselves more deeply aware of God's constant and sustaining presence in our lives.

Like Paul on the road to Damascus, sometimes we need to be knocked down so that the Lord can raise us up, because "if the Lord does not build the house, in vain do its builders labor."[33] Sometimes God must humble us in order to exalt us. With contrite and humble hearts open to God's will, He uses our limitations and weaknesses to show forth His majesty. By the power of God we can no longer make excuses: "God can't possibly want to do anything with me. What do I have to give?" "I'm single and raising three children." "I'm retired and can't do much anymore." "I'm just trying to survive to the next paycheck." "I don't have a college education." "I'm permanently disabled." "I'm taking medication for clinical depression." What the Lord promised Paul, he also promises us: " 'My grace is sufficient for you, for my power is made perfect in weakness.' I will all the more gladly boast of my weaknesses, that the power of Christ may rest upon me. For the sake of Christ, then, I am content with weaknesses, insults, hardships, persecutions, and calamities; for when I am weak, then I am strong."[34]

To obey means to become "weak" before God. Obedience is a free act of love on our part in which the mind and the heart resolutely submits to God's will in faith. However, because of our inherent sinfulness, which hinders the work of God in the interior life, the gift of grace must necessarily precede the obedience of faith so that it becomes easier for us to accept and believe the truth. It is when we

---

[32] Ibid. For a detailed study of the pope's understanding of the relationship between faith and reason, see John Paul II, Encyclical Letter *Fides et Ratio* (Faith and Reason), September 14, 1998.

[33] Ps 127:1.

[34] 2 Cor 12:9–10.

use our free will to give ourselves to God fully and completely, when we are no longer blinded by the darkness of immorality, selfishness, and pride, that our minds and hearts are opened to the light of truth and "seek to know and do God's will".[35] Obedience to God is the source of life and blessing; it is listening to God's voice and allowing that voice to change our lives; it is freely submitting "to the word that has been heard, because its truth is guaranteed by God, who is Truth itself".[36]

We begin this journey of deepening our spiritual lives as men just as Jesus did—in the desert with Satan. But we do not go into battle unarmed: we have the weapons of prayer and fasting—prayer, which gives us strength, and fasting, which empties us so that God can fill us. Becoming more and more aware of God's active, loving presence in our lives helps us to become more aware of our own sinfulness and have a more fruitful experience of reconciliation with God, who is Love and Mercy.

Between my second and third years of graduate school, I had an opportunity to study theology in Rome. All expenses were covered except for the air fare, which I could not afford. When I told my mother what I was planning to do, she gladly gave me the money.

However, a day or two before purchasing the plane ticket, I received a phone call from my mother. She informed me that my younger brother was in prison, was in serious danger of losing temporary custody of his son, and that I was to send my airfare money to bail my brother out of jail.

This news did not sit well with me, and I was sorely disappointed. I reminded my mother that I was the one who was "Mr. Responsible", which was the nickname given to me by my family as a teenager. I was the one who became an Eagle Scout. I was the one who left the monastery to run the house and take care of the family while she recovered from open heart surgery. I was the first person in the family to go to college and now had the opportunity of a lifetime to study theology in Rome. I was the one who spent most of my life putting others first and myself second.

I also reminded my mother that my brother dropped out of high school, that he quit the Navy, and that he had three children from

[35] CCC 1814.
[36] CCC 144.

three different women and never really put forth the effort to be a real father to them. He was the one who, through his entire life, thought only of himself. I told her that this is an opportunity for my brother to realize the seriousness of life, and that imprisonment may be the key to turning his life around. My mother listened patiently to my plea and, in the end, made the decision that any mother would: she told me how proud she was of me, that she loved me, and then ordered me to send the money.

But what hurt me more than not going to Rome was that I did not even receive so much as a "thank you" from my brother or any acknowledgment of the sacrifice that was made for him.

Many parallels in our lives as men can be found in the parable of the prodigal son.[37] The parable is about sin and forgiveness, yet we often do not like to hear about or talk about sin, because it is so personal. Sin makes us uncomfortable. Sin embarrasses us. Sin opens deep wounds that are often painful. If talking about sin bothers us, then we should look at the Cross. Jesus took all of our sins upon Himself: He was uncomfortable; He was embarrassed; His body endured deep wounds that were painful. Jesus took our sins personally. He is the Lamb of God who takes away the sins of the world. There is nothing we can ever do, there is no sin too great, and there is no hurt too deep that cannot be forgiven by the rich mercy and healing power of God's life-giving love.

In the parable, the younger son asks his father to give him the share of his estate. God, in His infinite wisdom and love, has given each of us a share of His estate as well: He made us in His image and likeness—called to serve, protect, and defend our families, the Church, and the culture. He has given us the fullness of truth in His Son. He has given us His Holy Spirit, the Lord and Giver of life. He has invited us into intimate and life-giving communion with Him.

The younger son goes off and squanders his inheritance, freely spending everything. Committing sin does not mean we are "bad" people. After all, in Genesis, God creates man and woman and says they are very good. Sin means that we are human, that we make mistakes—sometimes really big, scary, and messy ones—and that

---

[37] See Lk 15:11–32.

we are still dealing with the effects of Original Sin. We inherently desire and are attracted to truth, goodness, and beauty but, at the same time, are inclined toward sin. Sin occurs when we freely choose to put us first and God second, and when we think we know more than God. All of us have sinned to some degree or another, and it is for our sins that Jesus gave His life on the Cross.

After the younger son spent everything, a famine struck and he found himself in dire need, supporting himself by tending swine. Serious sin empties us of God's life, and creates a famine, a desert, within us. We wallow in the pig pen of overindulgence and self-gratification. We hit bottom. This is the point when we realize that we are not the center of the universe and truly begin to find answers to the big questions of life.

The younger son then "comes to his senses" and acknowledges his sinfulness. This is the most difficult part of our journey to forgiveness as men: admitting that we are wrong. As hard as it may be, we must lift up our Crosses and follow Jesus. We must foster a deeply personal relationship with Jesus Christ, the pillar of our salvation, through whom we can begin to understand the depths of the Father's loving kindness. If we follow Christ's example and allow ourselves to be open to the Father, who is rich in mercy, we can "evoke in the soul a movement of conversion, in order to redeem it and set it on course toward reconciliation".[38] A man's response to God's love and mercy must be that of the prodigal son: recognition of our sinfulness, humility before the Father, and the conversion of our hearts, minds, and wills. If the power of the Eucharist is to have any effect on our lives, we must first acknowledge our human weakness and need for the healing power of God's life-giving love. We must die to sin so that we can live in truth.

The younger son confesses his sins saying, "Father, I have sinned against heaven and before you."[39] "Those who approach the sacrament of Penance obtain pardon from God's mercy for the offense committed against him."[40] This is why the son does not simply pray to God to have his sins forgiven: he goes to his father just as we

---

[38] RP 20.
[39] Lk 15:21.
[40] CCC 1422.

go to our father—our priest.[41] Priestly absolution refers to the fact that Christ "entrusted the exercise of the power of absolution to the apostolic ministry which he charged with the 'ministry of reconciliation'".[42] In John's Gospel we read, "Jesus said to them again, 'Peace be with you. As the Father has sent me, even so I send you.' And when he had said this, he breathed on them, and said to them, 'Receive the Holy Spirit. If you forgive the sins of any, they are forgiven; if you retain the sins of any, they are retained.' "[43] "God remains the principal agent in the forgiveness of sin, but He now acts through ministers chosen and authorized by Himself."[44] In the Sacrament of Reconciliation, the priest is the tool and instrument that God has chosen to use for our help and for our salvation.

The father runs to embrace his son while he is still a long way off. Likewise, we do not have to wait until we feel close enough to God to turn back to Him and ask for forgiveness. We don't have to wait for the right time. We just need to head in the right direction, just a little way, and the Lord will run to meet us with His grace.

> But if a wicked man turns away from all his sins which he has committed and keeps all my statutes and does what is lawful and right, he shall surely live; he shall not die. None of the transgressions which he has committed shall be remembered against him; for the righteousness which he has done he shall live.... Cast away from you all the transgressions which you have committed against me, and get yourselves a new heart and a new spirit!... For I have no pleasure in the death of any one, says the Lord GOD; so turn, and live.[45]

---

[41] It was always understood that the priest was the one who interceded for, and made atonement to God on behalf of, the people. Leviticus 5:1–4, for example, lists a series of sins that one could commit and then, beginning in verse 5, states: "When a man is guilty in any of these, he shall confess the sin he has committed, and he shall bring his guilt offering to the LORD for the sin which he has committed ... and the priest shall make atonement for him for his sin" (vv. 5–6). Cf. Lev 4:13–20; 4:22–26; 4:27–31; 4:32–35; 5:5–13; 5:11–18; 6:22–29; 12:6–8; 14:15–31; 16:20–24, 32–34; 19:20–22; Mt 16:18–19; 18:18, 2 Cor 5:18–20; and Jas 5:13–16. Over and over again, we see that when the Jews needed their sins forgiven they went to the priest. Jesus Christ is the true High Priest, and He has given the authority to forgive sins in His name to His earthly priests.

[42] CCC 1442.

[43] Jn 20:21–23.

[44] Clarence McAuliffe, S.J., *Sacramental Theology* (St. Louis: B. Herder, 1958), 232.

[45] Ezek 18:21–22, 31–32.

The story of the prodigal son also tells us that the elder brother, who has been faithful to the father, cannot comprehend or accept the forgiveness shown by the father to the repentant son.[46] Once we begin to live our lives in communion with God and His will, in a spirit of reconciliation and penance, the world, still mired in self-centeredness, confusion, and anger, will reject us and our way of thinking. We must stand firm in the face of this adversity and use it as an opportunity to fulfill our prophetic mission to evangelize. By spreading the Gospel message, we become extensions of Christ to others; we become lights to those who are in darkness. Our words may often fall on deaf ears, and we may appear to accomplish nothing, but therein lies the mystery of Christ. Someone "in the world" who listens to Christ's message through us may, by the grace of God and in God's own time, begin the process that leads to conversion, reconciliation, and the loving acceptance of what is true, good, and beautiful.

Finally, the father says to his eldest son, "[Y]our brother was dead, and is alive; he was lost, and is found."[47] A few years ago, I attended my high school reunion in Newark, New Jersey. When my brother found out I was coming home, he absolutely insisted that I stay with him. He picked me up at the airport, and we drove back to his apartment. He had purchased a brand-new bed just for me. He had a hot breakfast ready and waiting for me every morning. He gave me unlimited use of his Lexus SUV. He had a very responsible and demanding job in which he excelled. He now took great and loving care of his children, making sure that they got to meet and spend time with their uncle. We stayed up until three in the morning most nights talking, playing guitars, and watching action-adventure and horror movies just as we did as kids.

---

[46] In *Reconciliatio et Paenitentia*, Pope John Paul II uses the parable of the prodigal son to show both the inexhaustible love and mercy of God the Father "who is always willing to forgive" (no. 5) and how man identifies with both sons in the parable. Humanity is both the prodigal son, who, in his sinfulness, separates himself from God and uses his free will to follow his own plans and designs, and the elder son: jealous, selfish, and hard-hearted in the face of the father's forgiveness, which he does not understand and cannot accept. Both sons, and indeed all of humanity, need a "profound transformation of hearts through the discovery of the Father's mercy" (no. 6). This reconciliation can only come in and through Jesus Christ, who liberates man from sin and reconciles man to Himself, and to all of creation, and who restores the "communion of grace with God" (no. 7).

[47] Lk 15:32.

I was deeply impressed with the change that had occurred in my brother's life. I was proud of him and asked him, "What made the difference?" He looked at me with a face that I had never seen from him before and he said, "I know how important that trip to Rome was for you, and I wanted to show you that the money didn't go to waste." The prodigal son had come home.

## Chapter Four

# Truth and Freedom

God created man a rational being, conferring on him the dignity of a person who can initiate and control his own actions. "God willed that man should be 'left in the hand of his own counsel,' so that he might of his own accord seek his Creator and freely attain his full and blessed perfection by cleaving to him." Man is rational and therefore like God; he is created with free will and is master over his acts.

— *Catechism of the Catholic Church*, no. 1730

What does it mean to be free—*truly* free? As we have seen from our study of the creation narratives in Genesis, man is made for covenant relationship with God. In this intimate exchange of love, true freedom is experienced when life-giving communion, which is freely given by God, is freely accepted and reciprocated by man. God, who is Eternal Love, would never forsake this relationship. He would never choose not to love man, since God is, within Himself, total, complete, and perfect Love. Man, on the other hand, as we have seen with our first parents, can choose to use his free will to reject God's love through sin.

God wants man to choose Him freely, and in giving him freedom, rooted in the obedience of faith,[1] man enjoys a special place on earth (the temporal order). If we were already in heaven (the transcendent order), we could no longer use our freedom to sin because, being in the presence of God, we would realize that we have found the One Good that fulfills all of our longings and desires. In this sense, every earthly good can be seen as either "more good"

[1] Cf. Rom 1:1–6.

or "less good" depending upon its compatibility with and orientation toward the Ultimate Good. Ideally, man's intellect, directed by his will and informed by his conscience,[2] actively pursues the best goods in order to satisfy our spiritual longing for the Ultimate Good. Since we directly confront the Ultimate Good only in heaven, we are free on earth in our particular choices to either embrace or refuse God's invitation to participate in His life.

There are two primary ways of understanding and defining the notion of "freedom": freedom as personal and subjective, or freedom as interpersonal and objective. Modern democratic societies pride themselves on being the ultimate example of liberty and personal freedom—of a way of "being" characterized by the popular adage "I am free to do what I want." This subjective freedom is contrary to the genuine, interpersonal freedom that Christ offers us, a freedom that invites us to life-giving love and intimate communion in the heart of the Trinity: "I have come ... not to do my own will, but the will of him who sent me."[3] Objective freedom means living, acting, and "being" in a way commensurate with God's truth rooted in the natural law.[4]

Our culture tells us that freedom means "independence"—that I don't need to subject myself to principles that are true in themselves but that truth can be changed to fit popular trends or my particular situation. John the Apostle, the disciple whom Jesus loved, reminds us that man's deepest truth and identity is to be in God: "God is love, and he who abides in love abides in God, and God abides in him."[5] The truth of God's ever abundant and merciful love is rooted in authentic freedom, a freedom "from" and a freedom "for": the freedom from sin so that we can be free for God.

---

[2] See chapter 3, footnote 23.

[3] Jn 6:38.

[4] The natural moral law states that there is a transcendent truth planted within us to which we have access by reason alone (cf. Rom 2:15). The natural law is designed to make us free since "human freedom finds its authentic and complete fulfillment precisely in the acceptance of the moral law given by God". Man, then, is truly free and genuinely happy when he uses his free will to align himself with the transcendent truths of the moral life "as the response due to the many gratuitous initiatives taken by God out of love for man" (VS 35, 10). For a fuller explanation of the natural law, see the section "Take the Helmet of Salvation" in chapter 8 of this book.

[5] 1 Jn 4:16.

Only in freedom can man direct himself toward goodness. Our contemporaries make much of this freedom and pursue it eagerly; and rightly so, to be sure. Often, however, they foster it perversely as a license for doing whatever pleases them, even if it is evil. For its part, authentic freedom is an exceptional sign of the divine image within man. For God has willed that man be left "in the hand of his own counsel" so that he can seek his Creator spontaneously, and come freely to utter and blissful perfection through loyalty to Him. Hence, man's dignity demands that he act according to a knowing and free choice [that] is personally motivated and prompted from within, neither under blind internal impulse nor by mere external pressure. Man achieves such dignity when, emancipating himself from all captivity to passion, he pursues his goal in a spontaneous choice of what is good, and procures for himself through effective and skillful action, apt means to that end. Since man's freedom has been damaged by sin, only by the help of God's grace can he bring such a relationship with God into full flower. Before the judgment seat of God each man must render an account of his own life, whether he has done good or evil.[6]

Free choice is a necessary prerequisite for spiritual freedom but is diminished (although not completely annihilated) in the person enslaved to sin. When we willingly use our freedom to conform ourselves to God's holy will—to be the person He created us to be and live in a way commensurate with this truth—then we are spiritually free. Spiritual freedom is realized when we lovingly accept God's grace in accord with who we are called to be in truth.[7] When we are spiritually free, we are liberated from our fallen condition and directed toward communion. At the center of God's plan for personal freedom is the creation of man in view of his insertion into Christ—that is, man is created in light of Christ so that man could participate in God's own Trinitarian life in a communion of mutual love. If freedom is willing conformity to the truth of man's being, then freedom is going to free our hopes, fears, dreams, joys, and sorrows—everything we have and everything we are—so that we truly can become brothers in Christ.

At first glance, living according to God's truth seems burdensome because following commandments and living according to a moral

[6] GS 17.

[7] See VS 84–87, esp. 85: "*The Crucified Christ reveals the authentic meaning of freedom; he lives it fully in the total gift of himself* and calls his disciples to share in his freedom" (emphasis in original).

code goes against society's view and understanding of freedom.[8] In God's design for authentic freedom, laws and commandments are at the service of the practice of love. In fact, the commandments are summed up in the Great Commandment of love: "[L]ove the Lord your God with all your heart, and with all your soul, and with all your strength, and with all your mind; and your neighbor as yourself."[9] Categorical resistance (and even mindless obedience) to the commandments is an imperfect freedom, a partial "slavery", until it becomes our delight to obey them. The truth is that "the more one does what is good, the freer one becomes. There is no true freedom except in the service of what is good and just. The choice to disobey and do evil is an abuse of freedom and leads to 'the slavery of sin.'"[10]

Man is created yearning for the fullness of freedom in God while still mired in concupiscent love.[11] Spiritual freedom comes when we

[8] Transcendent truth is not heteronomous, that is, it is not something extrinsically forced upon us without any regard for our uniqueness as persons. Rather, true freedom is built upon a participated theonomy, which says that objective truth found in the natural law—which may seem alien to us at first—is in reality designed for our total and complete happiness. This is a law that comes from God, and our inmost being willingly partakes in this law which is ultimately friendly to our nature, as opposed to the law being imposed from without against our free will. See VS 18, 41, 43, 48, 71, 78, 79, 95–96, esp. 41: "*Human freedom and God's law meet and are called to intersect*, in the sense of man's free obedience to God and of God's completely gratuitous benevolence towards man. Hence obedience to God is not ... a *heteronomy*, as if the moral life were subject to the will of something all-powerful, absolute, extraneous to man and intolerant of his freedom.... Others speak ... of *theonomy*, or *participated theonomy*, since man's free obedience to God's law effectively implies that human reason and human will participate in God's wisdom and providence" (emphasis in original). Moreover, there is no tension or opposition between individual freedom and a common, transcendent nature. Secular culture, which wants to divorce the two, says, "If I'm really free, how can there be a common, transcendent nature, which is binding?" As we have seen, within the very nature of man himself is a universality that does not ignore the individuality and uniqueness of each person. A transcendent principle in the moral life says that every individual, regardless of age, race, sex, etc., has an equal dignity. This can be known in its fullness by the truths of revelation, a portion of which can be known by reason alone. In Romans 1:19–20 and 2:14–16, Saint Paul says that everyone can know the basic truths of the natural, moral law without revelation. Therefore, secular culture cannot claim invincible ignorance for certain evils, because they should know by virtue of the natural law written in their hearts that certain actions are wrong or, at least, intrinsically disordered.

[9] Lk 10:27.

[10] CCC 1733. See also Jn 8:31–38.

[11] "In consequence of original sin human nature, without being totally corrupted, is wounded in its natural powers. It is subject to ignorance, to suffering, and to the dominion of death and is inclined toward sin. This inclination is called *concupiscence*" (*Compendium of the Catechism of the Catholic Church*, Official English Translation, 3rd printing [Washington, D.C.: USCCB, 2006], no. 77; emphasis in original).

willingly conform to the truth of who we are—to love with the love of Christ—but sin impedes our efforts to make this choice. Because of his fallen nature, man becomes frustrated in discovering that he cannot always live according to the absolute truth of God's will. Hence, he comes face-to-face with the realization that he is vulnerable—that apart from God he is finite and imperfect—and he equates this vulnerability with weakness. In turning toward and aligning himself with subjective truth, which he perceives as a strength, man fails to recognize that his freedom is, in a very real way, betraying his openness to the True and Greater Good.

Put another way, when man learns that relationship with God requires adherence to objective moral norms, his inclination to sin leads him to conclude that objective truth is a prohibition against freedom. As a result, he turns inward. Rather than choosing the transcendent good of absolute truth that *strengthens* his relationship with God (man as "other-centered"),[12] man exercises his free will to reject God's truth and merciful love (man as "self-centered"). As a result, concupiscence leads man to choose transient temporal "goods" rooted in relativism and subjective truth. In choosing the lesser good, man's freedom acknowledges his choice to sin. The more man freely chooses to sin and place his own truth above God's truth, and the more sin becomes a habit and vice, the more man becomes enslaved to the fleeting goods of this world; he becomes bound to disordered love and constrained by disordered attachments. In this way sin establishes an addictive pattern that keeps men from conforming to the truth of their being. Herein lies the irony: a man becomes enslaved by the very same subjective and relativistic principles that he thinks makes him free. A man's participation in pornography, masturbation, contraception, and his capitulation to greed and lust are just a few tangible examples of this reality.

Consequently, free choice itself must be set free. It is the crucified Christ who sets freedom free so that it may realize its perfect end: covenant relationship. Men need the indwelling love of Christ to

---

[12] For example, in 2 Cor 12:9–10, we read, "'My grace is sufficient for you, for my power is made perfect in weakness.' I will all the more gladly boast of my weaknesses, that the power of Christ may rest upon me. For the sake of Christ, then, I am content with weaknesses, insults, hardships, persecutions, and calamities; for when I am weak, then I am strong."

set us free from the bondage of sin, which comes through the Spirit, who leads us into all truth, for it is the truth that sets us free.[13]

Consider this example. As you enter a room, you notice a violin lying on a table. One of the strings has been removed from the violin and is laid on the table next to the violin. Our culture would tell us that the string on the table is free: it is no longer subject to the "rules and regulations" of the violin and can now do whatever it wants. In other words, the string is no longer bound by the constraints of the violin (the fingerboard, bridge, and tuning pegs) and can now "be itself". But what is the string now free to do? Absolutely nothing! By separating itself from the body of the violin, the string has now becomes useless.

What does this mean for us as men? When we choose subjective truth by separating ourselves from the body of objective truth—from the moral laws and commandments designed not to enslave us but to free us to love fully and completely—we journey down the somber path to emptiness and nothingness. We become slaves as we yield to every carnal desire that makes us feel good, fueled by the whimsical capriciousness of the culture. We become caricatures and poster boys for Satan's mendacity as he sits back and laughs in our faces.

From the Church's perspective, the violin string is not truly free because its full potential is not being actualized; by not freely choosing to be part of the whole, by allowing itself to be freed from that which makes it truly unique—from that which is true, good, and beautiful—the string can never fully be what it was created to be. The Church teaches that by freely submitting ourselves to God's law, to God's loving care, protection, and divine providence, and by making a complete gift of ourselves to the Giver of all gifts, we truly can be godly men. It is only when the string is tethered to the body of the violin, when it is tuned to the unique and proper pitch that it was designed for, and when it is played in harmony with the other strings, that the full potential of not only the string but the entire instrument can be truly realized and fully appreciated.

---

[13] Cf. Jn 8:31–38; cf also *VS* 87: "Jesus, then, is the living, personal summation of perfect freedom in total obedience to the will of God. His crucified flesh fully reveals the unbreakable bond between freedom and truth, just as his Resurrection from the dead is the supreme exaltation of the fruitfulness and saving power of a freedom lived out in truth."

This is why adherence to the Church's teaching, especially in the area of conscience and the moral life, bears tremendous fruits for men who are willing to give themselves over in love to God's law. Whether in the intimate expression of our sexuality, rooted in the lifelong covenant between a husband and a wife, or whether in the intimate expression of celibacy, which anticipates the eternal wedding feast in heaven, God allows His children to participate in His creative, life-giving work. This is the Father's gift to us: to allow us to love as He loves—to allow us to give ourselves to Him fully, completely, and freely, just as Christ poured out His love for us fully, completely, and freely on the Cross.

"By embracing in His human heart the Father's love for men",[14] Jesus showed us that by *freely* choosing to do the Father's will, by using our freedom to choose the good, even suffering and death cannot overpower God's love for us. God literally loves us to death. "In his suffering and death, [Christ's] humanity became the free and perfect instrument of [the Father's] divine love which desires" our salvation.[15] The Father sent His only Son, our Lord Jesus Christ, who is true God from true God, to die in order to show us that in *freely* giving up that which is most precious to us, our very lives, in order to do the Father's will, God will give us everlasting life. "For God so loved the world that he gave his only-begotten Son, that whoever believes in him should not perish but have eternal life. For God sent the Son into the world, not to condemn the world, but that the world might be saved through him."[16] God sent His Son, Jesus the carpenter, to give us the tools of grace, faith, and His own Body and Blood to strengthen us as we carry the Cross in our own lives. Jesus shows us that even in the darkest hour of our lives, God's love knows no end. Even in the hardships of everyday life, God's love knows no bounds. Even in our suffering and death, God's love holds nothing back. It is in these moments—in the total offering of ourselves in love to the Other, in the sublime moment of complete giftedness—that we discover the true meaning of freedom in the Cross of Jesus Christ.

Jesus dwells in man through His Spirit, where He simultaneously accuses and consoles. The Holy Spirit reveals man's sinful nature to

---

[14] *CCC* 609.
[15] Ibid.
[16] Jn 3:16–17.

him and brings him face-to-face with his sins so that he does not continue living a lie. The Spirit then shows mercy and opens man to the
life of Christ. Man's response to the Spirit is to love, and it is through
love that man follows and lives in Christ. In imitation of Christ, man
must bear his Cross; he must pour himself out and sacrifice himself in
love, which is the culmination of freedom.

Christian freedom is the highest pinnacle and the summit of
authentic freedom, not only because "Jesus asks us to follow Him
and to imitate Him along the path of love",[17] but also because "following Christ is the essential and primordial foundation of Christian
morality."[18] Our freedom can also be used poorly when we ignore
our authentic freedom and make ourselves arbiters of good and evil.
When we "disregard the dependence of human reason on Divine
wisdom ... as an effective means for knowing moral truths", we
are left with "the expression of a law which man in an autonomous
manner lays down for himself and which has its source exclusively
in human reason".[19] Moreover, freedom's reliance solely on man's
reason has the opposite effect on the dignity of the individual person.
Whereas the union of human and divine reason leads to the elevation
of human nature, the separation of the two leads to dehumanization.

Satan's pleasure principle—where he takes pleasure out of its proper
context of orientation toward the Ultimate End and elevates it as an
end in itself—is what makes sin so dangerous: we become addicted to
the pleasure. What complicates matters even more is that we live in
a society that promotes and encourages participation in activities that
dehumanize us. The basic tenet of dehumanization states that some
men are not made in the image and likeness of God and, therefore,
have no inherent value and dignity. Contemporary culture uses the
principle of dehumanization to rationalize and justify sinful actions
based in subjective, relativistic truth. For example, when two angry
men are preparing to fight, they often get ready for the encounter
by using dehumanizing language toward each other. The purpose of
this verbal exchange is to strip the other person of his humanity so
that you will not see him as a person. At the point when you have
sufficiently dehumanized the person in your mind, that is, when you

---

[17] VS 20.
[18] VS 19.
[19] VS 36.

have mentally stripped him of his dignity as a person and no longer see him as you see yourself, you are convinced and feel justified in committing an act of violence against him.

In 1857 the Supreme Court in the case of Dred Scott vs. John F. Sanford ruled that black people were property and not human beings. Chief Justice Taney, in his majority opinion, wrote, "[Slaves] had for more than a century before been regarded as beings of an inferior order, and altogether unfit to associate with the white race, either in social or political relations; and so far inferior, that they had no rights that the white man was bound to respect; and that the negro might justly and lawfully be reduced to slavery for his benefit." He continues, "A perpetual and impassable barrier was intended to be erected between the white race and the one which they had reduced to slavery ... and which they then looked upon as so far below them in the scale of created beings, that intermarriages between white persons and negroes ... were regarded as unnatural and immoral, and punished as crimes". After citing the section of the Declaration of Independence that says, "We hold these truths to be self-evident: that all men are created equal; that they are endowed by their Creator with certain unalienable rights", Justice Taney adds insult to injury by stating, "It is too clear for dispute that the enslaved African race were not intended to be included.... The unhappy black race were separated from the white by indelible marks ... and were never thought of or spoken of except as property."[20]

Compare this with the constant and unwavering position of the Magisterium of the Church, who has condemned slavery outright.[21]

---

[20] All excerpts are from "Chief Justice Taney: Mr. Chief Justice Taney Delivered the Opinion of the Court", American History from Revolution to Reconstruction and Beyond, accessed January 14, 2015, http://odur.let.rug.nl/~usa/D/1851-1875/dredscott/dred3.htm.

[21] See Fr. Joel S. Panzer, The Popes and Slavery (New York: Alba House, 1996), and Mark Brumley, "Let My People Go: The Catholic Church and Slavery", This Rock, July/August 1999, 16–21. A number of Catholic Church antislavery documents in Latin were reprinted by Dr. Jaime Luciano Balmes, El Protestantismo Comparado Con El Catolicismo (Barcelona, Spain: Brusi, 1849), translated into English by C.J. Hanford and Robert Kershaw, in European Civilization: Protestantism and Catholicity Compared (Baltimore: Murphy, 1850). Examples that Dr. Balmes cited include data from the following years: A.D. 441 (censuring slavers); A.D. 549 (church buildings as refuges for escaping slaves); A.D. 566 (excommunication-of-slavers proviso); A.D. 583 (Church issuance of freedom papers); A.D. 585 (use of Church property to free slaves); A.D. 595 (freeing entrants to monastic life); A.D. 616 (liberty restoration proviso); A.D. 625 (banning new slaves; use of Church property to free current slaves); A.D. 666 (banning shaving slaves); A.D. 844 (use of Church property to free slaves); and A.D. 922 (defines slave trade as homicide).

Pope after pope, including Popes Adrian I, Pius II, Eugene IV, Gregory XIV, Innocent XI, Benedict XIV, Pius VII, and many others, have strongly advocated against slavery, describing it as immoral, inhuman, and "the enemy of the human race [Satan]".[22] In 1537, 320 years before the Dred Scott Supreme Court decision, Pope Paul III excommunicated those who enslaved the Indians of the Americas.

In 1973 the Supreme Court, in the infamous Roe vs. Wade decision, legalized abortion at all stages of pregnancy. In his majority opinion, Justice Blackmun argued that an examination of common law shows that no one really agrees on when a human life begins— that medical advances have now made the procedure safer for women, and that the mother is more important than the child she is carrying. He adds that if abortion is not allowed, there could be detrimental effects to society. Justice Blackmun states, for example, that the woman's "mental and physical health may be taxed by child care", that "maternity, or additional offspring, may force upon the woman a distressful life and future", and "the continuing stigma of unwed motherhood may be involved." But the most insidious reason he gives is "this right of privacy [found in the 14th Constitutional Amendment] is broad enough to encompass a woman's decision whether or not to terminate her pregnancy" while freely admitting that the Court "need not resolve the difficult question of when life begins. . . . The judiciary, at this point in the development of man's knowledge, is not in a position to speculate as to the answer."[23]

It would seem logical that, before making a decision of such magnitude and permanence, determining the truth of when life begins would be of primary importance and, until such time that it can be determined, one should err on the side of an innocent life. Unfortunately, in our society, choice outweighs truth.

If "no one knows when life begins" is one of the tenets that supports the Roe vs. Wade decision, then one of the legs of the abortion platform is now severely weakened. Since 1973, the scientific discovery of deoxyribonucleic acid, the material that carries the genetic information in chromosomes (commonly referred to as DNA), has

---

[22] Paul III, Encyclical Letter *Sublimus Dei*, May 29, 1527, http://www.papalencyclicals .net/Paul03/p3subli.htm.

[23] All excerpts are from "U.S. Supreme Court Roe v. Wade, 410 U.S. 113 (1973)", Priests forLife.org, accessed January 14, 2015, http://www.priestsforlife.org/government/supreme court/7301roevwade.htm.

shown conclusively, irrefutably, and beyond any doubt that a fetus, from the moment of its conception, is a baby—a human being. Only human beings have human DNA.

Science proves what the Catholic Church has known all along: that life begins when God says it begins—at conception. God has made this abundantly clear in Scripture: "Before I formed you in the womb, I knew you". "For it was you who created my being, knit me together in my mother's womb ... Already you knew my soul, my body held no secret from you when I was being fashioned in secret.... Every one of my days was decreed before one of them came into being."[24] Holy Mother Church teaches that all "human life must be respected and protected absolutely from the moment of conception. From the first moment of his existence, a human being must be recognized as having the rights of a person, among which is the inviolable right of every innocent being to life."[25]

In recent years, the Supreme Court has also decided that any kind of sexual act—when freely chosen by consenting adults—has the same moral value as the marital act. Justice Anthony Kennedy stated that "when sexuality finds overt expression in intimate conduct with another person, the conduct can be but one element in a personal bond that is more enduring."[26] Justice Kennedy was half right: sexual intimacy is one element in an enduring bond, but the other half of the equation includes sex within the context of the marriage covenant established by God, and because marriage imitates and reflects God's life in the Trinity, the intimate bond of love between husband and wife must also necessarily be life-giving.

Once again, the Supreme Court has reflected the "anything goes" attitude of our society, where the fly-by-night relationships of reality television rule the day. In one fell swoop, the Court has placed marriage infidelity, pornography, and homosexuality—which are not created by God—on the same level as the Book of Genesis, where God creates man and woman and then blesses their relationship, uniting then in the one-flesh union of intimate, loving, and life-giving communion. On this point, the truth and beauty of our faith

[24] Jer 1:5; Ps 139:13, 14b, 15, 16b.
[25] CCC 2270.
[26] Lawrence vs. Texas, No. 02.102, Opinion of the Court (June 26, 2003), Law.Cornell .edu, p. 6, http://www.law.cornell.edu/supct/pdf/02-102P.ZO.

is clear: "The intimate community of life and love which constitutes the married state has been established by the Creator and endowed by Him with its own proper laws.... God Himself is the author of marriage.... Marriage is not a purely human institution ... [and] the vocation to marriage is written in the very nature of man and woman as they came from the hand of the Creator."[27]

Christian freedom is inexorably tied to our faith in Jesus Christ: "If you continue in my word, you are truly my disciples, and you will know the truth, and the truth will make you free.... [E]very one who commits sin is a slave to sin.... So if the Son makes you free, you will be free indeed."[28] As our relationship with Jesus grows and deepens, the question we must ask ourselves as men of faith is, "Now that I know the Church's teachings are objectively true, how do I now live my life in harmony with that truth?"

When I served as the director of a university public-safety department, one of my responsibilities was to speak to incoming freshmen about safety and security on campus. I reminded them that they were now adults and would be treated as such. I told them that, as adults, they will be held accountable for their decisions and responsible for their actions. I explained that the institutional policies and procedures to which they are now subject were designed to help create and maintain safe living and learning environments for all members of the community. From the freshmen's perspective, it may have seemed that these rules inhibited their freedom, but, in fact, just the opposite is true: the rules protect them and guide them into making good decisions so that they can be truly free and fully themselves.

As Catholic men, we sometimes approach solidarity with God's laws and commands with a freshman-like mentality where the truths of our faith, protected and defended by the teaching authority of the Church, seem restrictive, confining, or narrow. We are so caught up in the desires and aspirations of this world that we do not fully appreciate the fact that, as children of God, we participate "in the light and power of the divine Spirit".[29] As we have seen, by the use of reason alone, we have the ability to look at the world around us

---

[27] CCC 1603.
[28] Jn 8:31–32, 34, 36.
[29] CCC 1704.

and understand the order of things established by the Creator. By using our freedom in conformity with the natural law, we become capable of directing ourselves toward our Ultimate End, finding our perfection in seeking and loving God's law, and aligning ourselves with God's truth.

"In sending his Son, the Father has far surpassed the goodness of his law-giving. His Word is no longer merely spoken as instruction for us [as was the case in the Old Testament]. Rather, that Word has now become flesh and is 'rooted in the heart.' "[30] If God's Word, living in us, is to have any power and meaning at all, then "it must not only be 'heard' but acted out, in order that the living Word of the Father might truly bear divine fruit worthy of God".[31] Jesus, who is alive in our hearts, does not inhibit but fulfills our freedom under the guidance of God's law, for the Word spoken to us through Moses and the prophets has now become firmly established within each of us. How, then, do we as men become witnesses of the faith that we profess?

This is the challenge that Jesus issues to the Pharisees again and again in the Gospels. They have externalized God's law to such an extent, that "it has reached a point where the law has become a 'meaningless' form of reverence for God."[32] Many of us, like the Pharisees, simply "go through the motions" of our faith and are satisfied with the "what" or "how to" of the faith without ever acknowledging the "why": Why does the Church teach that abortion and euthanasia are completely unacceptable and incompatible with our faith? Why is it so important to go to Confession before receiving the Eucharist? Why do we all kneel after the "Holy, Holy" until after the "Great Amen"? It is the answer to these and many other questions about our faith that fosters a deeper and fuller sense of relationship and communion with God and with each other. We must never stop asking ourselves why we believe what we believe. The why of our faith leads us closer to the summum bonum, and the more we do what is good, the freer we become.

Jesus admonishes the Pharisees for putting too much emphasis on the outward expressions of their faith and reminds us that faith must

---

[30] Hans Urs von Balthasar, *Light of the Word: Brief Reflections on the Sunday Readings* (San Francisco: Ignatius Press, 1993), 232.

[31] Ibid.

[32] Ibid., 233.

be lived from the inside out. The way we live and express our faith on the outside should be a reflection of our interior life rooted in the crucified Christ. In the Eucharist, we are strengthened by the Word and nourished by His Body and Blood, which empowers us to glorify the Lord by our lives. Living in harmony with God's law should fill us not with anxiety but deep, inexpressible joy—with the same ineffable delight that filled David's heart when he prayed, "They are happy whose life is blameless, who follow God's law! They are happy who do his will, seeking him with all their hearts.... I take delight in your statutes; I will not forget your word."[33]

As we seek the path God has destined for our lives, we must take a step back and seriously question our efforts to grow deeply in our faith. We must ask difficult questions and pursue meaningful answers. The prevailing culture of death, with its witch's brew of moral relativism, sexual immorality, and subjective truth, will attempt to influence and shape our consciences with lies disguised as freedom, to be sure. If, however, we are open to truth, we will come to a deep and abiding faith in God, but not before our faith has been tested, for there is no Resurrection without Crucifixion—there is no Easter Sunday without Good Friday.

When this difficult period comes, we must keep our eyes fixed on the Cross. We will not find real truth in a society that places "the self" at the center of all meaning and existence. We will not find real truth in stubbornly opposing the Church's teaching in faith and morals. We will not find real truth by getting drunk or high. We will not find real truth in using a member of the opposite sex as an object for pleasure and gratification. This is not who we are.

Saint Paul lays the foundation for getting us back on track: "[A]s for you, man of God ... aim at righteousness, godliness, faith, love, steadfastness, gentleness. Fight the good fight of the faith; take hold of the eternal life to which you were called".[34] Our spirituality as men must flow from the Sacred Heart of Jesus and His call to live the Gospel with both fervor and humility. We must willingly and lovingly lay down our lives in service to our brides, whether they be our wives, the Church, or the culture, in imitation of the saints and in witness to the awesome power and testimony of Christ crucified.

[33] Ps 119:1–2, 16.
[34] 1 Tim 6:11–12.

There are no "good people" in heaven—only saints, and we are all called to be saints.[35] In order to become saints, we do not need to be great theologians like Saints Augustine and Thomas Aquinas. We do not need to be martyrs like Saints Stephen and Lawrence. We do not need to be great leaders like Saints Louis and Benedict. We do not even need to perform great works of charity like Saints Vincent de Paul and Martin de Porres. To become saints we must allow ourselves to be totally consumed by the fire of God's absolute love. We become saints by fulfilling Christ's command to go "all in", to love the Lord Our God with our whole being.

> For whoever would save his life will lose it; and whoever loses his life for my sake and the gospel's will save it. For what does it profit a man, to gain the whole world and forfeit his life? For what can a man give in return for his life? For whoever is ashamed of me and of my words in this adulterous and sinful generation, of him will the Son of man also be ashamed, when he comes in the glory of his Father with the holy angels.[36]

Jesus' call to sainthood begins with His command to "be perfect, as your heavenly Father is perfect."[37] Holiness is a calling by God to share in His very life through desiring and striving for spiritual perfection in love. The way of holiness molds, shapes, and forms us into the Body of Christ—into Jesus Himself. Likewise, virtue is a "habitual and firm disposition to do the good. It allows the person not only to perform good acts, but to give the best of himself. The virtuous person tends toward the good with all his sensory and spiritual powers; he pursues the good and chooses it in concrete actions. The goal of a virtuous life is to become like God."[38] Holiness leads to virtue and, when we use our freedom to cooperate with God's grace, gives us the moral fortitude and courage to be the men who God created and calls us to be.

---

[35] "To the Church of God which is at Corinth, to those sanctified in Christ Jesus, called to be saints together with all those who in every place call on the name of our Lord Jesus Christ ..." (1 Cor 1:2). Cf. Rom 1:7; 2 Cor 1:1; Eph 1:1, 15; Phil 1:1; Col 1:2, 4; Philem 1:7.

[36] Mk 8:35–38.

[37] Mt 5:48.

[38] CCC 1803.

Becoming a holy and virtuous man of God always involves a receptive listening to both the Word of God and to the Church. This includes fervent and constant prayer because it is only through prayer that we can come to know God better, and in knowing Him better we love Him better, and in loving Him better we find our true happiness in Him.[39] We must make an effort daily to place ourselves in the presence of the Lord through prayer so that our spirituality is firmly rooted in Christ crucified and our Catholic faith. The more men act under the influence, assistance, and grace of the Holy Spirit in seeking to know and to do God's holy will through a life of prayer, the more we grow in holiness and the closer we come to sainthood.

We know that we need to pray but often struggle to maintain an active and fruitful prayer life amid the busyness and chaos of the world around us. We know that God calls us to live according to His law, yet we struggle every day to say yes to God: to end bad habits and vices, and control sinful desires. Sometimes our weakness overwhelms us and the Cross feels so heavy that we buckle under its weight. Yet, it is when we are down that the Lord lifts us up, and it is when we are not looking that the Lord seeks us.

In the Gospels, Jesus draws a vivid picture of what a saint looks like.[40] It is truly striking how Jesus' saint looks nothing like us! Virtuous acts of humility, gentleness, righteousness, mercy, purity of heart, peacemaking, and standing up for truth are all frowned upon by our culture. The "I'm free to do and think as I please" and "Truth is whatever I want it to be" society we live in believes that saints have no real value and that becoming a saint is a waste of time. If we think of our world as a vineyard, the culture will try to convince us that the rotting fruit it produces—that reeks of moral and spiritual death and decay—is actually good for us, failing to mention that when we eat of this fruit we will become violently ill and will inevitably die with only Satan and the damned to keep us company.

Jesus tells His saints that theirs is the kingdom of heaven—that they will be comforted and satisfied, that they will see God and be called His children. To be saints, we must let God work in us; we must

---

[39] Cf. Thomas Merton, O.C.S.O., *Praying the Psalms* (Collegeville, Minn.: Liturgical Press, 1956), 12.

[40] See Mt 5:1–12.

take our hands off the steering wheel and let God drive. We must empty ourselves of sin so that God can fill us with His love. We must die to the ways of this world so that Christ can live in us.

Christ tells us that the seeds of sainthood are rooted in the rich soil of the greatest commandments: love of God and love of our neighbor. The world is the field in which the Word of God is sown. Through our efforts as evangelizing men of God—as sowers of the seed of the Gospel of Jesus Christ in the lives of others—the world will bear succulent, rich fruit. Yet, we may not know what fruit we are producing, because it is God who picks and distributes the fruit of our labors. We may never know how someone was touched by something we said. We may never know how things turned out after someone came to us for advice. We may never know how someone's life was changed when he met Jesus in us. But as His saints, we know that God's love has been poured into our hearts by the Holy Spirit, and it is in this outpouring of love into our hearts that the God who wishes to reveal Himself can achieve His purpose and goal.[41]

"In order to enjoy the merciful love of Jesus, it is necessary to humiliate ourselves, to acknowledge our nothingness, and this is a thing that many are unwilling to do. God wants humility of heart. When He sees that we are convinced of our nothingness ... and appeal to Him, He stoops towards us and gives with divine generosity."[42] Following Christ means going with Him into the Father's vineyard, the world, to share in the work of redemption.[43] In this world of sin and darkness, poor and humble saints shine brightly. Through them, the light of Christ ignites our hearts and inspires men to respond lovingly to the Father's tender embrace. In our love of God and neighbor we too become saints, for which we should rejoice and be glad for our reward will be great in heaven.

This loving relationship with God reaches the deepest level of intimacy and interpersonal communion when we receive him Body and Blood, Soul and Divinity, in the Most Blessed Sacrament of the Eucharist. "In each of our lives Jesus comes as the Bread of Life—to

[41] See Hans Urs von Balthasar, *You Crown the Year with Your Goodness: Sermons through the Liturgical Year* (San Francisco: Ignatius Press, 1989), 209.

[42] François Jamart, O.C.D., *Complete Spiritual Doctrine of St. Thérèse of Lisieux*, trans. Walter van de Putte, C.S.Sp. (New York: Alba House, 2001), 31–32.

[43] See von Balthasar, *Crown the Year*, 211.

be eaten, to be consumed by us. This is how He loves us.... In loving and serving, we prove that we have been created in the likeness
of God, for God is Love and when we love we are like God. This is
what Jesus meant when He said, 'Be perfect as your Father in heaven
is perfect.' "[44]

The reality of Christ's presence in the Eucharist is at the heart and
soul of what it means to be Catholic. The Eucharist is the principal
source of strength and nourishment for our souls precisely because it
is Christ Himself whom we receive. The power of the Eucharistic
Christ—present at the Holy Sacrifice of the Mass and in Adoration—
gives us the perseverance and resolve to stand up to the convictions
and truths of our faith: to be the disciples that Christ calls us to be.
The Eucharist is not just important to evangelization; the Eucharist
*is* evangelization!

The Eucharist exists to make us the Body of Christ, to make us
the sacramental representation of Jesus Christ on earth. Our being
changed into Christ is what the Eucharist is all about, and "because
of this, the unity of the Church has a greater depth than any human
union could ever hope to achieve.... The Eucharist is the intimacy
of the union of each person with the Lord."[45] Thus, it is in eating and
drinking the Body and Blood of Christ that we truly become what
we receive; and in receiving the Eucharistic Christ, we receive the
grace that gives us the courage to say with Saint Paul, "I have been
crucified with Christ; it is no longer I who live, but Christ who lives
in me."[46]

Many men are beginning to realize that what society presents as
"truth" ultimately leaves them with a feeling of emptiness and longing. With the Holy Spirit's help, they are returning to the Catholic
faith. Their experience within the culture has helped them to realize
that faith is not "warm and fuzzy" like a child's favorite blanket.

---

[44] Blessed Mother Teresa of Calcutta, "The Spirituality of Bl. Mother Teresa of
Calcutta—In Her Own Words", in section entitled "Mother Teresa of Calcutta Eucha-
ristic Quotes", Acfp2000.com, accessed June 22, 2012, http://www.acfp2000.com/Saints
/Mother_Teresa/Mother_Teresa.html.

[45] Joseph Cardinal Ratzinger, "Eucharist, Communion and Solidarity" (lecture, Bishops'
Conference of the Region of Campania, Benevento, Italy, June 2, 2002), http://www.vatican
.va/roman_curia/congregations/cfaith/documents/rc_con_cfaith_doc_20020602_ratzinger
-eucharistic-congress_en.html.

[46] Gal 2:20.

Faith is neither an enduring family tradition nor a fond memory that makes us feel good during Christmas and Easter. Our faith is something that is lived out every single day of our lives, where Christ the Servant becomes the heart and the center of who we are as men. This is where our true freedom and identity lies: in a spirituality that allows us to be self-gift and that leads us into the heart of the Trinity.

Truth will come when we persistently ask God for it. When we pray, we must knock, seek, and ask. We should converse with God just as we would with an intimate friend. We must not be afraid to share openly with the Father of Mercy our sorrows and joys, our hopes and fears, our aspirations and dreams, for His love and His truth will never fail. When truth does come, let us proclaim with great joy: "I love the Lord for He has heard the cry of my appeal; for He turned His ear to me in the day when I called Him."[47] This is the peace that true freedom brings.

---

[47] Ps 116:1–2.

*Chapter Five*

# Theology of the Body

The body is the revelation of the person and the laws that God has written into our biology are the laws that he has written into our very person.

—Christopher West[1]

"Trevor" is a husband and father who, like many of us, struggles to find meaning and purpose in his life while balancing the delicate relationship between work and family. What complicates matters is that, after being married for a while, Trevor became bored and thought he could make life more interesting by indulging in a little pornography. "After all," he thought, "what's the big deal? It's not like I'm cheating on my wife. In fact, I'm not hurting anybody. Besides, it'll help me relieve stress and make me feel better about myself. And the best part: it's free!" So, like many men, Trevor journeyed down the slippery precipice of Internet porn.

After a few months, when Trevor's marriage was in serious trouble, he came to see me and we talked for over two hours. In an email to me afterward, he wrote, "I told my wife what you told me. We both cried. I really wish I could give her everything, all of me. I realize now how much she loves me, how much she has been loving me while I am still dwelling in this sexual mud and sin. How could I have given up everything that was good and beautiful for pleasures? I am not very intimate with my wife, and I would rather spend time with my computer and indulge in all the sleaze than to engage in any emotional or intimate moments with her. Through all of this, she keeps loving me and wants to help me. Why can't I love her? What's

[1] Christopher West, "The Sacramentality of Marriage", in *Naked without Shame: Sex and the Christian Mystery* (Carpentersville, Ill.: The Gift Foundation, 2000), Audio Cassette, tape no. 6.

91

wrong with me? I am afraid. I can't run away from God and I need to trust in Him to help me. I hope it is still possible to save my marriage. I hope I will have the courage to break away from these sexual bonds and face life as it is, and find meaning in it. I hope I can love and, if I could, love my wife."

Trevor is infected with the disease of pornography addiction, but if we men are honest with ourselves, Trevor's situation becomes ours when we substitute "pornography" with whatever prevents and inhibits us from being the men Christ calls us to be. Trevor's life brings into clear relief that the opposite of love is not hate—the opposite of love is emptiness.

Instead of recognizing Christ within the rhythm of the life to which we have been called, instead of serving our wives and children, our Church and this culture, with the sacrificial love of the Sacred Heart of Jesus, instead of working hard at deepening and strengthening our faith life, we men allow ourselves to be shaped and influenced by the culture: by a way of thinking and being that does not care about the truth of Jesus Christ, that could care less about the freedom of His Cross, and that finds no meaning in the life-giving love of the Holy Spirit. We replace the fullness of self-donating love with the emptiness of a culture that mocks us.

Society's insistence on the right to exercise autonomy over and against our bodies (and even the bodies of others) has reduced the meaning of the body from that which reflects and expresses the person to a mere organic shell. This kind of thinking has opened the door to the cultural acceptance and progressive legalization of abortion, assisted suicide, euthanasia, and human cloning. The Church reminds us, however, that there is an inherent dignity of the body rooted in the transcendent truth of the natural law written onto our hearts by God—a law that is true, good, and beautiful, as well as welcoming to our nature and designed for our happiness.

The body is not meant for immorality, but for the Lord, and the Lord for the body. And God raised the Lord and will also raise us up by his power. Do you not know that your bodies are members of Christ? Shall I therefore take the members of Christ and make them members of a prostitute? Never! Do you not know that he who joins himself to a prostitute becomes one body with her? For, as it is written, "The two shall become one." But he who is united to the Lord becomes one spirit with him. Shun immorality. Every other sin which a man commits is outside the body; but the immoral man sins against his own body. Do you not know that your body is a temple of the Holy Spirit within you, which you have from God? You are not your own; you were bought with a price. So glorify God in your body.[2]

The fundamental significance of love for the individual person is perhaps best summarized by the evangelist John: "God is love, and he who abides in love abides in God, and God abides in him.... We love, because he first loved us."[3] Hence, love is essential to the individual person because man is "called to communion with God. This invitation to converse with God is addressed to man as soon as he comes into being. *For if man exists, it is because God has created him through love, and through love continues to hold him in existence.* He cannot live fully according to truth unless he freely acknowledges that love and entrusts himself to his Creator."[4] God's sustaining and life-giving love affects a man at every level of his being: physically, emotionally, and spiritually.

On the physical level, sexuality is a fundamental component of personality, that is, one of the means of expressing and living out human love. As the image of God, man is created for love, and in the marriage covenant this love is made manifest in sexual intimacy, which "includes right from the beginning the nuptial attribute, that is, the capacity of expressing love, that love in which a person becomes a gift and—by means of this gift—fulfills the meaning of his being and existence."[5] Human sexuality, through which we participate in the mystery of loving communion with God, can never find its full expression apart from the intimate partnership of life and love established by the Creator in marriage. Through this sacramental bond of unity and love, "the conjugal act preserves in its fullness the sense of true mutual love",[6] which is an expression of God's divine life within us.

---

[2] 1 Cor 6:13–20.
[3] 1 Jn 4:16, 19.
[4] *CCC* 27 (emphasis added).
[5] Pope John Paul II, *The Theology of the Body: Human Love in the Divine Plan* (Boston: Pauline Books and Media, 1997), 63.
[6] Ibid., 432.

Insofar as it entails sincere self-giving, growth in love is helped by the discipline of the feelings, passions, and emotions. Saint Thomas Aquinas tells us that love is the root of all other passions because there is no passion in the soul of man that is not founded on love of some kind. The *Catechism of the Catholic Church* reiterates both Aquinas and Saint Augustine when it states that " 'to love is to will the good of another.' All other affections have their source in this first movement of the human heart toward the good. Only the good can be loved. Passions 'are evil if love is evil and good if it is good.' "[7] On this point, Joseph Pieper notes that loving someone or something means finding him or it *probus* (good).[8] True love, which perfects a man in his totality as an individual person, becomes realized in him when he seeks and loves what is intrinsically true and ultimately good. Love is perfected in a man inasmuch as it leads to his Ultimate End, which is the Beatific Vision and union with God.

The gift of love is transformed through the power of Christ's redeeming grace, and we become partakers in His divine nature: "As an incarnate spirit, that is a soul which expresses itself in a body and a body informed by an immortal spirit, man is called to love in his unified totality."[9] Love entails a total self-giving, an act of selflessness that unites us to Christ crucified and opens our hearts to accept God's divine and loving will. Without love, a man "remains a being that is incomprehensible for himself; his life is senseless."[10] The fundamental nature of love itself, inherent within that symbiotic relationship between man and God, is spiritual communion. The spiritual dimension of love must be understood in light of Christ's redemption of the world, which calls us to God's grace and love in relationship, for to be truly human means to be related in love.

Sacrificial love leads to self-mastery. "If the person is not master of self—through the virtues and, in a concrete way, through chastity—he or she lacks that self-possession which makes self-giving

---

[7] *CCC* 1766.

[8] See Joseph Pieper, *About Love* (Chicago: Franciscan Herald Press, 1974).

[9] John Paul II, Apostolic Exhortation *Familiaris Consortio*, On the Role of the Christian Family in the Modern World, November 22, 1981, no. 11 (hereafter cited as *FC*).

[10] John Paul II, Encyclical Letter *Redemptor Hominis* (The Redeemer of Man), March 4, 1979, no. 25.

possible."[11] Chastity is "the successful integration of sexuality within the person and thus the inner unity of man in his bodily and spiritual being".[12] It is a moral virtue, a spiritual power that frees love from selfishness and aggression.

> We must commit ourselves to a progressive education of the will, to a progressive education of our feelings and emotions. Continence is not only and not even principally the ability to abstain. Such a role would be defined merely as negative. There is also a positive role of self-mastery. It is the ability to direct the respective reactions both as to their content and their character.[13]

Saint Peter acknowledges the connection between sacrificial love and man's participation in the life of God when he writes that God's

> divine power has granted to us all things that pertain to life and godliness, through the knowledge of him who called us to his own glory and excellence, by which he has granted to us his precious and very great promises, that through these you may escape from the corruption that is in the world because of passion, and become partakers of the divine nature. For this very reason make every effort to supplement your faith with virtue, and virtue with knowledge, and knowledge with self-control, and self-control with steadfastness, and steadfastness with godliness, and godliness with brotherly affection, and brotherly affection with love.[14]

To the degree that a man weakens chastity, his love becomes more and more selfish, that is, a love reduced to satisfying a desire for pleasure that separates love from sex and seeks only the apparent good. This is why disordered sexual expressions are sinful offenses against God: "It is failure in genuine love for God and neighbor caused by

---

[11] Pontifical Council for the Family, *The Truth and Meaning of Human Sexuality: Guidelines for Education within the Family*, December 8, 1995, no. 16, http://www.vatican.va/roman_curia/pontifical_councils/family/documents/rc_pc_family_doc_08121995_human-sexuality_en.html.

[12] *CCC* 2337.

[13] Christopher West, "Love and Fruitfulness", in *Naked without Shame*, tape no. 7.

[14] 2 Pet 1:3–7.

a perverse attachment to certain goods. It wounds the nature of man and injures human solidarity."[15]

Sexuality reaches its ultimate fulfillment when it is a participation in the mystery of God's life and love. Disordered sexual expressions within any other context (e.g., pornography, contraception, fornication, masturbation, homosexuality, oral copulation that leads to a completed sexual act, etc.), even within the covenant of marriage, are not part of God's plan or design and are, therefore, intrinsically evil and gravely sinful actions. This is serious business. Any such acts committed with full knowledge (you know that the action is wrong) and deliberate consent of the will (you freely choose to do the action anyway) are mortally sinful and place your eternal salvation at risk.

In the Book of Genesis we see that marriage is the primordial or "protosacrament". God creates man in His own image, male and female, to be completely equal in dignity. He blesses this relationship and commands them to be fruitful and multiply. This relationship right from the start images God's own Trinitarian life and is a mutually self-giving relationship focused on an axis of love, where love is the heart and the center of our existence manifesting itself through the giving of life. The loving and life-giving dimensions are woven into the fabric of our being, and trying to separate or force love and life apart is like trying to segment or compartmentalize God Himself.

This is one of the dangers of the culture for male spirituality: the deliberate separation of love from life in contradiction to what it means to be made in the image and likeness of God. Through an active prayer life and a vibrant Eucharistic faith, we must strive to foster and deepen the relationship of love and life that mirrors the love of God the Father. In covenant relationship, forged in the sacrifice of the crucified Christ, the Eucharist must be the heart and center of a man's spiritual union with God.

These tenets of authentic male spirituality apply to all men, no matter their state in life. Priests and religious live out the covenant union of the marriage feast of heaven, foreshadowed in the gift of celibacy, right here on earth.[16] The call to celibacy for the sake of the kingdom flows from a man's free choice in partnership with God's

---

[15] CCC 1849.
[16] Cf. Rev 19:7–9.

grace. The celibate state, through which a man consecrates himself to God in a special way, cannot be properly understood without referring to spousal love through which a person becomes a gift for the other. In celibacy, a man, who represents Christ the Bridegroom, shares this gift with "all people who are embraced by the love of the Spouse".[17] In this sense, celibacy manifests perfect conjugal love marked by fidelity to the Church in mutual self-donation. Men as husbands are to love their spouses with the same sacrificial love that Christ has for the Church, and since spousal love is also life-giving, all men are called to be spiritual fathers in whom "the mystery of man's masculinity, that is, the generative and fatherly meaning of His body, is also thoroughly revealed".[18]

Saint John Paul II was not afraid to confront challenges to authentic sexual expression. In the 1995 Encyclical Letter *Evangelium Vitae*, he states that "human life, as a gift of God, is sacred and inviolable.... The meaning of life is found in giving and receiving love, and in this light human sexuality and procreation reach their true and full significance."[19] Although this deeply profound and pregnant insight is intended to be a compendium of the Church's doctrine on human sexuality in general, these principles can apply to male spirituality specifically.

Throughout his pontificate, John Paul II developed an understanding and appreciation of the true nature and proper ordering of sexual intimacy by examining modern society's secular humanist perspective regarding married love and fidelity. He seamlessly integrated the perspectives of Thomistic philosophy and phenomenology regarding the role of sexuality in individual perfection. He then defended the proper ordering of sexuality to the conjugal love of man and woman, which is sanctified in the Sacrament of Marriage, and where the physical intimacy of the spouses becomes a sign and pledge of spiritual communion.[20] Finally, Pope John Paul II juxtaposed contemporary societal perspectives with the Church's understanding

---

[17] *MD* 21.

[18] John Paul II, *Theology of the Body*, 81.

[19] John Paul II, Encyclical Letter *Evangelium Vitae* (The Gospel of Life), March 25, 1995, no. 81.

[20] See *CCC* 2360.

of three disordered expressions of human sexuality: contraception, homosexuality, and pornography. We will now explore the Holy Father's approach to love and sexuality as described above through the lens of male spirituality.

Love is a constant theme in modern culture. Modern music, cinema, the Internet, and television constantly assault our senses with stories and features about love. Unfortunately, the attributes of authentic love—that is, the values of fidelity, exclusiveness, dependability, stability, childbearing, the establishing of a nuclear family, and love of children—are downgraded, while the values of sexual compatibility, erotic passion, and emotional ecstasy are given special attention.[21] In modern speech, the term "making love" has become synonymous with sexual intercourse, its value measured in terms of erotic intensity and sexual climax. This understanding of "lovemaking" makes no attempt to characterize sexual intercourse as an expression of genuine self-giving and sharing of life. It completely ignores the fact that sexual love forms bonds of communion with others in caring, faithful, and lifelong relationships based upon selflessness, sincerity, and fidelity. Modern society has, in essence, separated love from sex, thus creating a chasm of moral ambiguity and confusion that weakens the conscience, ennobles concupiscence, and nurtures disordered desires and carnal appetites within a man's heart. The restoration of a true and proper sense of sexual expression must begin by reuniting love and sexuality so that the unity between sex and faithful lifelong love, the unity between sex and procreation, and the unity between sex and marriage are revived. Sex, then, will be rooted in the solid foundation of God's divine love, and it is this love which will allow man to "recognize the voice of God which urges him 'to do what is good and avoid what is evil' ".[22]

Men must return to their senses. In order to develop a proper understanding of human sexuality, a man must first develop an

---

[21] "The decline of traditional models has left ... an eclipse of the truth about man which, among other things, exerts pressure to reduce sex to something commonplace. In this area, society and the mass media most of the time provide depersonalized, recreational and often pessimistic information [about the true meaning of sexuality]. Moreover, this information ... is influenced by a distorted individualistic concept of freedom, in an ambience lacking the basic values of life, human love and the family" (Pontifical Council for the Family, *Truth and Meaning of Human Sexuality*, no. 1).

[22] *CCC* 1706.

appreciation of the dignity of the human person, which "is rooted in his creation in the image and likeness of God".[23] Since this divine image is present in every man, "the human person participates in the light and power of the divine Spirit."[24] The power of the Holy Spirit infuses a man's soul, enlightening his intellect and will, and man finds perfection in seeking and loving what is true and good.[25] As the image of God, man is created for love, and this love is made manifest in sexual intimacy since "sexuality affects all aspects of the human person in the unity of his body and soul."[26] Sex, therefore, is a good "considered as desirable or capable of perfecting the agent".[27] Sexual love that is ordered toward the *objective good* perfects a man in his totality as a person. Sexual love that is ordered toward the *apparent good* answers to some particular craving or desire in a man, but does not perfect his nature considered in its totality.[28] The intrinsic nature of human sexuality is properly ordered toward the objective good "which makes itself heard in conscience and is fulfilled in the love of God and of neighbor".[29]

> The more the two [husband and wife], in their different aspects, find a proper unity in the one reality of love, the more the true nature of

[23] *CCC* 1700.

[24] *CCC* 1704.

[25] Cf. *GS* 15. "Sense pleasure ... cannot be man's supreme good because it perfects the body only: it actualizes the potentialities of, and satisfies only a part of the human being.... To find the ultimate good or final end of man, we have to turn to the supernatural vision of God which is attainable only in the next life" (F. C. Copleston, *Aquinas* [Baltimore: Penguin Books, 1965], 203–4). Cf. Thomas Aquinas, *Summa Theologica*, Ia, IIae, 2, If.

[26] *CCC* 2332. This is not to diminish the richness, beauty, and truth of celibacy, which is an expression in the temporal order of the intimacy and communion of love that we shall experience at the wedding feast of the Lamb in heaven.

[27] Copleston, *Aquinas*, 189.

[28] Ibid., 190–93, esp. 190.

[29] *CCC* 1706. "The person is thus capable of a higher kind of love than concupiscence, which only sees objects as a means to satisfy one's appetites; the person is capable rather of friendship and self-giving, with the capacity to recognize and love persons for themselves. Like the love of God, this is a love capable of generosity. One desires the good of the other because she or he is recognized as worthy of being loved. This is a love which generates communion between persons, because each considers the good of the other as his or her own good. This is a self-giving made to one who loves us, a self-giving whose inherent goodness is discovered and activated in the communion of persons and where one learns the value of loving and of being loved" (Pontifical Council for the Family, *Truth and Meaning of Human Sexuality*, no. 9).

love in general is realized. Even if *eros* is at first mainly covetous and ascending, a fascination for the great promise of happiness, in drawing near to the other, it is less and less concerned with itself, increasingly seeks the happiness of the other, is concerned more and more with the beloved, bestows itself and wants to "be there for" the other. The element of *agape* thus enters into this love, for otherwise *eros* is impoverished and even loses its own nature.[30]

Pope John Paul II's phenomenological approach to human love and sexuality envisions sex not as something purely biological but as a component of the innermost being of the individual person. He sees sexuality as a physical giving of oneself to another, which reaches its true and full meaning when it expresses itself in the intimate communion of persons through the sacramental sign of marriage.

> Love is a gift of God, nourished by and expressed in the encounter of man and woman. Love is thus a positive force directed towards their growth and maturity as persons. Love is also a precious source for the self-giving which all men and women are called to make for their own self-realization and happiness. In fact, man is called to love as an incarnate spirit, that is, soul and body in the unity of the person. Human love hence embraces the body, and the body also expresses spiritual love ... realized in a truly human way only if it is an integral part of the love by which a man and a woman commit themselves totally to one another until death.[31]

In the marriage covenant, "love includes the human body", and in the profound encounter of conjugal love and fidelity, "the body is made a sharer in spiritual love."[32] Sexuality has love as its intrinsic end, and its meaning must be understood in light of Christian revelation: "Sexuality characterizes man and woman not only on the physical level, but also on the psychological and spiritual, making its mark on each of their expressions. Such diversity, linked to the complementarity of the two sexes, allows thorough response to the design of God according to the vocation to which each one is called."[33]

---

[30] *DCE* 7.

[31] Pontifical Council for the Family. *Truth and Meaning of Human Sexuality*, no. 3 and *FC* 11. Cf. *Evangelium Vitae*, no. 43.

[32] *FC* 11.

[33] Pontifical Council for the Family, *Truth and Meaning of Human Sexuality*, no. 13.

When love is lived out in marriage, both spouses, "through this union, experience the meaning of their oneness[34] and attain to it with growing perfection day by day".[35] Love between a man and a woman is achieved when they give themselves totally to each other in the marriage covenant, where God has willed that life is to be conceived, nurtured, and developed.[36] Sexual giving, then, belongs to married love alone where "the physical intimacy of the spouses becomes a sign and a pledge of spiritual communion."[37] The conjugal act has two inseparable aspects: union and procreation.[38]

> By its intimate structure, the conjugal act, while most closely unit-ing husband and wife, capacitates them for the generation of new lives, according to the laws inscribed in the very being of man and of woman. By safeguarding both these essential aspects, the unitive and the procreative, the conjugal act preserves in its fullness the sense of true mutual love and its ordination towards man's most high calling to parenthood.[39]

Sacred Scripture provides keen insights into the nature of human sexuality[40] and its proper ordering in the Sacrament of Marriage.[41]

---

[34] See Mt 19:6.

[35] GS 48.

[36] Pontifical Council for the Family, *Truth and Meaning of Human Sexuality*, no. 14. "Spouses are a community of lovers, whose loving acts, joined with the creative power of God, may pour forth into the creation of a new life" (Janet E. Smith, *Humanae Vitae: A Generation Later* [Washington, D.C.: Catholic University of America Press, 1991], 46).

[37] CCC 2360.

[38] "Humans have procreative sexual intercourse, intercourse wherein they cooperate with God to bring into existence a new immortal being, whose growth in love and understanding of God they undertake and guide" (Smith, *Humanae Vitae*, 45). Cf. Paul VI, Encyclical Letter *Humanae Vitae* (Of Human Life), July 25, 1968, nos. 8, 9, and 12.

[39] John Paul II, *Theology of the Body*, 432. John Paul II echoes the sentiments of Vatican II: "[Conjugal love] involves the good of the whole person.... This love is uniquely expressed and perfected through the marital act.... Hence the acts themselves which are proper to con-jugal love and which are exercised in accord with genuine human dignity must be honored with great reverence" (GS 49, 51).

[40] See Lev 20:11, 17, 21; Rom 1:18; 6:12–14; 1 Cor 6:9–11; 2 Cor 7:1; Gal 5:16–23; Eph 4:17–24; 5:3–13; Col 3:5–8; 1 Thess 4:1–18; 1 Tim 1:8–11; 4:12; and 2 Pet 1:4.

[41] See Gen 1:27–28; 2:18; 4:1–2; 5:1–2; Mt 5:27–28; 9:15; 19:3ff.; Mk 2:11–20; 10:2ff.; Lk 5:34–35; Jn 3:29. Cf. 2 Cor 11:2; Eph 5:27; and Rev 19:7–8.

It provides the foundation for the Church's teaching on sexual intimacy:[42] "The biblical Word of God several times urges the betrothed and the married to nourish and develop their wedlock by pure conjugal love and undivided affection."[43] Pope John Paul II examines a number of Scripture passages that discuss the nature of love and sexuality, paying particular attention to the Sermon on the Mount in chapter 5 of the Gospel of Matthew[44] and the creation account in chapter 2 of the Book of Genesis.[45] The Holy Father's anthropology of man is rooted in Sacred Scripture: "Thanks to [the biblical narratives] we have been able to find the nuptial meaning of the body and rediscover what it consists of as a measure of the human heart such as to mold the original form of the communication of persons."[46]

One of the recurring tenets of moral relativism is the association of personal freedom with bodily choice, often expressed as "my body, my choice". This leads to a mindset that separates love and life, thus creating, as in the case of Trevor, a void and emptiness within a Catholic man's heart. Now distant from an intimate and personal relationship with God, a man fills this emptiness with disordered passions, leading him to ambivalence and agnosticism, rationalizing his behavior, and justifying his stance against Church teaching along the way. In effect, he has become his own god and a slave to the culture of death.

The first decade of the twenty-first century has generated the most vicious attack on conscience the world has ever seen. "The day before he was elected Pope Benedict XVI, Cardinal Joseph Ratzinger warned the world of a 'Dictatorship of Relativism.'... It is true that

---

[42] For example, John Paul II's commentary on Genesis notes that "the formulation of Genesis 2:24 indicates that human beings, created as man and woman, were created for unity. Formed in the image of God, also inasmuch as they form a true communion of persons, the first man and the first woman must constitute the beginning and the model for that communion for all men and women who, in any period, are united so intimately as to be one flesh" (John Paul II, *Theology of the Body,* 50).

[43] *GS* 49. Cf. Gen 2:22–24; Tob 8:4–8; Prov 5:15–20; 31:10–31; Song 1:2–3, 16; 4:16; 5:1; 7:8–14; 1 Cor 7:3–6; Eph 5:25–33. Pope John Paul II adds, "[Biblical catechesis] is necessary in order to discover the depths of Christ's words and to explain [its] significance to the human heart [which is] so important for the theology of the body" (John Paul II, *Theology of the Body,* 110).

[44] See John Paul II, *Theology of the Body,* 103–11.

[45] See ibid., 29–77, esp. 29–51.

[46] See ibid., 125.

relativists are now brazenly attempting to dictate to consciences.... The Dictatorship of Relativism is now demanding that when religious faith comes into conflict with non-faith, faith must give way. When belief comes into conflict with unbelief, belief must give way. When religion comes into conflict with anti-religion, religion must step down."[47]

Moral relativism professes political correctness and values-neutral education that promote the very ideas that, left unchallenged, will ultimately erode the spiritual foundation upon which our faith is built, all in the name of "tolerance" and "diversity", and at the expense of authentic truth and freedom.

When Pope Benedict XVI visited Africa, he said, "AIDS cannot be overcome by the distribution of condoms. On the contrary, they increase the problem. The Church teaches that fidelity within heterosexual marriage, chastity and abstinence are the best ways to stop AIDS."[48] In response, a writer for *US News and World Report* stated that the pope's comment was "one of the most horrifically ignorant statements made by a world leader" and that "his opposition to condoms conveys that religious dogma is more important to him than the lives of Africans."[49]

What is the truth? "Condoms have never been shown to reduce HIV infection rates and AIDS deaths in general-population epidemics like those in sub-Saharan Africa. Paradoxically, the more condoms AIDS activists send to Africa, the more widespread the disease has become."[50]

"In South Africa, which has strongly promoted condoms as the best way to prevent AIDS, the number of free condoms distributed to the public rose rapidly between 1994 and 1998, from 6 million to

[47] John Mallon, "Conscience and the Dictatorship of Relativism: Of the Modern Thought Which Claims to Set People Free but Actually Enslaves Them", *Inside the Vatican*, accessed January 14, 2015, http://www.insidethevatican.com/articles/conscience.htm.

[48] Fr. John Zuhlsdorf, "US News and World Report Attacks the Pope", *Fr. Z's Blog*, March 18, 2009, http://wdtprs.com/blog/2009/03/us-news-world-report-attacks-the-pope/.

[49] Bonnie Erbe, "Pope's Dangerous AIDS Message in Africa: No Condoms", *US News and World Report*, March 18, 2009, http://www.usnews.com/opinion/blogs/erbe/2009/03/18/popes-dangerous-aids-message-in-africa-no-condoms.

[50] Sue Ellen Browder, "Dirty Little Secret: Why Condoms Will Never Stop AIDS in Africa", *Holy Spirit Interactive*, accessed January 14, 2015, http://www.holyspiritinteractive.net/columns/guests/suebrowder/dirtysecret.asp.

198 million. The total number of condoms distributed in South Africa during 1998 was nearly 210 million."[51] "Did this giant increase curb the pandemic? On the contrary: statistics released by South Africa's government in 2005 revealed that death rates skyrocketed from an average of 870 deaths a day in 1997 to 1,370 deaths a day in 2002—a 57 percent increase."[52]

"In Botswana, condom sales rose from 1 million to 3 million between 1993 and 2001. Meanwhile, HIV prevalence among urban pregnant women rose from 27 percent to 45 percent. During the same period in Cameroon, condom sales increased from 6 million to 15 million, while HIV prevalence [tripled] from 3 percent to 9 percent."[53]

Edward C. Green, director of the AIDS Prevention Center at the Harvard Center for Population and Development Studies, agreed with Pope Benedict when he stated that "the best evidence we have supports the Pope's comments." Mr. Green went on to explain that "we have found no consistent associations between condom use and lower HIV-infection rates, which, 25 years into the pandemic, we should be seeing if this intervention was working. . . . The best and latest empirical evidence indeed shows that reduction in multiple and concurrent sexual partners is the most important single behavior change associated with reduction in HIV-infection rates."[54]

*Masturbation.* Many men, as a direct result of poorly formed consciences, freely choose to wallow in the stench of moral relativism through the deliberate misuse of the sexual faculty. Masturbation is one of the most prevalent offenses against the dignity of the body and chastity.

> By *masturbation* is to be understood the deliberate stimulation of the
> genital organs in order to derive sexual pleasure. Both the Magisterium
> of the Church, in the course of a constant tradition, and the moral

[51] Ibid.

[52] Ibid. In addition, deaths of individuals ages fifteen to forty-nine (when people are most sexually active) more than doubled.

[53] Ibid. Cf. Norman Hearst and Sanny Chen, "Condom Promotion for AIDS Prevention in the Developing World: Is It Working?" *Studies in Family Planning* 35, no. 1 (March 2004): 39–47.

[54] Quoted in Kathryn Jean Lopez, "From Saint Peter's Square to Harvard Square", *National Review Online*, March 19, 2009, http://www.nationalreview.com/articles/227110 /saint-peters-square-harvard-square/kathryn-jean-lopez.

sense of the faithful have been in no doubt and have firmly maintained that masturbation is an intrinsically and gravely disordered action. The deliberate use of the sexual faculty, for whatever reason, outside of marriage is essentially contrary to its purpose. For here sexual pleasure is sought outside of the sexual relationship which is demanded by the moral order and in which the total meaning of mutual self-giving and human procreation in the context of true love is achieved.[55]

Despite the Church's clear and unambiguous teaching in this area, men try to minimize their culpability by rationalizing away the seriousness of this sin. It's easy to see why, given the proliferation of this practice by organizations like Planned Parenthood[56] and publications like *Men's Health* magazine.[57] A few excerpts from the Planned Parenthood teen website and Menshealth.com should suffice to make this point abundantly clear.

> Masturbation can't make you blind, crazy, or stupid. It can't damage your body or stunt your growth. In fact, masturbation can actually be good for you.

> "We are programmed ... to need orgasms," says Gloria Brame, Ph.D., a clinical sexologist in Athens, Ga. "It's a fundamental aspect of men's health, right up there with brushing your teeth."

> "It relieves stress and keeps everything about your body—your heart rate, blood pressure, reproductive system, brain chemistry—in very good shape," Brame says.

> Regularly flushing your system ... keeps your semen healthy and prevents the build up of prostate cancer-causing chemicals.

> Sexual intercourse doesn't provide the same benefit because it puts you at risk of contracting a sexually transmitted infection.

The truth about masturbation is—as in Trevor's case—"with repetition, your brain can learn to prefer sexual fantasy and masturbation to real sexual intimacy with your spouse. In fact, your brain's 'arousal circuitry' can become so dominantly wired for 'self-sex' that

---

[55] *CCC* 2352.
[56] See http://www.plannedparenthood.org/teens/sex/masturbation.
[57] See http://www.menshealth.com/health/health-and-sexual-benefits-masturbation.

physical intimacy with your spouse can become increasingly difficult and eventually virtually impossible."[58] As long as the beauty of the Church's teaching—along with a virtuous respect for our bodies and the dignity of women—is not proclaimed from the pulpit, plainly expressed in catechesis at the parish level, and passed down from father to son, the sin of masturbation (and pornography, which is closely associated with it) will continue to destroy men's consciences, and turn our hearts and lives away from the Lord of love and truth.

Regarding the theology of the body, the accusation of "physicalism" (also called "biologism") is often levied against the Magisterium, claiming that the teaching authority of the Church has taken biological laws—laws written into human nature—and built moral laws out of them. The Church, according to the revisionists, takes something that is good in itself and actualizes a moral law. For example, the human life span—from conception to death—has a number of biological laws that we align ourselves with on a daily basis, such as heartbeat, breathing, digestion, etc. We see the inherent good of the biological process and make a moral decision not to interrupt it. The accusation of physicalism says that the Church has taken that moral law and made it absolute, thereby restricting the freedom to control our own bodies.

The revisionist claim is that the Church takes the text of the body and reads it literally, thereby removing man's personal freedom to exercise dominion over nature and biology in the process. Since there are biological laws at work in the fertility cycle, for example, the Church has taken the biological law and tells you that, at every step, you have to follow this biological law and not interfere with it, which takes away your freedom. Therefore, since acts like sterilization, contraception, homosexuality, in vitro fertilization, cloning, and other acts that interrupt the normal, healthy reproductive process are not allowed, the Church has taken biological laws and turned them into absolute moral laws that restrict individual choice and freedom.

The revisionists claim they respect the "premoral" goodness of these biological laws, and, once placed in a moral setting, you employ proportionalism in order to determine whether and how you are

---

[58] "Physical Effects of Masturbation", Reclaim: God's Plan for Sexual Health, accessed January 14, 2015, http://www.reclaimsexualhealth.com/Education-Resources/Masturbation/.

going to act over and against these "natural inclinations".[59] This concept is summarized by John Paul II in *Veritatis Splendor*.

> According to certain theologians, this kind of "biologistic or naturalistic argumentation" would even be present in certain documents of the Church's Magisterium, particularly those dealing with the area of sexual and conjugal ethics. It was, they maintain, on the basis of a naturalistic understanding of the sexual act that contraception, direct sterilization, autoeroticism, pre-marital sexual relations, homosexual relations and artificial insemination were condemned as morally unacceptable. In the opinion of these same theologians, a morally negative evaluation of such acts fails to take into adequate consideration both man's character as a rational and free being and the cultural conditioning of all moral norms. In their view, man, as a rational being, not only can but actually *must freely determine the meaning* of his behaviour.... Still, they continue, God made man as a rationally free being; he left him "in the power of his own counsel" and he expects him to shape his life in a personal and rational way. Love of neighbor would mean above all and even exclusively respect for his freedom to make his own decisions. The workings of typically human behaviour, as well as the so-called "natural inclinations", would establish at the most— so they say—a general orientation towards correct behaviour, but they cannot determine the moral assessment of individual human acts.[60]

The revisionist argument begs the following question: What kind of norms would the Church have if, in fact, she were truly biologistic and physicalist? No technological change or intervention would be allowed, so the Church would discourage the use of eyeglasses and hearing aids. You could follow your passions, so premarital sex and polygamy would be acceptable. Gluttony would be tolerable. Fasting would be outlawed. Celibacy would be considered evil. Couples would be encouraged to have as many children as is physically possible. Clearly, this is not the perspective of Holy Mother Church.

---

[59] Traditional Catholic moral theology teaches that good intent and difficult circumstances can never make an intrinsically evil act into a good act. A "premoral" act is an act evaluated in light of circumstance and intent before it is determined to be intrinsically evil. "Premoral" means prior to an agent involved in a moral setting. Proportionalism suggests that right or wrong actions are determined by evaluating the positive or negative results of the action. Thus, good and evil reside in the results of an action and not in the action itself.

[60] *VS* 47 (emphasis in original).

Instead, the Church teaches that the body speaks a personal language. Dwelling within our biology is a transcendent language and meaning that speaks in and through the body. When one listens to the language of the body, the body is speaking on both a biological level (e.g., "I'm hurting, please help me") and on a personalist level ("Human life is an extremely valuable gift, and my life has unique meaning"). It takes a person to read, listen to, and understand the language of the body, and then align himself with what that language is saying. Without both body and person working integrally together, the language of the body would be meaningless.

The spiritual and immortal soul is the principle of unity of the human being, whereby it exists as a whole—*corpore et anima unus*—as a person. These definitions ... remind us that reason and free will are linked with all the bodily and sense faculties. *The person, including the body, is completely entrusted to himself, and it is in the unity of body and soul that the person is the subject of his own moral acts.* The person, by the light of reason and the support of virtue, discovers in the body the anticipatory signs, the expression and the promise of the gift of self, in conformity with the wise plan of the Creator. It is in the light of the dignity of the human person—a dignity which must be affirmed for its own sake—that reason grasps the specific moral value of certain goods towards which the person is naturally inclined. And since the human person cannot be reduced to a freedom which is self-designing, but entails a particular spiritual and bodily structure, the primordial moral requirement of loving and respecting the person as an end and never as a mere means also implies, by its very nature, respect for certain fundamental goods, without which one would fall into relativism and arbitrariness. *A doctrine which dissociates the moral act from the bodily dimensions of its exercise is contrary to the teaching of Scripture and Tradition.*[61]

---

[61] *VS* 48–49 (emphasis in original). Prior to his ascent to the Chair of Peter, the cardinal-archbishop of Krakow wrote extensively about the personal language of the body: "If the author of *Humanae vitae* noted 'the unsurpassable limits to the possibility of man's dominion over his own body and over their functions,' arguing that 'these limits cannot be determined except with the respect due to the integrity of the human organism and its functions,' he considers the body not as an autonomous being, with its own structure and dynamic, but as a component of the whole man in his personal constitution; therefore he appeals to the 'principle of totality' in a context of the global vision of man. The respect due to the body, particularly in its procreative functions—functions rooted in the whole specific somatic quality of sex—is respect for the human

*Contraception.* The challenges to *corpore et anima unus* are significant. Whenever I mention the word "contraception" in a homily, you can see eyes start to roll, arms start to fold, and minds and hearts begin to shut down. The looks on some men's faces seem to say, "Here we go again. Another lecture on what the Church won't let me do." And people wonder why more priests and deacons will not preach on this and other exigent issues. The beauty of the Church's teaching on sexual morality and the value of human life needs to be proclaimed boldly and courageously so that the truth can begin to form minds and wills in accord with the natural law implanted in our hearts by God—so that we can actually live our faith and not simply pay lip service to it.

The "contraceptive mentality", which permeates much of modern society, undermines both the unitive and procreative dimensions of sacramental marriage. Contraceptives separate sexual intercourse from its inherent openness to life-giving love and increase the propensity and the temptation to separate sex from fidelity, permanence, and exclusive relationship. In essence, contraceptives facilitate the separation of sex from love, and, therefore, a contraceptive act of intercourse ceases to be an act of love.

Contraception is the choice, *by any means, to sterilize a given act of intercourse.* In other words, a contracepting couple chooses to engage in intercourse [the unitive dimension] and, knowing that it may result in new life [the procreative dimension], they intentionally and willfully suppress their fertility. Herein lies the key distinction

---

being, i.e., for the dignity of the man and the woman. This personal dignity is precisely what determines those 'unsurpassable limits to the possibility of man's dominion over his own body and over its functions.' To think and to act correctly, we cannot confine ourselves to any partial aspect that one or another particular science with the greatest 'technical' efficacy suggests. We must, on the other hand, integrate these aspects continually in order to reach the integral vision of man, the personal subject. Only on the basis of this vision can we correctly judge the one or the other technique of action (in this case we are dealing directly with the so-called technique of contraception) that assert themselves in the field of particular sciences—e.g., those techniques that interfere efficiently in the bio-physiological processes themselves" (Karol Cardinal Wojtyla, "The Anthropological Vision of *Humane Vitae*", trans. William E. May, Christendom Awake, April 30, 2008, http://www.christendom-awake.org /pages/may/anthrop-visionjpII.htm; originally published as Karol Cardinal Wojtyla, "La Visione Antropologica della *Humane Vitae*", *Lateranum* 44 [1978]: 125–45).

between Natural Family Planning (NFP) and contraception: NFP *is in no way contraceptive.* The choice to *abstain* from a fertile act of intercourse is completely different from the willful choice to sterilize a fertile act of intercourse. NFP simply accepts from God's hand the natural cycle of infertility that He has built into the nature of women.[62]

Vatican II reminds us that harmonizing married love with the responsible transmission of life, which respects the total meaning of mutual self-giving and procreation in the context of true love, is possible only in the virtue of married chastity.[63] "[Contraception] leads not only to positive refusal to be open to life but also to a falsification of the inner truth of conjugal love, which is called upon to give itself in personal totality."[64] Pope Paul VI confirms the Church's constant teaching in *Humanae Vitae*,[65] a recurring theme in the teaching of Saint John Paul II[66] and a hermeneutic in the Magisterium of Karol Cardinal Wojtyla:

These unsurpassable limits of man's dominion over his own body are rooted in the profound structure of personal being and stand in relationship to a specific value, that is, the personal value of man. It is absolutely indispensable to put these structures and values into evidence, if our aim is the interior correctness in the conjugal act that is destined, above all, to realize the "communion of beings" (see

[62] Archbishop Charles J. Chaput, "Of Human Life: Addendum—Some Common Questions", July 22, 1998, answer to question no. 2, http://www.archden.org/archbishop/docs/of_human_life.htm (emphasis added).

[63] See *GS* 51.

[64] *FC* 32. For a detailed anthropological analysis of *Humane Vitae*, see Wojtyla, "Visione Antropologica della *Humane Vitae*".

[65] "Excluded is every action that, either in anticipation of the conjugal act or in its accomplishment or in the development of its natural consequences, would have as an end or as a means, to render procreation impossible" (Paul VI, *Humanae Vitae*, no. 14).

[66] "In the conjugal act, it is not licit to separate the unitive aspect from the procreative aspect because both the one and the other pertain to the intimate truth of the conjugal act" (John Paul II, *Theology of the Body*, 398). In addition, "When couples, by means of recourse to contraception, separate these two meanings [unitive and procreative] that God the Creator has inscribed in the being of man and woman and in the dynamism of their sexual communion, they act as 'arbiters' of the divine plan and they 'manipulate' and degrade human sexuality—and with it themselves and their married partner—by altering its value of 'total' self-giving. Thus the innate language that expresses the total reciprocal self-giving of husband and wife is overlaid, through contraception, by an objectively contradictory language, namely, that of not giving oneself totally to the other" (*FC* 32).

*Humanae Vitae*, no. 8). It is this that creates the basis for a just criterion in this matter. Man cannot exercise power over his own body by means of interventions or techniques that, at the same time, compromise his authentic personal dominion over himself and that even, in a certain way, annihilate this dominion. This way of exercising dominion over one's own body and over its functions, although effected with a method elaborated by man's intelligence, is in contrast with the profound and "global" "given" that man is himself, namely, a person with dominion over himself and that this dominion over himself enters into the integral definition of his freedom. The encyclical *Humanae vitae* justly exhorts us to see that sound freedom triumphs over license (see no. 22).[67]

*Homosexuality.* In his inauguration speech at the start of his second term, President Obama made the following remarks regarding the redefinition of marriage in the United States: "Our journey is not complete until our gay brothers and sisters are treated like anyone else under the law.... For if we are truly created equal, then surely the love we commit to one another must be equal as well."[68] This statement typifies the "equal means being the same" principle of moral relativism. It fails to recognize the fundamental and intrinsic unity within the complementarity of man and woman, it diminishes and undermines authentic sexual expression rooted in the love and life embrace of covenant relationship to subjective feelings mired in concupiscence, it distorts the meaning of "rights" and "freedom" to fit political rhetoric, and it completely ignores the natural law.

Many people often misunderstand or misrepresent the Church's teaching on homosexuality. The Church is *not* against homosexuals. She never has been and never will be. The *Catechism of the Catholic Church* says, "Basing itself on Sacred Scripture, which presents homosexual acts as acts of grave depravity, tradition has always declared, 'homosexual acts are intrinsically disordered.' They are contrary to the natural law. They close the sexual act to the gift of life. They do not proceed from a genuine affective and sexual complementarity.

[67] Wojtyla, "Anthropological Vision of *Humane Vitae*".

[68] President Barack Obama, Inaugural Address at the U.S. Capitol, Washington, D.C., January 21, 2013, http://www.whitehouse.gov/the-press-office/2013/01/21/inaugural-address-president-barack-obama.

Under no circumstances can they be approved".[69] The Church's teaching on homosexuality is rooted in biblical principles.[70] Both the Bible and the Church's tradition condemn homosexual *acts*, not persons, and prohibit other acts that violate the natural law such as fornication, adultery, and abortion.

Human sexuality and openness to the transmission of new life are intricately woven into the fabric of our nature, both physically and spiritually. Men and women are, literally, made for each other. The physical nature of men and women perfectly complement each other according to God's divine plan. That plan, articulated in the first chapter of Genesis, says that men and women are made in God's image and likeness (see v. 26). God is Love and Life itself, and He created men and women to share His divine life, to be His spiritual children. Love *and* life are, therefore, intrinsic and essential to the complementarity between men and women.

Again (and this cannot be overemphasized), homosexual acts themselves are objectively and gravely immoral—*not the person* with a homosexual orientation—because there is no communion of body and spirit, which facilitates openness to the procreation of new life. Homosexuality undermines the truth, fullness, and wholeness of sexual communion.

This does not mean that persons with homosexual tendencies are "bad people" and are "going to hell". This kind of thinking is fueled by ignorance and misunderstanding, and because of the Church's consistent teaching, Catholics are often accused of discrimination against people of homosexual orientation. This is simply not true. The truth is that the Church recognizes the dignity of every person and condemns social discrimination in all its forms. The *Catechism* continues, "[Homosexuals] must be accepted with respect, compassion, and sensitivity. Every sign of unjust discrimination in their regard should be avoided. These persons are called to fulfill God's will in their lives and, if they are Christians, to unite to the sacrifice of the Lord's Cross the difficulties they may encounter from their condition."[71]

---

[69] *CCC* 2357.

[70] Most notably, Gen 19:1–19; Lev 18:22–25; 20:13; Rom 1:24–27; 1 Cor 6:10; and 1 Tim 1:10.

[71] *CCC* 2358.

Clearly the Church, in accord with her social teaching, acknowledges and affirms the dignity of every person. She recognizes the innate tension inherent in loving the sinner and hating the sin and, like Mary at the wedding in Cana, directs us to her Son who suffered and died for our sins. Saint Paul summarizes this point beautifully when he says, "I rejoice in my sufferings for your sake, and in my flesh I complete what is lacking in Christ's afflictions for the sake of his body, that is, the Church".[72] In other words, homosexuals must be loved, respected, and encouraged to participate in Christ's Paschal Mystery by uniting the Cross of same-sex attraction to the suffering Christ and to cooperate with God's will by living chastely.

Some homosexual advocates claim that homosexuality is a "gift" and that God "made me this way". This is simply not true. The following story from John's Gospel illustrates this point.

> As he [Jesus] passed by, he saw a man blind from his birth. And his disciples asked him, "Rabbi, who sinned, this man or his parents, that he was born blind?" Jesus answered, "It was not that this man sinned, or his parents, but that the works of God might be made manifest in him." ... As he said this, he spat on the ground and made clay of the spittle and anointed the man's eyes with the clay, saying to him, "Go, wash in the pool of Siloam" (which means Sent). So he went and washed and came back seeing.[73]

Why did Jesus perform this miracle and, in fact, any miracles at all? If the man was born blind, then, according to the homosexual argument, blindness is "the way God made him" and is his "gift". Yet, Jesus did not say to him, "Sorry, I can't help you. You were born blind, which is the way my Father in heaven made you." His blindness was not his fault just like someone born with fetal alcohol syndrome, Trisomy 13, or spina bifida cannot be blamed for his condition. The man was "born that way" because of a defect of nature that can be attributed to the continuing effects of Original Sin, *not* a gift from God.

Jesus became incarnate in the womb of the Blessed Virgin Mary and died on the Cross so that we "may have life, and have it

[72] Col 1:24.
[73] Jn 9:1–3, 6–7.

abundantly."[74] Through Christ's Passion, death, and Resurrection, and in cooperation with the grace of the Holy Spirit, God heals, elevates, and perfects our human nature, sometimes in extraordinary ways. Men and women are, by nature, designed to see, hear, walk, and be attracted to the opposite sex. We are not naturally homosexual. Even if scientists found a genetic propensity toward homosexuality, what would this prove? Simply that, like the man born blind, something (not someone) is wrong, not right. Thus, when Jesus heals the man born blind, He is restoring the man to the nature that God originally intended from the beginning.

God made us, and He knows that dwelling within the bodies He gave us is a transcendent language and meaning that speaks in and through our bodies. Therefore, we must discern whether the strong urges and longings we feel are concupiscent tendencies, which are carnal appetites whose end is self-gratification, or the language of the body, through which the Holy Spirit infuses man's soul, enlightening his intellect and will, and endowing him with the capacity and freedom to direct himself toward his true good.[75] Consequently, homosexual persons are called to chastity, and it is the Church's sincere hope that, "by the virtues of self-mastery (and) ... by prayer and sacramental grace, they can and should gradually and resolutely approach Christian perfection".[76] The same holds true for a spouse remaining chaste within marriage, a single person remaining chaste until marriage, and a priest or religious remaining chaste in celibacy.

In addition, comparing the rights of women and minorities to homosexual rights is like comparing apples to oranges. This argument is often made from a defective sense of justice, saying that homosexual unions are a "civil right" and must be implemented for the sake of "tolerance", "diversity", and "equality", which misses the point entirely.

Being a woman or a minority is not a personal lifestyle choice. Being a female or of a different nationality does not change the reality of marriage as a union between one man and one woman, and any children that may come from that union that serves as the foundation and nucleus of culture and society. Being a certain race or sex does

---

[74] Jn 10:10.
[75] See CCC 1704–5.
[76] CCC 2359.

not violate the natural moral law that comes from God. The natural law states that there is a transcendent truth planted within us to which we have access by reason alone (see Rom 2:15). The natural law is designed to make us free since "human freedom finds its authentic and complete fulfillment precisely in the acceptance of the moral law given by God."[77] Man, then, is truly free and genuinely happy when he uses his free will to align himself with the transcendent truths of the moral life "as the response due to the many gratuitous initiatives taken by God out of love for man".[78] Let's look at a few examples of how these principles translate into human law.

It is required that all persons operating a motor vehicle wear a seat belt. By its very nature, the seat-belt law denies drivers the personal choice of whether or not to wear a seat belt. In this case, individual rights are subjugated for the common good since seat belts save lives and lessen the impact of rising medical costs.

Abortion and euthanasia, legal in some states, are clear violations of the natural law. Abortion takes the life of innocent, unborn children in the womb, and euthanasia violates the principle of justice, its core tenet being that some individuals have more value and worth than others based on their utility and efficacy. Even though these gravely sinful actions are legal, that does not make them right. They clearly violate the rights and dignity of persons. Christians have a moral obligation not to follow them.

Many countries in the world have eliminated slavery and apartheid laws. These laws were wrong because all people are intrinsically valuable persons who are not by nature property. Slavery and apartheid were about racial segregation, selective discrimination, and brutal oppression based on skin color. Laws that are in the best interest of the public are not based on individual rights, preferences, or any other subjective criteria but on the objective truths of the natural law. The redefinition of marriage attempts to change the true nature of covenant relationship between one man and one woman—and any children produced by that union—as an institution that serves the public interest and common good, and reduces it to an individualized lifestyle decision.

[77] VS 35.
[78] Ibid.

Furthermore, "equality before the law must respect the principle of justice which means treating equals equally and what is different differently, that is, to give each one his due in justice. This principle of justice would be violated if de facto unions were given a juridical treatment similar or equivalent to the family based on marriage. If the family based on marriage and de facto unions are neither similar nor equivalent in their duties, functions and services in society, then they cannot be similar or equivalent in their juridical status."[79]

Traditional marriage is falling like dominoes around the world as many governments fail to make the distinction between public and private interest. Society and the public authorities must protect and encourage what is in the best interest of the public, and the State must only guarantee freedom to pursue private interest. In issues of public interest, public law intervenes, and issues of private interests must be referred to the private sphere. Marriage and the family are of public interest; they are the fundamental nucleus of society and should be recognized and protected as such. So-called alternative lifestyles are personal, private matters, and public authorities should not get involved in this private choice. De facto unions are the result of private behavior and should remain on the private level.[80]

The redefinition of marriage negates the necessity of mothers and fathers, and reduces parenting to a cliché: all you need is love. "[Children] would be deprived of the experience of either fatherhood or motherhood. Allowing children to be adopted by persons living in [homosexual] unions would actually mean ... that their condition of dependency would be used to place them in an environment that is not conducive to their full human development."[81]

The reality is that there are a number of families who do not have a mother and a father raising their children together (as in the case of death or divorce, for example). These situations, however, are a

[79] Pontifical Council for the Family, *Family, Marriage and "De Facto" Unions*, July 26, 2000, no. 10, http://www.vatican.va/roman_curia/pontifical_councils/family/documents/rc_pc_family_doc_20001109_de-facto-unions_en.html.

[80] See ibid., no. 11.

[81] Congregation for the Doctrine of the Faith, *Considerations regarding Proposals to Give Legal Recognition to Unions between Homosexual Persons*, June 3, 2003, no. 7, http://www.vatican.va/roman_curia/congregations/cfaith/documents/rc_con_cfaith_doc_20030731_homosexual-unions_en.html.

matter of *circumstance*, not design. "The fact that some married couples do not have children either because of infertility or personal decision does not determine the purpose of marriage. Exceptions do not invalidate but prove the rule; individual practices do not invalidate the objectives of an institution; variations do not nullify a norm. The inherent biological fact remains that marriage between a man and a woman will usually result in children which no shift in the realm of ideas, social trends or new technologies can change."[82] Marriage is about promoting the relationship of husbands, wives, and children for the benefit and continuation of society, not about affirming the choice of one's partner in life.

> Business dealings are regulated, but the law does not set terms for our relationships or allow us to sue over their neglect. There are no civil ceremonies for forming friendships or legal obstacles to ending them. Why is marriage different? The answer is that friendship does not affect the common good in structured ways that warrant legal recognition and regulation; marriage does. This is the only way to account for the remarkable fact that almost all cultures have regulated male-female sexual relationships. These relationships alone produce new human beings. For these new and highly dependent people, there is no path to physical, moral, and cultural maturity without a long and delicate process of ongoing care and supervision—one to which men and women typically bring strengths, and for which they are better suited the more closely related they are to the children. Unless children do mature, they will never become healthy, upright, productive members of society; and that state of economic and social development we call "civilization" depends on healthy, upright, and productive citizens. But regularly producing such citizens is nearly impossible unless men and women commit their lives to each other and any children they might have. So it is a summary, but hardly an exaggeration, to say that civilization depends on strong marriages.[83]

Being raised by a mother and a father who are married, however imperfect they may be, is a fundamental right that every child

---

[82] *Same-Sex Marriage—Why Not? A Primer Questions and Answers from the Canadian Bishops' Conference*, http://www.cccb.ca/site/Files/QandA-on-Marriage.html.

[83] Sherif Girgis, Ryan T. Anderson, and Robert P. George, *What Is Marriage? Man and Woman: A Defense* (New York: Encounter Books, 2012), 38.

deserves and is in the child's best interest. "Marriage itself constitutes the most human and humanizing context for welcoming children, the context which most readily provides emotional security and guarantees greater unity and continuity in the process of social integration and education."[84]

"The word 'marriage' isn't simply a label that can be attached to different types of relationships. Instead, 'marriage' reflects a deep reality—the reality of the unique, fruitful, lifelong union that is only possible between a man and a woman. Just as oxygen and hydrogen are essential to water, sexual difference is essential to marriage. The attempt to 'redefine' marriage to include two persons of the same sex denies the reality of what marriage is. It is as impossible as trying to 'redefine' water to include oxygen and nitrogen."[85]

> Today, many people see marriage as merely an *adult centric* institution because there is a cultural rift in the connection between marriage and children. For example, many children are born to unwed parents and couples who get married decide never to have children. As a result, an *adult centric* culture states that marriage is merely the public recognition of a committed relationship between loving adults. This describes something just for adults—a private relationship with no public benefit. In reality, marriage is a *family centric* institution and is the foundation of a stable family life. Therefore, marriage unites a man and a woman with each other and any children born from their union. This is what marriage is and does. *Family centric* marriage serves at the foundation of family life and society. It incorporates the common human desire of every person to know and be cared for by his or her own mother and father. Family centric marriage has a public interest and is in the best interest of every child without exception.[86]

---

[84] Pontifical Council for the Family, *Family, Marriage and "De Facto" Unions*, no. 26. Cf. Mark Regnerus, "How Different Are the Adult Children of Parents Who Have Same-Sex Relationships? Findings from the New Family Structures Study", *Social Science Research* 41 (2012): 752–70.

[85] "Frequently Asked Questions", answer to question no. 4 in the section entitled "The Meaning of Marriage and Sexual Difference", Marriage: Unique for a Reason, accessed January 15, 2015, http://www.marriageuniqueforareason.org/faq/#sec1q4.

[86] "Explaining the Reality of Marriage in Secular Terms", in the section entitled "Two Conflicting Understandings", Catholics for the Common Good, accessed January 22, 2013, www.ccgaction.org/swc/realityofmarriage.

People can love whomever they want. The Church does not impose morality on anyone. She proposes principles rooted in objective truth and natural law oriented toward the good of all society. The Church's teachings are not based on popular opinion or cultural trends.

Catholic men need to understand how important this is. Exclusive attention to the individual, his intentions and choices, without referring to the social and objective dimension, oriented to the common good, is the result of an arbitrary and unacceptable individualism that is blind to objective values, violates the dignity of the person, and is harmful to the social order. Therefore, it is necessary to promote an authentic male spirituality "that will help not only believers but all men of good will to rediscover the value of marriage and the family. In the *Catechism of the Catholic Church*, we read: 'the family is the original cell of social life. It is the natural society in which husband and wife are called to give themselves in love and in the gift of life. Authority, stability and a life of relationships within the family constitute the foundations for freedom, security and fraternity within society.' "[87]

*Pornography.* One of the most pervasive and dangerous forms of dehumanization in today's society is pornography. It is arguably the quintessential example of sex separated from love and tenderness, as well as human nobility and dignity. There is no question or doubt that pornography is one of the most destructive elements to authentic Catholic male spirituality.

> Pornography consists in removing real or simulated sexual acts from the intimacy of the partners, in order to display them deliberately to third parties. It offends against chastity because it perverts the conjugal act, the intimate giving of spouses to each other. It does grave injury to the dignity of its participants (actors, vendors, the public), since each one becomes an object of base pleasure and illicit profit for others. It immerses all who are involved in the illusion of a fantasy world. It is a grave offense.[88]

Pornography desecrates sexuality but is often viewed by contemporary society as harmless, playful, liberating, and progressive. It

---

[87] Pontifical Council for the Family, *Family, Marriage and "De Facto" Unions*, no. 12. Also, see *CCC* 2207, 2332ff.

[88] *CCC* 2354.

constitutes an assault on the dignity of the person, on the respect due to the human body, and on the reverence due to sexuality. Pornography, at its core, turns sex into a consumer product and places it in a context of lovelessness, exploitation, and pleasure devoid of commitment. The Lord Jesus addresses the seriousness of the sin of lust and its implications in Matthew's Gospel: "You have heard that it was said, 'You shall not commit adultery.' But I say to you that every one who looks at a woman lustfully has already committed adultery with her in his heart. If your right eye causes you to sin, pluck it out and throw it away; it is better that you lose one of your members than that your whole body be thrown into hell. And if your right hand causes you to sin, cut it off and throw it away; it is better that you lose one of your members than that your whole body go into hell."[89]

Saint John Paul II recognizes that pornography "is not the effect of a puritanical mentality or of a narrow moralism.... It is a question of an extremely important, fundamental sphere of values. Before it, man cannot remain indifferent because of the dignity of humanity, the personal character, and the eloquence of the human body."[90] This is why pornography is so destructive to the person: it pollutes and ultimately destroys charity, which is the fundamental mystery of personal loving communion, which we, as the image of God, share with Him. It deafens us to the call of love and communion, which God has inscribed in the humanity of man and woman as our primary vocation.[91] The whole meaning of true freedom directed toward self-giving in communion and friendship with God and others is lost.[92]

It is critical to understand how pornography destroys the *corpore et anima unus* relationship in men. Simply stated,

> pornography is the most misunderstood and underestimated drug in the history of the world. And while this drug is not injected or ingested, but enters the brain through the eyes and ears, it is just as powerful and its devastating effects are just as real. Referring to pornography as a drug is not metaphorical. Internet pornography triggers such a radical flood of neurochemicals in the brain, that it has been compared to

[89] Mt 5:27–30.
[90] John Paul II, *Theology of the Body*, 225.
[91] See *FC* 11.
[92] See *MD* 7, 18.

cocaine. At the simple click of a button or tap of a screen, we have instant and unlimited access to images that trigger a response in the human brain similar to street drug use. Pornography viewing triggers the brain into releasing a flood of it's [sic] own endorphins and other potent neurochemicals such as dopamine, serotonin and norepineph-rine. These internal chemicals produce a powerful rush or high very similar to street drugs. People across the globe are turning to pornog-raphy as their drug of choice for escape and self-medication because it can be accessed from virtually anywhere; it's often completely free of charge; and it is designed to encourage anonymity and secrecy.[93]

The Most Reverend Robert W. Finn, bishop of the diocese of Kan-sas City, in his pastoral letter on pornography, notes that the

use of pornography is a serious sin against chastity and the dignity of the human person. It robs us of sanctifying grace, separates us from the vision of God and from the goodness of others, and leaves us spir-itually empty. Attraction to pornography and its gratifications is a false "love" that leads to increasing emotional isolation loneliness [sic] and subsequent sexual acting-out with self and others. It depends on the ex-ploitation of other persons: frequently the desperate or poor, or the innocent young. Use of pornography has cost persons their jobs, their marriages and families. Traffickers in Child Pornography may end up in prison. It has often been associated with and has contributed to, acts of sexual violence and abuse.... In the misuse of our sexuality human weakness and selfishness can manifest themselves, sometimes in terrible ways. Human sexuality is a gift but not a toy. It is a gift to be respected and directed toward its proper end: loving and personal communion with others.[94]

"Pornography is fraudulent because it depicts 'love' without love. Since the other person is not loved, pornography requires deper-sonalization and anonymity. With pornographic sex, substitution is

[93] "Pornography Creates a Chemical Dependency", Reclaim: God's Plan for Sexual Health, accessed January 15, 2015, http://www.reclaimsexualhealth.com/Education -Resources/Pornography/.

[94] Bishop Robert W. Finn, "Blessed Are the Pure in Heart: A Pastoral Letter on the Dig-nity of the Human Person and the Dangers of Pornography", February 21, 2007, introduction and chapter 1, http://www.diocese-kcsj.org/_docs/Pastoral-02-07.pdf.

not only acceptable, it is essential. As theologian Josef Pieper said, pornography removes the fig leaf from the genitals and places it over the human face. Pornography strips its participants of more than their clothes; it strips them of their humanity."[95]

Our spiritual fathers on earth, our bishops, are—slowly but surely—beginning to address this issue. They recognize the destructive power of pornography in the lives of men and its detrimental effects on the family and society. The Most Reverend Paul S. Loverde, bishop of the diocese of Arlington, writes powerfully in a pastoral letter that,

> in my forty years as a priest, I have seen the evil of pornography spread like a plague throughout our culture. What was once the shameful and occasional vice of the few has become the mainstream entertainment for the many—through the Internet, cable, satellite and broadcast television, cell phones and even portable gaming and entertainment devices designed for children and teenagers. Never before have so many Americans been so tempted to view pornography. Never before have the accountability structures—to say nothing of the defenses which every society must build to defend the precious gift of her children—been so weak. This plague stalks the souls of men ... ravages the bonds of marriage and victimizes the most innocent among us. It obscures and destroys people's ability to see one another as unique and beautiful expressions of God's creation, instead darkening their vision, causing them to view others as objects to be used and manipulated. It has been excused as an outlet for free expression, supported as a business venture, and condoned as just another form of entertainment. It is not widely recognized as a threat to life and happiness. It is not often treated as a destructive addiction. It changes the way men and women treat one another in sometimes dramatic but often subtle ways. And it is not going away.[96]

*Conclusion.* Modern society often views the supreme expression of communion between man and woman in the sexual act as

---

[95] Robert R. Reilly, "The Politics of Porn", Catholic Education Resource Center, accessed January 15, 2015, http://www.catholiceducation.org/en/marriage-and-family/sexuality/the -politics-of-porn.html. Published as Robert R. Reilly, "The Politics of Porn", *Crisis*, December 1998, pp. 34–37.

[96] Bishop Paul S. Loverde, "Bought with a Price: Pornography and the Attack on the Living Temple of God", Arlingtondiocese.org, December 2006, introduction, http://www .arlingtondiocese.org/documents/bp_boughtwithaprice.pdf.

something casual and trivial. The true meaning of human sexuality must be rooted in the objective good that seeks to perfect man in his totality. It must also be properly ordered to and sanctified in the sacramental bond of marriage, where the practice of chastity, through which conjugal love finds its fullest expression in mutual self-giving and openness to new life, gives dignity and value to the person. Human sexuality, through which we participate in the mystery of loving communion with God, is both unitive and pro-creative. Hence, the disordered sexual expressions found in mastur-bation, contraception, homosexuality, and pornography undermine the intrinsic nature and purpose of human sexuality. Ultimately, sexuality can never find its full expression apart from the intimate partnership of life and love established by the Creator in marriage, where the husband and wife become one heart and one soul, and together obtain their human perfection.[97] Sex is only what it is meant to be if it is an exchange of the love of God and a participa-tion in the mystery of God's life and love. If it's not that, then it's not sex as God intends it to be.

Celibacy is also a participation in the mystery of God's life and love, although realized differently in the celibate man. It is a beau-tiful expression of intimacy with God on earth that quintessentially anticipates our relationship with Christ in the heavenly wedding feast. It is a sacrificial love that gives itself freely and completely in service to the Church for love of Christ, who "taught us to love him by first loving us, *even to death on the cross*".[98] Celibacy is an image of Christ's life of prayer and contemplation through which a man seeks the face of the Lord and yearns for Him. In pondering this mysterious encounter with God throughout his lifetime, the celi-bate man uncovers deeper levels of love and communion that move him closer to the Father's heart. As he moves closer to the Father's heart, the echo of God's heartbeat reverberates in his soul, stirring the Holy Spirit within him as he listens attentively to the Lord. At its core, celibacy is love lived from the Cross where God speaks to men through His Son.

[97] See *CCC* 2364 and Paul VI, *Humanae Vitae*, no. 9.
[98] William of St. Thierry, "On the Contemplation of God", Monday of the Third Week in Advent, Office of Readings, *Liturgy of the Hours*, vol. 1 (New York: Catholic Book Pub-lishing, 1975), 271 (emphasis in original).

For you to speak thus in your Son was to bring out in the light of day how much and in what way you loved us, for you did not spare your own Son but delivered him up for us all. He also *loved us and gave himself up for us*.... Everything he did and everything he said on earth, even enduring the insults, the spitting, the buffeting—the Cross and the grave—all of this was actually you speaking to us in your Son, appealing to us by your love and stirring up our love for you.[99]

The movement toward an authentic Catholic male spirituality with regard to human sexuality can be summarized in Luke's account of Christ's encounter with the Gerasene demoniac.

Then they arrived at the country of the Gerasenes, which is opposite Galilee. And as he stepped out on land, there met him a man from the city who had demons; for a long time he had worn no clothes, and he lived not in a house but among the tombs. When he saw Jesus, he cried out and fell down before him, and said with a loud voice, "What have you to do with me, Jesus, Son of the Most High God? I beg you, do not torment me." For he had commanded the unclean spirit to come out of the man. (For many a time it had seized him; he was kept under guard, and bound with chains and shackles, but he broke the bonds and was driven by the demon into the desert.) Jesus then asked him, "What is your name?" And he said, "Legion"; for many demons had entered him. And they begged him not to command them to depart into the abyss. Now a large herd of swine was feeding there on the hillside; and they begged him to let them enter these. So he gave them leave. Then the demons came out of the man and entered the swine, and the herd rushed down the steep bank into the lake and were drowned. When the herdsmen saw what had happened, they fled, and told it in the city and in the country. Then people went out to see what had happened, and they came to Jesus, and found the man from whom the demons had gone, sitting at the feet of Jesus, clothed and in his right mind; and they were afraid. And those who had seen it told them how he who had been possessed with demons was healed. Then all the people of the surrounding country of the Gerasenes asked him to depart from them; for they were seized with great fear; so he got into the boat and returned. The man from whom the demons had gone begged that he might be with him; but he sent him away,

[99] Ibid., 271–72 (emphasis in original).

saying, "Return to your home, and declare how much God has done for you." And he went away, proclaiming throughout the whole city how much Jesus had done for him.[100]

After the Fall in the Garden of Eden, the man hid himself from God's presence because he was naked and afraid (see Gen 3:9–10). When men freely choose to live in our own reality and order our lives in accord with what everybody else does and not in harmony with a well-formed conscience oriented toward the rich and beautiful truths of the Catholic faith, we are naked in our sins and hide ourselves from God. Afraid to love, we live among the tombs of a relativistic, secular way of being.

Yet the truth of who we are as men cries out for an encounter with the Living God. When we encounter authentic Catholic teaching with regard to our sexuality as men—as we make our way back on the road to authentic freedom after having our lives stuck in the muddy byways of sin—we make attempts to reconnect our faith with our everyday lived experience: "What does this teaching have to do with me?" If we are to find the true joy and peace for which our hearts long, we must humbly lay our minds and wills before the Lord.

After the encounter with Christ in the Sacrament of Reconciliation, filled with the Holy Spirit and firmly resolved to make our relationship with God our most important priority in life, we become free. As long as we continue to form our consciences in truth, partner and pray with other godly men, and continue to learn and grow in our faith, we remain free—clothed in Christ's righteousness and in our right mind.

Having put on the mind of Christ and transformed by His love, we can begin to evangelize—to share our experience of Christ with others and to declare how much God has done for us.

On that day, you will say: I give you thanks, O LORD; though you have been angry with me, your anger has abated, and you have consoled me. God indeed is my savior; I am confident and unafraid. My strength and my courage is the LORD, and he has been my savior. With

[100] Lk 8:26–39.

joy you will draw water at the fountain of salvation, and say on that
day: Give thanks to the LORD, acclaim his name; among the nations
make known his deeds, proclaim how exalted is his name. Sing praise
to the LORD for his glorious achievement; let this be known throughout all the earth. Shout with exultation, O city of Zion, for great in
your midst is the Holy One of Israel![101]

---

[101] Is 12:1–6 (NAB).

## Chapter Six

# Fatherhood

The notion of fatherhood in many families has been reduced to a biological fact.... Since human fatherhood, as a reflection of the Fatherhood of God, was designated to be the pillar of the family, the disappearance of esteem for fatherhood has led to the collapse of that pillar and to the disintegration of the family ... and inexorably is leading to the disintegration of society itself.... The spirit of anti-fatherhood has entered even the Catholic Church.

— Msgr. Joseph A. Cirrincione, *St. Joseph, Fatima and Fatherhood*[1]

Reality check: many Catholic men view regular Sunday Mass attendance as a burden and not an opportunity. How are men as husbands and fathers supposed to lead their families when they will not allow the Lord to lead them? Why don't we look forward to experiencing the Living God in word and sacrament with the same zeal and enthusiasm we have when watching sports? The truth is that there is a serious disconnect between the faith of Catholic men and their everyday lives. Let's be honest: these men don't know why they attend Mass, do not acknowledge or care about Christ's presence in the Eucharist, and, therefore, cannot effectively be the husbands and fathers God calls them to be. Most of these men are natural law practitioners who are often described by their wives as being "really good guys", but their wives are at a loss to explain why their husbands will not go to Mass with them and the children.

To get at the heart of the problem and find meaningful solutions, we must first situate Catholic fatherhood within the context

[1] Msgr. Joseph A. Cirrincione, with Thomas Nelson, *St. Joseph, Fatima and Fatherhood: Reflections on the Miracle of the Sun* (Rockford, Ill.: Tan Books, 1989), 40.

of encountering Jesus Christ in covenant relationship in the Eucharist, in the loving and life-giving communion of sacramental marriage, and in the priesthood. Once fatherhood is firmly ensconced within the heart of Christ's Paschal Mystery, we can then begin to develop a true understanding and appreciation of the great privilege God the Father has bestowed on men by allowing us to borrow His sacred name.

*Fatherhood within the Context of Covenant Relationship.* Humans are by nature relational beings because we image the Trinitarian God, who reveals Himself to us for the purpose of establishing a relationship. Therefore, the Church as the Bride of Christ and God's sign and instrument to humanity must, at her core, be the locus of continuity that tirelessly invites mankind into a relationship with God the Father, thus fostering unity and solidarity among her members. From a faith perspective, the only true *koinonia* (communion) that individuals enter into is the oneness they experience in loving God and their neighbor as themselves. It is the relational nature of God, revealed to us most fully in Jesus Christ, who reveals our own nature to ourselves "and restore(s) the unity of all in one people and one body".[2] This unity is expressed in a special way through the family, who forms a community of persons and "is thus the first human 'society.' It arises whenever there comes into being the conjugal covenant of marriage, which opens the spouses to a lasting communion of love and of life, and it is brought to completion in a full and specific way with the procreation of children: the 'communion' of the spouses gives rise to the 'community' of the family. The 'community of the family is completely pervaded by the very essence of 'communion.' "[3]

When the Church looks at how the actual grace of Christ is not only represented but communicated, it looks first and foremost to the dynamics of sacraments, primarily to the Eucharist, which is the "efficacious sign and sublime cause of that communion in the divine life, and that unity of the People of God by which the Church is kept in being".[4] In the Church, which is the Mystical

---

[2] *CCC* 813. This same paragraph adds, "It is the Holy Spirit, dwelling in those who believe and pervading and ruling over the entire Church, who brings about that wonderful communion of the faithful and joins them together so intimately in Christ that he is the principle of the Church's unity."

[3] John Paul II, *Letter to Families, 1994, the Year of the Family*, February 2, 1994, no. 7.

[4] *CCC* 1325.

Body of Christ, "the life of Christ is poured into the believers, who, through the sacraments, are united in a hidden and real way to Christ who suffered and was glorified."[5] The Eucharist is the essential dynamic of communion, relationship, and integration that binds individual Christians to each other and to Christ. The Eucharist is the supreme moment of unity in the Church, and the privileged and defining moment of *koinonia*. The Church could not continue to mediate the grace it possesses without the Eucharist, which forms the Church and brings the Church, in her fullest dimension, into being.

The Eucharist is also the requisite component of faith because in the Eucharist all of the impetus and impulses of faith reach their right and proper expression. The Holy Eucharist, Vatican II tells us, is "the fount [source] and apex [summit] of the whole Christian life".[6] It is the source of faith because it is the most profound encounter with God possible to a Christian, and it is the summit of faith because it is the supreme experience of God possible in this world.

Since sacramental marriage is essentially a spiritual life, it can be said that the Eucharist is the source and summit of Christian marriage as well. For those spouses who imbibe the Church's teaching on the true nature of marriage, who embrace sacramental marriage as a divine vocation from God, who understand that the married life means using every avenue possible to grow closer to Christ—fully aware that Christ Himself is present in the Eucharist—it makes sense that the Eucharist should be central to the married life of a Catholic. Thus, the heart of the family and, in fact, the entire life of the Church flows from the Eucharistic Christ. The Body and Blood of Christ nourishes the loving and life-giving dimensions of family life, strengthens family unity and stability, and fosters growth in holiness that fuels our desire to know and to do God's will. Modeled on the life of the Holy Family, where Jesus was prepared for His mission on earth, a Eucharist-centered family life prepares children to respond faithfully to the Lord's voice through their life's vocation.

All too often, however, Catholic spouses deliberately ignore one of the critical elements of living eucharistically: the Church's teaching on conjugal morality. It has been shown that 51 percent of all

[5] LG 7.
[6] LG 11; cf. CCC 1324.

marriages end in divorce, and this number is the same among Catholics who practice contraception, sterilization, and selective abortion.[7] Spouses who fail to recognize the received Tradition on sacramental marriage also fail to nurture a deep love for Christ in the Holy Eucharist. The better spouses understand the Eucharist's role in Christian marriage, the more they will be able to love Christ both present in the Eucharist and in one another throughout their married lives.

The Sacrament of Marriage, rooted in the Eucharist, concretizes the essential truth of *koinonia* in an absolutely tangible and meaningful way in the conjugal act between husband and wife:

> Since the Christian family united in Christ is a reflection of the Trinitarian *communion of Persons*, the conjugal union is a sign or sacrament of the love of the Trinity. It is therefore a holy and blessed act similar to the priest's consecration of the Eucharist at Mass. When a couple engages in this holy act while, at the same time, not giving themselves in love, the conjugal embrace is no longer a reflection of the love of the Trinity. A holy, sacred sign is desecrated. Such desecration, if knowingly and willingly done, is a sacrilege. It is comparable to a priest's desecration of the holy Eucharist. Thus, contracepting couples act contrary to the filial communion of persons and in so doing they give grave offense to God and to each other.[8]

The intimate union of man and woman, where they give themselves to one another in mutual and exclusive relationship as husband and wife, is by no means merely something biological but speaks to the innermost being of the individual person. Human sexuality is bodily, but our bodies are not impersonal machines or playthings: the body reveals the person. Since the body, whether male or female, is the expression of the person, it follows that a man and a woman in giving their bodies to one another give their persons to one another. This exchange also occurs when we receive the Eucharistic Christ, who gives His Body and Blood, Soul and Divinity, to us, and we give ourselves to Him in return. A husband's and wife's bodily gift

[7] See Janet E. Smith, "Paul VI as Prophet", in *Why Humanae Vitae Was Right: A Reader*, with a foreword by John Cardinal O'Connor (San Francisco: Ignatius Press, 1993), 526–27.

[8] Richard M. Hogan and John M. LeVoir, *Covenant of Love: Pope John Paul II on Sexuality, Marriage, and the Family in the Modern World*, 2nd ed. (San Francisco: Ignatius Press, 1992), 256.

to each other is the outward, sacramental sign of the communion of persons existing between them, which is an image of the communion of Persons we know as the Trinity: the Father, Son, and Holy Spirit.

In the conjugal act, the spouses image the life-giving power of the Eucharist as a loving response to God's design "by means of the reciprocal personal gift which is proper and exclusive to them. [The] husband and wife tend toward that communion of their beings whereby they help each other toward personal perfection in order to collaborate with God in the begetting and rearing of new lives."[9] In the breaking and eating of the Eucharistic bread, the spouses enter into profound and intimate relationship and communion with Christ and with one another through the gift of sacramental grace.[10] This total gift of self by the Eucharistic Christ to His Church is mirrored in the cardinal act of worship between husband and wife, namely, the conjugal act:

> This "worship" signifies the self-surrender of spouses. Thus spousal "worship" is taken up into the sublime action of worship, Christ the Bridegroom immolating himself for his spouse, the Church. A Eucharistic quality may be discerned in the loving awe with which spouses ought to offer such "worship" to one another. Thus the redemptive and Eucharistic "giving thanks" dimensions of the Sacrifice of the Mass are reflected in two members of the worshipping Mystical Body, made "one flesh" in this sacrament.[11]

The married couple, as a living witnesses to the reality of Christ's real presence in the unity and communion of persons, is transformed into Christ by the Eucharist. Through the eating of the Body and Blood of the Lord, they receive a deeper share of what they are

---

[9] Paul VI, Encyclical Letter *Humanae Vitae* (Of Human Life), July 25, 1968, no. 8.

[10] "Conjugal communion constitutes the foundation on which is built the broader communion of the family.... This communion is rooted in the natural bonds of flesh and blood, and grows to its specifically human perfection with the establishment and maturing of the still deeper and richer bonds of the spirit: the love that animates the interpersonal relationships of the different members of the family constitutes the interior strength that shapes and animates the family communion and community" (*FC* 21).

[11] Peter J. Elliott, *What God Has Joined: The Sacramentality of Marriage* (New York: Alba House, 1990), 158. Cf. *FC* 56: "Christian marriage, like the other sacraments, 'whose purpose is to sanctify people, to build up the body of Christ, and finally, to give worship to God,' is in itself a liturgical action glorifying God in Jesus Christ and in the Church."

already through Baptism: the Body of Christ.[12] Together, the married couple forms a lifelong,[13] self-donating, and indissoluble union of love: a "communion of persons intended to bear witness on earth and to image the intimate communion of persons within the Trinity".[14]

Through the power of Christ's redemptive death, which is both actualized in the Eucharist and symbolized in the marriage covenant, the husband and wife—as the domestic church, as an intimate community of conjugal life and love, and as the quintessential incarnation of the larger Church—"are elevated and assumed into the spousal charity of Christ, sustained and enriched by His redeeming power".[15]

In the sacramental encounters of Eucharist and marriage, the spouses are brought closer to that oneness and *koinonia* with God and each other that they were destined for before the Fall. Jesus Himself by coming to restore our broken relationship with the Father gives spouses the strength and grace to live their marriage vocation. Christ, in a deeply personal way, gives Himself to spouses through the Eucharist "to which Christian marriage is intimately connected."[16]

---

[12] "The married couple are priests by their baptism. Their priestly offices are activated in the sacrament of matrimony and especially in the Eucharist. John Paul suggests that the prayer of the married couple must be the prayer of the domestic church, of the familial communion of persons. It should be as a communion, as one flesh, that spouses pray" (Hogan and LeVoir, *Covenant of Love*, 277). Cf. *CCC* 1396: "Those who receive the Eucharist are united more closely to Christ. Through it Christ unites them to all the faithful in one body—the Church. Communion renews, strengthens, and deepens this incorporation into the Church, already achieved by Baptism."

[13] "The sacrament of Matrimony can be regarded in two ways: first in the making and then in its permanent state. For it is a sacrament like to that of the Eucharist, which not only while it is being conferred, but also while it remains, is a sacrament; for as long as the married parties are alive, so long is their union a sacrament of Christ and his Church" (Elliott, *What God Has Joined*, 112, citing Pius XI, *Casti Connubii*, December 31, 1930, no. 110, citing St. Robert Bellarmine, *De controversiis*, Tom. III, *op. cit.*, cap. vi, p. 628).

[14] William E. May, *Marriage: The Rock on Which the Family Is Built* (San Francisco: Ignatius Press, 1995), 65.

[15] Ibid., 106. May continues, "The Church's understanding of marriage as a sacrament in the precise sense of a created, visible reality that signifies and makes efficaciously present in the world the invisible reality of God's redemptive grace is rooted in its understanding of Christian marriage as a reality that not only *signifies*, as do all true marriages, the life-giving, love-giving, grace-giving union of Christ with his Bride, the Church, but also *inwardly participates* in this union" (107; emphasis in original).

[16] *FC* 57. On this point, Peter Elliott notes the following insightful quote by St. Robert Bellarmine: "If Marriage already entered into and celebrated is truly considered, one cannot deny that those couples who are living together in a conjugal society and union are an external material symbol representing the indissoluble union between Christ and his Church; in a similar way, in the Sacrament of the Eucharist, after the consecration has taken place, the

The gift of the Eucharist intensifies the graces given to the couple both in their Baptisms and in the marriage covenant:

> The Eucharistic Sacrifice, in fact, represents Christ's covenant of love with the Church, sealed with His blood on the Cross. In this sacrifice of the New and Eternal Covenant, Christian spouses encounter the source from which their own marriage covenant flows, is interiorly structured and continuously renewed. As a representation of Christ's sacrifice of love for the Church, the Eucharist is a fountain of charity. In the Eucharistic gift of charity the Christian family finds the foundation and soul of its "communion" and "mission": By partaking in the Eucharistic bread, the different members of the Christian family become one body, which reveals and shares in the wider unity of the Church. Their sharing in the Body of Christ that is "given up" and in His Blood that is "shed" becomes a never-ending source of missionary and apostolic dynamism for the Christian family.[17]

The Eucharist, then, assists spouses in living out their marriage covenant. The Eucharist strengthens the couple's faith and opens their hearts to the life-giving power of God's love, which enriches and deepens their conjugal communion. "It is in the Eucharist that the couple is strengthened to continue their struggle for holiness and to sanctify their family."[18] The man and the woman, who by their marriage covenant are no longer two but one flesh, are renewed and fortified by the Eucharist and are better equipped to live out their sacramental marriage in loving solidarity where they "render mutual help and service to each other through an intimate union of their persons ... [and], through this union, they experience the meaning of their oneness and attain to it with growing perfection day by

---

consecrated species remain, which are a sensible and external symbol of internal spiritual nourishment" (Elliott, 106, quoting St. Robert Bellarmine, *De controversiis*, Tom. III, *op. cit.*, cap. vi, p. 628).

[17] *FC* 57.

[18] Hogan and LeVoir, *Covenant of Love*, 276. Peter Elliott adds, "The Eucharistic way in which their Marriage covenant is structured and continuously renewed can be understood as the strengthening of their 'one flesh' with the Eucharistic Lord. 'The unity of the new covenant which marriage signifies is accomplished in Jesus' sacrifice and actualized for us in the Eucharist'. Their love becomes that of the self-giving Bridegroom whose broken Body and outpoured Blood seals the Eternal Covenant. Within that Covenant, their own nuptial covenant can become a self-giving union and communion, leading them to eternal life" (Elliott, *What God Has Joined*, 186–87).

day.''[19] The family that results from this union "draws its inner solidity from the covenant between the spouses, which Christ raised to a sacrament. The family draws its proper character as a community ... from that fundamental communion of the spouses which is prolonged in their children.''[20]

In the marriage covenant, the spouses share in the priestly mission of Jesus Christ by offering up their lives and labors to God through and with Jesus at every Eucharist;[21] their entire married and family life, sincerely offered up in and through the Eucharistic heart of Jesus, becomes a sacrifice acceptable to the Father by the merits of Jesus Christ. On Calvary, blood and water flowed from the pierced heart of Jesus, which is the fount of sanctity and the symbol of all the superabundant merits and veritable graces that are available, in a special way, to married couples who are open to receive our Eucharistic Lord. Just as Christ opened His arms on the Cross in complete and loving surrender to the Father's will, husbands and wives, in sacramental Communion, open themselves up to a total self-giving of one to the other through mutual consent and through self-surrender in the conjugal act.[22]

> Jesus Christ, Priest and Bridegroom of the Church, consecrated himself at the Last Supper as Priest and as Victim.... As Bridegroom seeking his beloved spouse, he consents to die out of love for her, to become her Victim-Spouse. Thus at the Last Supper, his nuptial consent is offered to the Father: "And for their sake, I consecrate myself, that they may be also consecrated in truth" (John 17:19). He sets himself apart as Victim for his beloved spouse, a consent fulfilled in "my body which will

---

[19] GS 48.

[20] John Paul II, *Letter to Families*, no. 8.

[21] "The Eucharist is fittingly joined to Marriage ... so that the first act of married life together may be the offering of that Sacrifice which they signify in their union. The first food that they share should be that Body and Blood 'given up' in Christ's offering of spousal love for his Church. The Nuptial Mass and first communion shared as husband and wife brings them into communion with the Sacrifice which they are called to live out each day as Christian spouses. This is meant to be the first of many Communions shared together, as spouses and as parents with children of the Church around them" (Elliott, *What God Has Joined*, xxiii–xxiv).

[22] "[The Sacrament of] Marriage is evident in the redemptive love of the Bridegroom. He sought his spouse by taking our human nature. He sacrificed himself as the second Adam to bring forth, cleanse and wed his beloved spouse so that, 'In this sacrifice there is entirely revealed that plan which God has imprinted on the humanity of man and woman since their creation; the marriage of baptized persons thus becomes a real symbol of that new and eternal covenant sanctioned in the blood of Christ'" (ibid., 32).

be given up for you …," "my blood which will be shed for you and for many," and in the "*Consummatum est!*" of the Cross. This consent and self-giving was specific, exclusive, and total for the beloved spouse. He set himself apart in consecration for her. Likewise, by consent and self-surrender in consummation, a Christian husband and a Christian wife set themselves apart, in consecration for one another.… By the sacred and exclusive nature of this consecration, Christian husbands and wives are bound to fidelity,… the fidelity of Christ Jesus who gave his body and blood so as to become one flesh with his Bride. A sublime truth is, therefore, both expressed and sealed when the spouses receive the Body and Blood of their Lord in the Nuptial Mass. The first Food of these two lives bound together underlines the mutual consecration of their bodies, their selves. His Holy Communion with them shows forth the "great mystery" to which they are raised by the bond of the Spirit [and] invites them to live in a perpetual communion of life and love.[23]

There are several major texts in Scripture from which one can draw parallels between sacramental marriage and the Eucharist. Saint John Paul II notes that in Ephesians 5:21–33, the Eucharist "draws its essential significance and its sacramental power from that spousal love of the Redeemer, by means of which the sacramentality of the Church itself is constituted above all".[24] The Eucharistic gift images the goods of the marriage covenant in that it embodies unconditional, self-giving love that is to be mutual, exclusive, and fruitful. Saint Paul reminds us of this fact when he describes the use of the sexual union and the "one flesh" of marriage as a warning against fornication.[25] As we have seen by their married union, spouses become "one body", just as we become one in the communion of the Eucharist.[26]

[23] Ibid., 151–53.

[24] Pope John Paul II, The *Theology of the Body: Human Love in the Divine Plan* (Boston: Pauline Books and Media, 1997), 142. The Holy Father refers specifically to Ephesians 5:29–30, which makes reference to Christ nourishing the members of His Body. He says that "in fact Christ nourishes the Church with his body precisely in the Eucharist."

[25] See 1 Cor 6:13–20.

[26] "Because there is one bread, we who are many are one body" (1 Cor 10:17). Peter Elliott notes that "the link between these two passages in 1 Corinthians is found explicitly in Ephesians 5:28–30: 'Even so husbands should love their wives as their own bodies. He who loves his wife loves himself. For no man ever hates his own flesh, but nourishes and cherishes it, as Christ does the church, because we are members of his body.' Marriage and the Eucharist come together in the mystery of the Church, already introduced by St. Paul in the earlier verses concerning Christ's headship in the Church (vv. 23–24), his spousal love unto death for her (v. 25), [and] her sanctification and perfection through his water and word (vv. 26–27)" (Elliott, *What God Has Joined*, xxv).

The Eucharistic words of Jesus at the Last Supper may also be seen in their nuptial meaning, which anticipate the "self-immolation" of the Bridegroom, freely giving up His Body and Blood for His beloved spouse.[27] This theme is easily connected back to Genesis, where Adam gave his own body for his spouse, Eve (see Gen 2:21–22). "Adam's cry is echoed, as it were, on the Cross: 'This is at last bone of my bone and flesh of my flesh' (Genesis 2:23). In the Paschal Mystery, the Redemption is at once Christ's work *for* us and his extension of himself in his Mystical Body which is his beloved bride."[28] Saint Paul, then, in the Ephesians 5 text, combines Adam's joyful proclamation in Genesis with the "great mystery" of the Bridegroom on the Cross to show both the redemptive and Eucharistic nature of the marriage covenant.[29] Saint John Paul II addresses this same theme from a Christian anthropology perspective:

> We find ourselves at the very heart of the Paschal Mystery, which completely reveals the spousal love of God. Christ is the Bridegroom because "he has given himself": his body has been "given," his blood has been "poured out" (cf. Luke 22:19–22). In this way "he loved them to the end" (John 13:1). The "sincere gift" contained in the sacrifice of the cross gives definitive prominence to the spousal meaning of God's love. As the Redeemer of the world, Christ is the Bridegroom of the Church. *The Eucharist is the Sacrament of our redemption.* It is *the Sacrament of the Bridegroom and of the Bride.* The Eucharist makes present and realizes anew in a sacramental manner the redemptive act of Christ, who "creates" the Church, his body. Christ is united with this "body" as the bridegroom with the bride. All this is contained in the Letter to the Ephesians. The perennial "unity of the two" that exists between man and woman from the very "beginning" [marriage as the primordial sacrament] is introduced into this "great mystery" of Christ and of the Church. It is *the*

---

[27] "The Bridegroom begins his ultimate nuptial progression, through death to resurrection, for the sake of his beloved spouse ... In the Jerusalem tradition handed on by Saint Paul, our Lord says: 'This is my body which is for you ... This cup is the new covenant in my blood' (1 Corinthians 11:24–25). In Luke, in the same tradition, the Body of Christ is 'given for you' (Luke 22:19)" (ibid., 24).

[28] Ibid., 29.

[29] See Eph 5:28–30.

*Eucharist* above all that expresses *the redemptive act of Christ the Bridegroom toward the Church the Bride.*[30]

When my wife and I were married, we made a permanent decision to love—to give ourselves to each other freely and completely. The life-giving bond that Colleen and I share is so powerful and so real that we had to give that love names: Claire, Angela, Benjamin, and Sophia. Children are the result of the central act of sacrifice and worship between a husband and wife, namely, the union of their bodies in the conjugal act, which, as we have said, mirrors the total gift of self by the Eucharistic Christ to His Church.

Marriage and, indeed, all the sacraments tell us something about who God is. Marriage, in fact, reflects the reality that the Father, Son, and Holy Spirit are of one divine nature, essence, and substance, for Scripture tells us: "God created man in his own image, in the image of God he created him; male and female he created them"[31], and again, "Then the man said, 'This at last is bone of my bones and flesh of my flesh; she shall be called Woman, because she was taken out of Man.' Therefore a man leaves his father and his mother and cleaves to his wife, and they become one flesh".[32] In creating husbands and wives, God has made two things very clear: first, the one-flesh union between a husband and wife reflects His own divine image and likeness, and second, the fact that husbands and wives are truly equal does not mean they are the same person or have the same role in the marriage.

We can understand the role of husbands and fathers within marriage by correctly interpreting chapter 5 of Saint Paul's Letter to the Ephesians, particularly verses 22–24: "Wives, be subject to your husbands, as to the Lord. For the husband is the head of the wife as Christ is the head of the church, his body.... As the Church is subject to Christ, so let wives also be subject in everything to their husbands."

---

[30] John Paul II, *Theology of the Body*, 481. Cf. *LG* 7–8. Peter Elliott notes that Pope John Paul II as Karol Cardinal Wojtyla states, "The love of Christ-the-Bridegroom stems directly from the cross and the sacrifice.... He is able to bring his Gift (*the Eucharist*) to the Church precisely because he has already given himself in the sacrifice of his blood" (Elliott, *What God Has Joined*, 30; emphasis in original).

[31] Gen 1:27.

[32] Gen 2:23–24.

Saint Paul is saying that wives should put themselves under the mission of their husbands. What is the mission of the husband? To "love your wives, as Christ loved the Church".³³ How did Christ love the Church? He gave Himself up for her. He died for her in service to her. Jesus tells us, "[W]hoever would be great among you must be your servant, and whoever would be first among you must be your slave; even as the Son of man came not to be served but to serve, and to give his life as a ransom for many."³⁴ The husband is the head of the home precisely because he is the chief servant and priest of his family. Men's role as husbands and fathers necessarily means that we must sacrifice everything: our bodies, our desires and wills, our hopes and dreams—everything we have and everything we are for the sake of our wives, children, the Church, and the culture. Living our fatherhood by the example of Christ on the Cross is what separates boys from men, what separates the men who are merely "daddies" from the real men who are truly fathers.

*Fatherhood and the Domestic Church.* There is no question that we are in a fatherhood crisis in our Church and world where many men have completely abdicated or simply ignored the responsibility of exercising moral and spiritual authority in the home. With no fathers to model faith-filled leadership and God-centered authority, our young men have grown up embracing moral relativism and secular ideology, and these have become their god. "As experience teaches, the absence of a father causes psychological and moral imbalance and notable difficulties in family relationships".³⁵

The apostle Paul lays the foundation for getting fathers back on track: "Christ did not send me to baptize but to preach the gospel, and not with eloquent wisdom, lest the cross of Christ be emptied of its power. For the word of the cross is folly to those who are perishing, but to us who are being saved it is the power of God. . . . [W]e preach Christ crucified".³⁶ The virtues of authentic Catholic fatherhood are the wellspring that flow from the Blood of the Cross from which we fathers must drink deeply in order to live the Catholic faith with fervor and humility through continuous acts of service and sacrifice.

³³ Eph 5:25.
³⁴ Mt 20:26–28.
³⁵ FC 25.
³⁶ 1 Cor 1:17–18, 23.

Our spiritual fatherhood is truly authentic when it is focused on Christ crucified. Hence, it is only through an authentic spirituality of fatherhood, a spirituality that imitates Christ—that meditates on God's Word and responds to that Word in faith and, through the Holy Spirit, makes us share in the Triune life—that we can foster and nurture growth in holiness. The more we act under God's spirit, the more we seek to know and to do God's holy will in our lives, the more we implore the assistance and grace of the Holy Spirit, the more we grow in holiness. The Lord Jesus is the quintessential model of holiness, and by following His perfect example, we grow in our love of God and our neighbor.

The Most Blessed Sacrament is the source of spiritual fatherhood because the Eucharist *is* Jesus Christ. It is not a symbol or representation of Christ but the reality of God with whom we are in intimate relationship: a relationship that "draws the faithful and sets them aflame with Christ's insistent love".[37] The Eucharist, therefore, is the fountain where we receive the strength, power, and grace to seek the Lord in faith. The Eucharist is the beginning of spiritual fatherhood and "is for the soul the most certain means of remaining united to Jesus".[38] It is a deepening of the relationship that began in Baptism, was deepened and strengthened in Confirmation, and realizes a level of intimacy in the Eucharist that is inherently supernatural and mysterious, yet inexhaustible. In the reception of the Eucharist, we literally become one with God in a way that is purposeful and real. It is the "fount" from which flows the definition of who we are as men in terms of our relationship with Christ, "who maintains and increases the Divine life in us".[39]

Strengthened by the Eucharist, fathers should personify and exude faith, that is, they should exhibit a clear awareness that their work on earth is, first and foremost, God's work. Therefore, men must foster ongoing growth in faith and personal formation, which must include daily prayer so that our spirituality is firmly rooted in personal relationship with the Holy Trinity and grounded in the Catholic faith.

Spiritual fathers must be aware of the influence of secular thought and culture, with its disordered values, ideologies, and disintegrated

[37] Vatican Council II, Constitution on the Sacred Liturgy, *Sacrosanctum Concilium*, December 4, 1963, no. 10.
[38] Columba Marmion, O.S.B., *Christ the Life of the Soul: Spiritual Conferences*, 11th ed., translated by a nun of Tyburn Convent (London: Sands, 1925), 261.
[39] Ibid., 263.

view of the person, and its profound influence within and upon our children today. Many of our teenagers and young adults are struggling to hold on to Catholic beliefs and practices. They do not feel deeply connected to the sacraments. They cannot see what the Catholic faith has to do with their daily lived experience. Many, because they have been poorly catechized in the faith, fall into the abyss of self-indulgence and self-gratification, embracing societal norms that place themselves at the center of all reality and truth, and at odds with the Catholic faith. In short, our youth and young adults have become fans of Jesus but not followers.

This view is in direct contrast to the life and mission of Jesus Christ and is, therefore, the antithesis of the life and mission of the Church. Solid faith formation led by the father within the family must occur and operate within the context of faith and Church, so that every family member is continually molded into the image of Christ for the purpose of salvation. Pride of place must be given to a systematic approach to disseminating the truth and beauty of Catholic teaching—firmly rooted in the foundational truths of the Trinity, the Incarnation, and grace as revealed to us in Sacred Scripture, passed down through Sacred Tradition, and protected by the Magisterium—that makes Jesus Christ come alive in the hearts of our young people (cf. Lk 24:32).

To this end, the father—as the chief servant of the family—must nurture an atmosphere of inclusion in all aspects of family and parish life so that youth and young adults "who by Baptism are incorporated into Christ and integrated into the People of God, are made sharers in their particular way in the priestly, prophetic, and kingly office of Christ, and have their own part to play in the mission of the whole Christian people in the Church and in the world".[40] Under the guidance and direction of strong, godly fathers, these young people of faith should participate fully in the evangelizing and sanctifying activity of the domestic church as well as the corporal and spiritual works of mercy, the renewal of the social order in the spirit of the Gospel, and the pastoral ministry of the parish.

In addition, the sacramental dimension of family life must be encouraged. The home and parish must embody a spirituality that

---

[40] CCC 897.

enhances and promotes devotion and active participation in the Eucharist, where "grace is channeled into us and the sanctification of men in Christ and the glorification of God, to which all other activities of the Church are directed as toward their goal, are most powerfully achieved."[41] This must be accompanied by a deeper appreciation and understanding of the reality of sin and the need for frequent reception of the Sacrament of Reconciliation.

All of this must originate and be fostered in the home, the domestic church and foundation of the parish community, where education in the fundamental truths of the faith are nurtured, fostered, and ensconced through family prayer—for example, Rosaries, Eucharistic Adoration, weekly attendance at Mass, recitation of the Liturgy of the Hours, and Scripture study. Families, led by truly spiritual fathers, are a special witness to God's loving plan in the world and the breeding ground for future generations of Catholic men and women. Hence, the church of the home, while always remaining faithful to the Magisterium, must work together as an evangelizing society to produce "shining witnesses and models of holiness" who emulate the love of Christ in the world.[42]

Relativistic ideology clouds the vision of secular society. The spiritual man must see clearly with the eyes of Jesus Christ, through the lenses of faith, hope, and love. This vision, in turn, must give spiritual strength to the faithful and concreteness to the domestic church, and it must extend charitably to the parish and broader community. We must live our lives "in harmony with [our] faith so that [we] can become the light of the world. We need that undeviating honesty which can attract all men to the love of truth and goodness, and finally to the Church and to Christ."[43]

*Fathers as Kings, Prophets, and Priests.* Inherent within Christ's masculinity are qualities natural to all Catholic husbands who, by cooperating with God's grace in their lives, make a gift of themselves in love. These include love-centered headship, servant-based leadership, and life-giving authority. These headship, leadership, and authority characteristics are modeled after Christ's kingly, prophetic, and priestly

---

[41] Vatican Council II, *Sacrosanctum Concilium*, no. 10.

[42] *LG* 39.

[43] Vatican Council II, Decree on the Apostolate of the Laity, *Apostolicam Actuositatem*, November 18, 1965, no. 13.

*munera*, realized both in the family, where children bring to realization the husband's role as father, and in the priesthood, where the priest serves in the person of Christ, the eternal Bridegroom giving life to Christ's Bride and God's children as a father of the Church on earth.

Christ has shown us the ideal of the king who surrenders all to serve with humility those entrusted to his care. Our Lord says, "[E]very one who exalts himself will be humbled, and he who humbles himself will be exalted".[44] Humility does not mean having low self-esteem, or being overly pious or holy, since true humility is not about us. Humility is love-centered headship.

Saint Louis trembled as he took the solemn oath as king of France. He asked God for courage, light, and strength to use his authority to defend the Church and serve his people well. He founded a hospital in Paris that housed three hundred patients, and he received poor and hungry people in his home on a daily basis. During Lent and Advent he cared for all who came, often waiting on them personally.

When Solomon became king of Israel, he asked God to give him "an understanding mind to govern your people, that I may discern between good and evil.... It pleased the LORD that Solomon had asked this. And God said to him, 'Because you have asked this, and have not asked for yourself long life or riches or the life of your enemies, but have asked for yourself understanding to discern what is right, behold, I now do according to your word.' "[45] In humility, King Solomon asked God for wisdom, and God gave him what he asked for, and so much more.

A husband most definitively assumes his responsibility as king when the family is completed by the addition of children, for not only must a father serve his children as he has been serving his wife, but he must now also serve his wife in new, nurturing, and protective ways. "Love for his wife as mother of their children and love for the children themselves are for the man the natural way of understanding and fulfilling his own fatherhood."[46] Thus, in fatherhood "the mystery of man's masculinity, that is, the generative and fatherly meaning of His body, is also thoroughly revealed".[47]

[44] Lk 14:11.
[45] 1 Kings 3:9–12.
[46] FC 25.
[47] John Paul II, *Theology of the Body*, 81.

Christ has shown us the ideal of the prophet, a man who witnesses daily to the awesome majesty, power, and glory of God in the world as a servant-leader. A father must be a prophet for his family, the Church, and the culture, meaning that his witness must be lived out and not simply preached, reinforcing the formational and sanctifying aspects of fatherhood.

> And he told them many things in parables, saying: "A sower went out to sow. And as he sowed, some seeds fell along the path, and the birds came and devoured them. Other seeds fell on rocky ground, where they had not much soil, and immediately they sprang up, since they had no depth of soil, but when the sun rose they were scorched; and since they had no root they withered away. Other seeds fell upon thorns, and the thorns grew up and choked them. Other seeds fell on good soil and brought forth grain, some a hundredfold, some sixty, some thirty. He who has ears, let him hear."[48]

When fathers share their love for the Catholic faith in response to the grace received in Baptism, they are sowers planting seeds. It is the Holy Spirit that allows the seed of faith to take root and grow in the hearts of those who hear and accept His invitation to life-giving communion, and if we freely and lovingly cooperate with what God wants to do in us, our lives will bear much fruit. Men must encourage their children, family members, parishioners, friends, fallen-away Catholics—everyone—never to stop learning about the faith, never to stop asking questions, and never to stop struggling, as well as to live the faith that we profess with great joy and enthusiasm! Living an authentic male spirituality inspires others to make the connection between the faith that they learn and the lived experience of that faith. Sometimes this means picking up our Crosses and following Christ with the understanding that living the truth means being countercultural. A father, as a sower of the seeds of faith "in the midst of a crooked and perverse generation, among whom" he shines as "a light in the world",[49] bears witness to the truth that Christ did not die so that His teachings could be changed by the culture; Christ died so that His love and His truth could change the world.

[48] Mt 13:3–9.
[49] Phil 2:15.

What is our response when we come face-to-face with truth? Do we allow the seed to fall to the ground and never take root deep within us, where "the evil one comes and takes away what is sown in his heart"?[50] Are we Catholic only to the point where we feel comfortable and ignore the Church's teaching on difficult issues? Are we prepared to learn the why of our faith before simply dismissing certain Church teachings that are at odds with the popular culture? Are we honest enough with ourselves to truly engage and struggle with what it means to be a faithful Catholic?

When we come face-to-face with truth, is the seed of faith sown on the rocky ground of our hearts, where it lasts only until some tribulation or persecution comes along? Do we accept the Church's teaching so long as it doesn't affect us directly? When we are faced with serious challenges in our lives that require moral strength and fortitude, are we able to say yes to Jesus Christ and no to outside forces that see Jesus only as "a great guy" and not the Savior of the world, that see all truth as relative rather than the only Son of God as "the way, and *the truth*, and the life"?[51] Jesus asks us to follow in His footsteps: to die and rise with Him. He did not put down His Cross, walk away, and take the easy way out—and neither should we!

Is the seed of God's love trying to grow amid the thorns of sin in our souls? Do the obligations of our faith, which free men to love as God loves, influence the way we think and act, or are we content with reducing our faith to myopic battles between Democrats and Republicans, or liberals versus conservatives? Do we accept the responsibility of life-giving love and communion that comes with being Catholic, or do we decide and define for ourselves what being Catholic means, influenced by a culture of death that chokes the Word and bears no fruit?

We are called to lives of holiness, lives that constitute the simplest and best way to perceive the beauty of truth, to experience the liberating force of God's love, and to acknowledge the value of unconditional fidelity to all of God's laws, even in the most difficult situations. Our Lord calls us to be His courageous servants of all that is true and good and beautiful. Deep inside our hearts we know it; let us not be afraid to live it! Let us strive to hear the Word of God and understand it; let us be rich and fertile soil so that God's life may grow in us.

[50] Mt 13:19.
[51] Jn 14:6; emphasis added.

Christ has shown us the ideal of the priest, who formally sanctifies the world and intercedes for His Bride, the Church. Fathers are called to the same role in the family, the domestic church. "One of the marvels of God's plan is that He has given fathers a priesthood and priests a fatherhood. Within the family, the father stands before God as a priest and mediator. Within the Church, the priest stands before his parish as a father. This is a powerful truth. And it is more than a metaphor. It is something profoundly sacramental, and built into the fabric of God's plan from the very beginning."[52]

In the days before global positioning systems, Mapquest, and Google Earth, men were stereotyped as reluctant to ask for directions. You know the scene: a couple is driving somewhere and, unable to find their destination, the wife turns to her husband and says, "Honey, maybe we should stop and ask for directions." The husband, dismayed that his wife would dare challenge his sense of direction, stubbornly says, "I know where I'm going!" This would go on and on until they eventually found the place or fell so far behind schedule that they would have no choice but to stop at the nearest gas station for directions.

Thanks to modern technology, those days are gone forever. In this day and age it's virtually impossible to get lost. However, a GPS may be able to get you from Portland to Chicago, Mapquest may be able to get you to your favorite downtown restaurant, and Google Earth may show you the best route from New York to Australia, but no amount of technology in the world will get you from earth to heaven!

What Jesus says in the Gospel of Matthew is true of many men today: we are "harassed and helpless, like sheep without a shepherd."[53] When a man would rather spend time looking at pornography or hanging out with the boys than have any meaningful relationship with his wife and children, he is lost. When a man approaches dating as a conquest, where the primary goal is to "hit it and quit it", he is lost. When a man becomes wealthy at the expense of the poor, he is lost. When a man under the influence of drugs or alcohol beats his wife, passing on a legacy of violence and abuse to his children, he is lost.

[52] Scott Hahn, "Going on Vacation: Why Fathers Are Priests and Priests Are Fathers", in *Scripture Matters: Essays on Reading the Bible from the Heart of the Church* (Steubenville, Ohio: Emmaus Road Publishing, 2003), p. 83.
[53] Mt 9:36.

Just as Jesus called laborers into the field to reap an abundant harvest of souls, He calls husbands and fathers who are lost to use the navigational tools of prayer, forgiveness, and mercy to find our way back to our Father in heaven. Just as Jesus called men to the priesthood to serve His Bride, the Church, the same Jesus calls men through Baptism to be priests of the domestic church, the church of the home. A husband and father should exercise his priestly ministry through "the offering he makes of himself and his daily activities".[54] This offering should be united to Christ's offering in the Eucharist "for their work, prayers, and apostolic endeavors, their ordinary married and family life, their daily labor, their mental and physical relaxation, if carried on in the spirit—and even the hardships of life, if patiently borne—all of these become spiritual sacrifices acceptable to God through Jesus Christ."[55] The main job of the priest is to offer sacrifice, and the Holy Sacrifice of the Mass should lead fathers to intimate and personal relationship with God, uniting them so closely to Christ that the Eucharist becomes the very soul and center of their spiritual and family life.

The priest of the home must accept the responsibility of living the Gospel by his words and actions. In a world filled with temptation and sin, living Gospel values can be challenging. It takes discipline and self-control to hone virtue and holiness within the family. As such, fathers should be the locus of order and life-giving authority in the home.

Discipline should *never* be done out of anger and frustration. The instrument of discipline should be a tool that is used to *disciple* our children, to bring them into a deeper, more loving relationship of covenant intimacy with Jesus. Christ-centered discipline includes both listening with an open heart, and establishing clear and unambiguous rules concerning unacceptable behaviors, firmly planted within the soil of patience and understanding. Consequences for violating the fourth commandment to honor our fathers and our mothers should be exercised with immediate and consistent disciplinary action. The parameters and rubrics around which discipline is structured and implemented should be decided by both the father and the mother, but the father, as the priest of the home, should be the

---

[54] John Paul II, Post-Synodal Apostolic Exhortation *Christifideles Laici* (The Lay Members of Christ's Faithful People), December 30, 1988, no. 14 (hereafter cited as *CL*).

[55] *LG* 34.

enforcer. If the father is not there at the time a disciplinary measure is employed, he must ensure that his children revere and respect their mother's decisions and actions in his absence.

Mothers are often more in tune with the emotional, psychological, and spiritual development of their children. Therefore, for their part, mothers must help fathers discern the most effective disciplinary approach for the children according to the character and personality of each child. When a dad makes a disciplinary decision and, for whatever reason, a mom disagrees with the action taken, she must never undermine her husband's authority by correcting him or negating his decision in front of the children. Disagreements regarding discipline should always be handled privately.

The priest of the home must accept the responsibility of living "the Gospel in faith and proclaiming it in word and deed, without hesitating to identify and denounce evil".[56] Christian parents are the primary and indispensable catechists of their own children. Fathers are not only called to preach the Gospel, but also, and above all, to *live* the Gospel by setting a good example for their children. If our children see us living the Catholic faith with fidelity and joy—on our knees praying, reading the Bible, leading the family in prayers and devotions—then we can be sure that our example will be worth more than a thousand words and have confidence that our love for Christ will be written into the hearts of our sons and daughters. When we do this, the Catholic faith will become more than a fond memory that fades with time. A father's living witness to covenant intimacy will become his enduring legacy, a precious gift for his children, and a sure sign of hope in God's endless mercy and love.

[*Priests as Husbands and Fathers of the Church on Earth.*][57] The crisis in the Church in the United States, brought on by the discovery of

---

[56] *CL* 14.

[57] This entire subsection that I have entitled "Priests as Husbands and Fathers of the Church on Earth", including "The Priest as Man", "The Priest as Husband", and "The Priest as Father", was written entirely by Monsignor John Cihak, S.T.D., published as "The Priest as Man, Husband, and Father", in *Sacrum Ministerium* 12, no. 2 (2006): 75–85. Monsignor Cihak's treatment of the subject of fatherhood as it relates to the priesthood is unparalleled. Consequently, rather than my trying to construct my own thesis around this topic as a non-priest, Monsignor Cihak has given his kind and generous permission to republish his article in its entirety in this book. All footnotes for this section (nos. 57–74) are from Monsignor Cihak's original work (emphasis added).

sexual abuse perpetrated by members of the clergy, indicates the need
for clergy reform and renewal. The need for the renewal of the clergy,
as for all Christians, is perennial and certain periods of the Church's
history have been more intense than others in this regard. Around
the year 1000 it was the reform of Pope St. Gregory VII, especially
in the area of celibacy among clergy. In the late 1500s, it was the
reform spearheaded by the Council of Trent and by St. Charles Borromeo, who established the seminary system for the formation of
priests. Some have proposed that the current crisis can be solved by
having women priests, married priests or part time priests.

The Church proposes another way. The clergy will be renewed in
this age, as in previous ages, only through a re-appropriation of the
very essence of priesthood.

The contemporary crisis, profoundly marked by sexual misconduct,[58]
in its essence is a problem rooted in the priest's *humanity*; more specifically, his fundamental human identity as man, husband, and father and
the relationships that necessarily flow from it.[59] The contemporary crisis, especially in its form as sexual misconduct, is driven by the priest's
rejection of his fundamental human identity in some manner. The first
vocation of Christians is to become holy, and for the priest his path to
holiness lies in loving with the fully human and priestly Heart of Jesus.
Jesus both reveals and exercises His priesthood in a fully human way,
and therefore His priests exercise the priesthood given them by Christ
in a fully human way. Since Christ's manhood is indispensable for His
priesthood, we can conclude that the manhood of His priests is equally

---

[58] It is important to observe from the beginning that clergy sexual abuse is not unique to the
United States although most of the media attention has been focused there. The media, moreover, has characterized the scandal as a problem of pedophilia. The studies commissioned by
the Bishops of the United States on clergy sexual abuse help to give us a better understanding
of the nature of the crisis, which is more nuanced than the media reports, and which I believe
supports the line of argumentation in the present article. The data from the John Jay Report
of 2004 indicate that a great majority of the priest offenders were not in fact pedophiles. Their
data stated that 81% of the sexual abuse victims were male (19% were female) with 78% of the
victims between the ages of 11–17. Moreover, 77% of the priest offenders molested adolescent
boys and 63% of the male victims were between the ages of 14–17. Thus a great majority
of the victims were actually post-pubescent adolescent boys. The study further states that a
majority of the priest offenders had one or two victims. Such statistics indicate that the sexual
abuse crisis is less a matter of pedophilia and more a matter of deep-seated homosexual tendencies. Cf. John Jay Report, section 4.3, at 69–70; Catholic Medical Association, *To Protect
and To Prevent: The Sexual Abuse of Children and Its Prevention*, 2006, 5–6.

[59] The priest's fundamental human identity also includes his identity as *son*, but this important dimension of his identity extends beyond the scope of this article.

indispensable in sacramentally representing Christ's priesthood.[60] Thus the current renewal of the priesthood will not happen by changing or modifying the priest's *function* but by renewing the *identity*, specifically the *human identity* of the priest.

The Church—in the documents of Vatican II (especially *Lumen gentium* and *Presbyterorum ordinis*) and in the ordinary magisterium of Pope John Paul II—has placed great emphasis on the inherent human *relationality* of the priest. By "relationality" we mean that man is essentially made to be in relationship with God and others. But how is he relational? The priest is relational following the pattern set by the Master. Jesus the priest is relational as *man*, as *husband* to the Church, and as *father* in generating spiritual life. The priest's relationality imitates Christ's. The priest relates in his humanity as man, as husband, and as father.

Some may characterize the renewal of the human identity of the priest by contrasting "cultic" priesthood and "pastoral" priesthood. They think that "cultic" priesthood, with its emphasis—I presume—on the priest's sanctifying office, must be deemphasized in favor of a "pastoral" priesthood in which the emphasis—again, I presume—falls on teaching and governing. I disagree with such a dichotomy for two main reasons. First, one does not find this manner of discourse in Vatican II or elsewhere in the Church's teaching. Second, the attempt to contrast "cultic" and "pastoral" presupposes wrongly that the three-fold *munera* of the priest (teaching, sanctifying, and governing) are somehow in competition with each other, or are exclusive of each other.

The Church instead takes a wider view. Such a solution does not reach deep enough. The problem is not "cultic" priests or "pastoral" priests, but *humanly relational* priests as men, as husbands and as fathers.[61] The Church ever since the Council has been emphasizing

---

[60] Cf. *Catechism of the Catholic Church*, no. 1577. [*CCC* hereafter.] For a more detailed study of the indispensability of the priest's manhood, cf. Manfred Hauke, *Women in the Priesthood?* (San Francisco: Ignatius Press, 1988); Robert Pesarchick, *The Trinitarian Foundation of Human Sexuality as Revealed by Christ According to Hans Urs von Balthasar. The Revelatory Significance of the Male Christ and the Male Ministerial Priesthood* (Tesi Gregoriana Teologia 63, Roma 2000).

[61] It may be argued that a candidate for the priesthood may take refuge in the cultic relationship of priesthood, in which the relationality is scripted according to rubrics, in order to avoid the difficult task of the constant relational improvisation required by the teaching and governing offices of the priesthood. Such refuge taking is understandable. It is much easier to be in a relationship that is already scripted, and fallen human persons tend to relate in a way that is more secure and requires the least amount of vulnerability. The solution to the problem of "hiding" in cultic relationality, however, lies not in de-emphasizing the cultic

the relationality that must be a part of *all* the priest's offices: the relationality he brings to his teaching, the relationality he brings to offering Holy Mass and dispensing the Sacraments, and the relationality he brings to shepherding Christ's flock. The priest pours out his life in sacrificial love by teaching, sanctifying, and governing as a man, as a husband, and as a father, patterned on the way Jesus lives His priesthood. The priest's pastoral charity flows from his inherent human identity as man, husband, and father, so that the divine love which shines out from Christ's own perfect humanity can also shine through the imperfect humanity of His priest. Thus the renewal of the priesthood today will address the priest's humanity, that is, who he is as man, husband and father.

[*The Priest as Man.*] First, the priest is a man. What does this mean? A man is made in the image and likeness of God, and thus is made for self-giving love. That is the meaning of his existence. God alone fulfills a man, yet the Lord has willed that this fulfillment happen through a man's relationship with *woman*, who is equal in dignity and complementary in mission.[62] This is an important point: man cannot achieve his fulfillment as man without woman, and vice versa. Man cannot attain fulfillment alone with God, which was revealed in Adam's solitude (Gen 2:20), nor can he do it in relationship only with other men. In the same way woman cannot attain her fulfillment alone or only with other women, but only through the complementary relationship with man.

The Church's teaching, therefore, is neither chauvinist nor feminist, but human—human as both masculine and feminine intrinsically related to each other in God. This is not a politically correct

---

relationship (the approach of some seminary formators) or by hiding in the cultic relationship (the approach of some candidates), but rather in going deeper into the candidate's relationality as a man. Trying to shape the candidate's relationality by emphasizing or de-emphasizing one of the *munera* does not get to the root of a candidate's difficulties in relating. Since relationships are founded upon trust, it seems best in my view for the formator to affirm the candidate's ability to relate in the cultic realm, and from that point to help him unpack the tremendous vulnerability that the Lord Jesus asks of His priest in the cultic realm. Then the candidate can be more easily led down into his ability or inability to relate as a man. Cultic relationality is necessary but not sufficient for a priest. However, it can be argued that the priest's cultic relationality is primary among the three *munera* because his relationality as priest is necessarily Christ's priestly relationality. Without a foundation in the cultic relationship, the priest's relationality easily becomes unfettered from Christ's priestly relationality and devolves into simply his own. The cultic relationality of the priest is Christ's total self-giving to the Father on the Cross. Christ's total self-giving in love seen clearly in the cultic realm sets the pattern for the priest's relationships in preaching and governing.

[62] Cf. *CCC* 371–72.

way of speaking, but this is Divine Revelation. Through this essential relationship with woman, a man in the order of nature becomes a husband and father. A man is fulfilled and perfected through spousal love and paternity. Furthermore, man is also comprised of body and soul, and against any heresy of Angelism or Jansenism, man's embodiment is good and holy. Man's embodiment is willed by the Lord in creation and is essential to man's ability to be in relationship.

Man and woman, made in the image and likeness of God, are called to become sharers in the divine nature.[63] Their destiny is to share eternal life with the Blessed Trinity and with all the angels and saints. Thus, man is to become holy, to become like God. He is called to a life of virtue, prayer, and total, self-giving love in imitation of the Father, Son, and Holy Spirit who reveal themselves as Persons in their self-giving love. Holiness is the universal vocation we receive in Baptism. To be a man is to live beyond oneself with others and for others.

Because of original sin, man is a sinner who bears the wounds of original sin and its effect of concupiscence. Choosing to love the way Jesus showed us, therefore, requires grace and often involves renunciation and suffering on our part. Jesus calls His followers to the narrow path that leads to life (Matthew 7:13–14; Luke 13:24), and His grace enables us to renounce our wills and to suffer well. The ability to renounce one's own will and to accept suffering in order to love lies at the root of what Pope John Paul II calls "affective maturity."[64] Affective maturity, or "responsible love" as he also terms it, is the ability to give oneself freely in love. Pope John Paul II stresses affective maturity as a fundamental and essential criterion to be able to relate to others. He writes, "We are speaking of a love that involves the entire person, in all his or her aspects—physical, psychic and spiritual—and which is expressed in the 'nuptial meaning' of the human body, thanks to which a person gives oneself to another and takes the other to oneself."[65] For most people, the affective maturity needed to love selflessly is gained through a struggle with one's concupiscence.

To be a Christian man, therefore, means to accept Jesus' invitation to enter into ongoing and life long conversion toward greater holiness. A man called to priesthood is one who practices saying "No" to his own disordered pleasures and selfish designs, and saying "Yes"

---

[63] Vatican II, *Dei Verbum*, 2.

[64] Cf. John Paul II, *Pastores Dabo Vobis [I Will Give You Shepherds]*, [March 25,] 1992, nos. 43–44. [*PDV* hereafter]

[65] *PDV* 44.

to the Lord's will and acting for the good of others. This process takes into account a man's failings, sinfulness, and weakness through which divine grace can shine. The man called to priesthood, therefore, is not a perfect man. God did not call angels to be priests, but men (Hebrews 5:1). Rather the priesthood will perfect him if he embraces it, strives to cooperate with the grace in it, and lives it in the way Jesus and His Bride intend it to be lived. The man as priest is an earthen vessel into which is poured divine treasure (2 Corinthians 4:7). Though not perfect and still a sinner, a man living the call to the priesthood demonstrates a sufficient capacity for self-sacrifice, and a willingness to struggle for self-mastery to become holy.

The struggle for holiness entails, furthermore, the pursuit of virtue, which often involves "long and exacting work,"[66] whereby man governs his passions and gains the freedom necessary for responsible love.[67] This means he is honest and able to admit, at least eventually, when he is wrong or fails. At the foundation of the priest's manhood, therefore, is his necessary and complementary relationship with woman whereby he becomes a husband and father in some manner, and his affective maturity revealed in and developed by sacrificial love whereby he grows in holiness.

[*The Priest as Husband.*] The second aspect of the priest's fundamental human identity is that of a husband. Jesus is the Head and Bridegroom of the Church. His relationship to the Church is *spousal.*[68] The priest is a husband by his participation in Christ's spousal relationship with His Bride the Church.[69] The priest's participation in Christ's spousal relationship to the Church is seen most clearly in the priest's words of consecration and absolution where the "I" of Christ and the "I" of the priest are one.

A priest strives to love the Church with the Heart of Jesus. His is a husband's love. The priest's spousal relationship with the Church

---

[66] *CCC* 2342.

[67] Cf. *CCC* 2337–339, 2342.

[68] Cf. Gen 2:21–25; John 19:34–37, Ephesians 5:23–25, Revelation 21:2.

[69] Cf. Vatican II, *Presbyterorum ordinis*, 2; *PDV.* 16, 22. The Church affirms her identity as Bride not only in her teaching but also in her Liturgy, for example, in the Easter *Exsultet*, in the Preface for the Dedication of a Church, and in the anamnesis of Eucharistic Prayer III. The priest as husband to the Church has a strong theological current in the Fathers. The other strong current in the Fathers is the priest as friend of the Bridegroom. I emphasize the first current while recognizing the importance of the second. The two currents are related. The first shows the priest that he indeed participates in Christ's spousal relationship to His Bride. The second current reminds the priest that he is not Christ, and thus his sharing in Christ's spousal relationship is participatory and not identical.

is the foundation for his promise of life-long celibate chastity. The priest's spousal relationship is expressed in the promises he makes at ordination of celibacy, obedience, and prayer, as well as in his striving after the evangelical counsels of poverty, chastity and obedience, which the diocesan priest does not vow explicitly but which nevertheless constitute the pastoral charity of Jesus' own priesthood. To participate in Christ's spousal relationship to the Church means that his life must conform to the way in which Christ loved his spouse: through the total sacrificial gift of Himself on the Cross. "Model your life on the mystery of the Lord's Cross," the priest is told at ordination when the bishop places the chalice and paten in his hands.

The priest's spousal love for the Church, like Christ's and that of all Christian marriages, is necessarily both *unitive* and *procreative* in a spiritual way. The priest strives to become one with his Bride the Church in imitation of the way Christ is one with His Bride. He offers her his mind (1 Corinthians 1:16) and his oneness with the Father (1 Corinthians 3:23). He nurtures, protects and loves her as His own flesh (Ephesians 5:28–30). The unitive aspect of his spousal love can be found in the Profession of Faith and Oath of Fidelity he makes before receiving Holy Orders. He swears before God that he will hold as his own what his Bride holds as her own, that he will allow her to define him and his convictions.

Another example of the unitive aspect is the reluctance, even difficulty, and amid great grief with which the Bride grants a dispensation from celibacy for a priest who wants to leave and marry because this entails a breach of the unitive aspect of the priest's spousal love for the Church.[70] The Bride's love is a jealous love. The procreative aspect of the priest's spousal love is evident in Baptism and Confession where the priest quite literally generates new spiritual life, or in offering Holy Mass which renews Christ's marital covenant with the Church.

As a husband the priest cherishes his Bride and gives himself generously to her. He willingly and joyfully spends his time, energy and resources on those entrusted to him. He protects them from harm. The priest's procreative love is seen in his zeal for the Gospel—that the members of his Bride will receive a living faith. Just as a father's task is not just procreation of children, but their education and formation as well, so too the priest is entrusted with the education and

---

[70] This point is made with priests of the Latin Rite in mind, but it also reveals the fittingness of the ancient tradition of obligatory continence for clerics. Cf. Stefan Heid, *Celibacy in the Early Church: The Beginnings of a Disciple of Obligatory Continence for Clerics in East and West* (San Francisco: Ignatius Press, 2000).

formation of the spiritual children he has begotten. The Church as Bride is concretized for the priest, first and foremost, in the Blessed Virgin Mary, who concretely shows a priest the feminine face of his Bride the Church.[71] Thus the man called to priesthood is a man who is capable of, and inclined toward, being a good husband and father in Christian marriage. He will strive to live his specific promises, as well as poverty, chastity and obedience, as the expression of his *spousal love* for the Church. His priestly ministry *unites* him ever more closely to his spouse, the Church, and generates new spiritual life in her.

[*The Priest as Father.*] The priest's manhood and spousal relationship with the Church also makes him a father. True love always generates life, and in the priest's case it is spiritual and eternal life. St. Charles Borromeo often gave conferences to his priests when he was Archbishop of Milan. In the opening lines of the conference he addressed to his diocesan synod on April 20, 1584, he writes:

> "She was with child and she cried out in her pangs of birth, in anguish for delivery." (Revelation 12:2) said John in the Apocalypse concerning the mother, of whom we proceed to speak. O what pain, O what wailing of Holy Church! She cries out with prayers in the presence of God, and in the presence of you through my mouth, pronouncing divine words to you. It seems that I am hearing her saying to her betrothed the Lord Jesus Christ what Rachel had formerly said to her husband Jacob, "Give me children or I shall die" (Genesis 30:1). I am truly desirous of the one to be born. Indeed I dread this sterility; so unless you come, Christ, and give to me many sons, I am precisely at this very moment about to die. This is the spirit of our most beloved mother, in whom we are principally gathered here. I especially long for this, so that we may have it.[72]

The implication of his words is that Holy Mother Church cries out to her Divine Bridegroom, and to the one who participates in Christ's spousal relationship, for children. The priest's spousal love is

---

[71] For this reason, I believe, *PDV* (cf. n. 46), the *Program of Priestly Formation, 5th ed.* (cf. nos. 26, 110, 125, 280) and the *Directory on the Ministry and Life of Priests* (cf. nos. 60, 68, 85) emphasize the importance of the priest's living and affective devotion to the Blessed Virgin Mary. The complementarity of woman is never abolished or left behind in the priest's free promise of celibacy. The complementarity of woman does not threaten the priest's celibacy, but actually supports it spiritually since her complementarity is necessary to his perfection as a man.

[72] *Acta Ecclesiae Mediolanensis*, Pars II, 20 April 1584, 347. [Translation G. O'Connor]

necessarily generative. Jesus' priest, therefore, is not a bureaucrat, a hired hand, a CEO, or a careerist, but a father.

We are used to calling priests "father," yet it is no metaphorical or poetic designation. The priest's fatherhood is real because it is a participation in divine fatherhood (1 Corinthians 4:15, Ephesians 3:15). Therefore the priest's fatherhood is constituted by our heavenly Father's fatherhood—total, complete self-giving. It is the Father who gives Himself away in generating the Son, and then to save us gives away what is most precious to Him, His Son. It is the Father who says that if we want to see Him to look upon the face of His Son (John 14:9)—what humility! As a father the priest does not abandon his family or use his family for his own benefit, but rather is the *first* to sacrifice for his family. He is eager to build and generate new spiritual life in his family.

Thus, the man called to priesthood strives to renounce his own desires and plans, and take up his ministry of prophet-priest-king as an expression of his *spiritual fatherhood*. His priestly ministry *generates* spiritual life in the Church. His priestly ministry leads his Bride along the path of deification, holiness, transformation into the likeness of Christ, the high priest.

In the current renewal of the clergy, the Church emphasizes in the teachings of Vatican II and Pope John Paul II that the priest is relational as a man, as a husband, and as a father. A renewal of this inherent relationality, which has always been part of the essence of Jesus' priesthood, will bring about the renewal in the priest's teaching, sanctifying and governing.

With this intense focus on the nature that is configured by the grace of the priesthood, we can begin to understand more deeply the Church's recent and more specific clarifications about the priesthood, for example, the reiteration of reserving priestly ordination to men alone, or of mandatory celibacy in order to adequately express Christ's spousal love as Bridegroom of the Church.[73] The focus on the priest as man, husband and father also underlies the recent clarification that men with "deep seated" homosexual tendencies cannot be admitted as candidates for the priesthood since such a tendency necessarily implies a rejection of the complementarity of woman, a rejection of

---

[73] John Paul II, *Ordinatio Sacerdotalis*, 1994. The tremendous symbolic value of the priest's free promise of celibacy in showing Christ's spousal relationship to the Church is a compelling reason why the Latin Church must exercise extreme caution in ordaining married men to the priesthood.

his spousal relationship with the Church and a rejection of his spiritual fatherhood.[74] This more recent clarification is not difficult to understand intellectually, especially in light of the Church's teaching on the human person, but perhaps can be a difficult clarification for some to accept.

The priest's fundamental human identity as man, as husband, and as father, given to man in his creation, is also revealed in Jesus himself, the Redeemer of man.[75] The priest's fundamental human identity is as man, husband, and father because Jesus relates in His priesthood as man, husband and father. The priest is called to be in a deep relationship in his fundamental human identity, which includes his weaknesses and vulnerability, so that his human personality—indeed his entire manhood—becomes a bridge for others to encounter Jesus Christ the Redeemer of man, and thereby lead them to the life of Heaven.

As regards his inherent relationality, the priest's first and foremost relationship is with Jesus Christ. The priest who is not in deep relationship with Jesus is not being fully honest about who he is called to be, and cannot safely guide others to Him. From that deep relationship with Christ, the priest can grow in relating to others in a more human manner, that they might profit from his deep relationship with Christ. It is in his weakness and vulnerability, imbued with divine grace, that the priest knows himself as dependent and in constant need of grace. His weakness reminds him that he is not an island, but needs help from on high and from others. Through his relationship with Christ and others and the awareness of his weaknesses, idiosyncrasies and pitfalls, the priest can be shaped in his human personality to be a bridge for others to Christ and to the divine life of Heaven. A reappropriation of the fundamental human identity of the priest is the path to authentic renewal today.

*Participating in the Fatherhood of God.*[76] Jesus says, "[E]very one who acknowledges me before men, I also will acknowledge before my Father."[77] Why, then, is there so much resistance to calling God "Father"? In the Mass, for example, we sometimes hear both

[74] Congregation for Education. *Instruction Concerning the Criteria for the Discernment of Vocations with regard to Persons with Homosexual Tendencies in view of their Admission to Seminary and Holy Orders*, 2005.

[75] Cf. *PDV* 43.

[76] This section entitled "Participating in the Fatherhood of God" was inspired by William E. May's "The Mission of the Father: 'To Reveal and Relive on Earth the Very Fatherhood of God'", in *Josephinum: Journal of Theology* 9, no. 1 (Winter/Spring 2002): 42–55.

[77] Mt 10:32.

worshippers and priests neuter the language of the Liturgy, deliberately excluding almost all references to God as "Father" in what seems to be a misguided attempt at political correctness or some foolish effort to affirm everyone.

Jesus is the only one who can truly call God "Father", yet—through His life, death, and Resurrection—He invites all of us to participate in His divine life and leads us into the Heart of Love, into a relationship of intensely personal, deeply loving, and fully life-giving communion as His brothers, as adopted children of our heavenly Father.

But why does Jesus never—not even once—refer to God as His heavenly mother? Was Jesus implying that men are superior to women or that God does not possess motherly attributes? Or is motherhood somehow less than fatherhood? Of course not! The Word of God in the Book of Genesis is quite clear on this point: "God created man in his own image, in the image of God he created him; male and female he created them. . . . [A]nd they become one flesh".[78] God made men and women totally and completely equal right from the beginning: equal but different; and it is in this unity within the complementarity of their being that we come to understand why God is Father.

Every Sunday in the Creed we pray, "I believe in one God, the Father, the Almighty, creator of heaven and earth". God the Father "in His deepest mystery is not a solitude, but a family since He has in Himself fatherhood, sonship, and the essence of the family, which is love."[79] When the apostles asked Jesus how to pray, He gave them the Our Father.[80] Christ instructs Mary Magdalene to go and proclaim to the apostles that God is "your Father".[81] The "our" and "your" hearken back to the earliest prayer of Israel, the Shema ("Hear, O Israel: The LORD our God is one LORD"),[82] where divine inspiration reveals that the Lord God wants to be known and loved, that He is a God of relationship. "From the point of view of universal human

---

[78] Gen 1:27; 2:24.

[79] "Homily of His Holiness John Paul II", Puebla de Los Angeles (Mexico), Palafox Major Seminary, January 28, 1979, http://www.vatican.va/holy_father/john_paul_ii/homilies/1979/documents/hf_jp-ii_hom_19790128_messico-puebla-seminario_en.html.

[80] See Mt 6:9–13 and Lk 11:2–4.

[81] "Jesus said to her, 'Do not hold me, for I have not yet ascended to the Father; but go to my brethren and say to them, I am ascending to my Father and your Father, to my God and your God' " (Jn 20:17).

[82] Deut 6:4. Cf. Deut 14:1–2.

experience, Israel recognized the divine fatherhood through wonder at creation and renewal of life.... The divine fatherhood in Israel's regard is marked by an intense, constant, and compassionate love."[83]

> By calling God "Father", the language of faith indicates two main things: that God is the first origin of everything and transcendent authority; and that he is at the same time goodness and loving care for all his children. God's paternal tenderness can also be expressed by the image of motherhood, which emphasizes God's immanence, the intimacy between Creator and creature. The language of faith thus draws on the human experience of parents, who are in a way the first representatives of God for man. But this experience also tells us that human parents are fallible and can disfigure the face of fatherhood and motherhood. We ought therefore to recall that God transcends the human distinction between the sexes. He is neither man nor woman: He is God. He also transcends human fatherhood and motherhood, although he is their origin and standard: no one is father as God is Father.[84]

In the Scriptures, God is called Father de facto but only referred to as "mother" analogously.[85] A mother by nature—without any loss whatsoever to her personal dignity and complementary uniqueness—

---

[83] John Paul II, "General Audience", January 20, 1999.

[84] *CCC* 239.

[85] Septuagint passages that refer to God as mother by analogy include Deuteronomy 32:10–11, 18; Psalms 22:10; 91:4; 131:2; Ruth 2:12; Hosea 13:8; and Isaiah 42:14; 49:15; 66:13. "These passages all *liken* YHWH to a woman in some fashion or another, but nowhere is YHWH spoken of as feminine *per se*. And even when feminine images or similes for God are employed, it is still very much a masculine YHWH to whom they are applied. This is clear from the consistent use of the masculine pronoun 'he' for God. YHWH is never 'she' or 'her,' even when feminine imagery is invoked. As theologian John W. Miller puts it: 'Not once in the Bible is God addressed as mother, said to be mother, or referred to with feminine pronouns. On the contrary, gender usage throughout clearly specifies that the root metaphor is masculine father'" (Mark Brumley, "Does the Bible Support the Feminine God/Dess?", EWTN.com, accessed January 16, 2015, http://www.ewtn.com/library/SCRIPTUR /FEMGODES.TXT, citing John W. Miller, *Biblical Faith and Fathering* [Mahway, N.J.: Paulist Press, 1989], p. 61; the article was taken from the March–April 1996 issue of *Catholic Dossier*). Septuagint passages that refer to God as father de facto include Deuteronomy 32:6; 1 Samuel 9:11; 16:6; 2 Samuel 7:14; 8:16; 1 Chronicles 17:13; 22:10; 2 Chronicles 29:1; Judges 9:1; Psalm 68:5; 89:27; Wisdom 2:16; 14:3; Tobit 13:4; Sirach 23:1, 4; 51:10; Isaiah 63:16; 64:8; Jeremiah 3:4, 19; 31:9; and Malachi 1:6; 2:10. Surprisingly, God as "Father" is used rarely in the Septuagint, only twenty-five times or so. The Israelites may have avoided its frequent use because of the cultural climate of the ancient Near East, where the name "father" was used in various fertility religions and carried heavy sexual overtones. See James B. Pritchard, ed., *Ancient Near Eastern Texts: Relating to the Old Testament*, 3rd ed., with supplement (Princeton,

receives from a father. God as "mother" implies that God is not the source of all that exists, omnipotent and eternal, but dependent upon an external, all-powerful entity for His divine Personhood. This is an important truth rooted in Catholic teaching on Trinitarian circumincession[86]—which has major implications for an orthodox Christology, and for understanding how an authentic Catholic male spirituality is rooted in Christ's Passion and death:

> Omnipotence has its ultimate root in the begetting of the Son and the spiration [generation] of the Spirit. There is thus an obvious connection between God's omnipotence and the fact that he is a Father. "... *God's power is one with his fatherhood*, it appears as an infinite donation of life." To link God's omnipotence with the mystery of Christ ... is to link it with the fatherhood of God.... God is creator for the same reasons that he is Father. He creates paternally, and his Son, who is his Wisdom, is at one and the same time creator along with him ... and the model for all creation—at once the "image of the invisible God" and "the first-born of all creation (Colossians 1:15)". Consequently, since creation has its origin in the mystery of God's fatherhood, its fulfillment can only be filial: It is only in being conformed to the Son, the image of the Father, that man will attain his perfection.[87]

Both men and women are called upon to image God, but, as Pope John Paul II taught, "women are more capable than men of paying

---

N.J.: Princeton University Press, 1969). In the New Testament, however, Jesus call God "Father" sixty-five times in the Synoptic Gospels and over one hundred times in the Gospel of John. The exact term Jesus used (*Abba*) is still found three times in the New Testament (Mk 14:36; Rom 8:15–16; Gal 4:6), but elsewhere the Aramaic term *Abba* is translated as *pater* in Greek (*pathvr*). The uniqueness of Jesus' calling God His Father is evident for several reasons. For one, the rarity of addressing God as *Abba* is striking. There is no evidence in pre-Christian Jewish literature that the Israelites addressed God as *Abba*. A second distinctive feature involves the intimacy of the name. *Abba* was a term little children used when they addressed their fathers. The nearest equivalent would be the English term "Daddy". Christ reveals man to Himself, and in that revelation, we enter into a profound intimacy and communion with God where His fatherhood "is no longer limited to showing his relationship with creatures, but expresses the fundamental relationship which characterizes his inner life.... God is a father in his very being; he is always a father since from all eternity he generates the Word who is consubstantial with him and united to him in the Holy Spirit" (John Paul II, "General Audience", March 10, 1999).

[86] See *CCC* 236, 2779–80.

[87] Jean-Pierre Batut, "God the Father Almighty: Thoughts on a Disputed Term", *Communio International Catholic Review* 26, no. 2 (Summer 1999): 293, 284 (emphasis in original).

attention to another person, and that ... the man—even though he shares in the parenting relationship—always remains 'outside' the process of pregnancy and the baby's birth; in many ways he has to learn his own 'fatherhood' from the mother."[88] The woman, in her way of embodying the likeness of God, points to God's immanence and "withinness" since motherhood involves a special communion with the mystery of life as it develops in the woman's womb. In general, a woman's identity is more interiorly focused, intimately linked to her being and "bodiliness" that points to God's "heart"—the *perichoresis* of the Divine Persons in the intimate exchange of love and life between the Father, Son, and Holy Spirit. The man, in his way of embodying the image of God, points to God's "otherness" and transcendence, where a man's identity, in general, is more exteriorly focused and closely associated with his actions—with the realization of himself in relation to the external world.

> The Fathers of the Church distinguish between theology (*theologia*) and economy (*oikonomia*). "Theology" refers to the mystery of God's inmost life within the Blessed Trinity and "economy" to all the works by which God reveals himself and communicates his life. Through the *oikonomia* the *theologia* is revealed to us; but conversely, the *theologia* illuminates the whole *oikonomia*. God's works reveal who he is in himself; the mystery of his inmost being enlightens our understanding of all his works. So it is, analogously, among human persons. A person discloses himself in his actions, and the better we know a person, the better we understand his actions.[89]

The intrinsic unity within the complementarity of man and woman, in light of Pope John Paul II's insight above, analogously points to the *oikonomia* ("male") and *theologia* ("female") relationship in the Trinity. Their bodies reveal their persons and, within the context of covenant union, tell us something about God's divine identity as the source of all love, intimacy, and communion.

There is no greater example of this unity within the complementarity of man and woman than that of Joseph and Mary. Mary

[88] *MD* 18.
[89] *CCC* 236.

participated in an intimate, life-giving relationship with God in an interior, bodily way that only a woman could. In becoming one with the child in her womb, she became one with God Himself. Joseph was outside of this relationship and had to learn his role as father— as the provider, protector, and servant of the Holy Family—through the Blessed Virgin Mary's motherhood. Mary "is the only productive principle with regard to the human nature of Christ, as much as God the Father is such with regard to the divine nature, and through this she possesses in her virginal motherhood the power of the male fatherhood.... She produces Christ in the flesh through a spiritual power without violation of her virginity, as much as the Father produces Him according to the spirit."[90]

*Saint Joseph: The Ideal Father.* God is the source of all that is. He is Being and Existence itself—the "Other" who cares deeply for those dependent upon Him. God the Father gave us Jesus Christ, the Living Eucharist, and the Holy Spirit who fills our hearts with love and enables us to share in the very life of God. In and with Jesus, we truly become sons of God and are able to call him our Father. He is rich in mercy, watching over His creation with prudent love, with a wise and loving plan for humanity. His Fatherhood is manifested in deeds—in what He does for His children.

When my wife and I are out with our children, she thinks primarily about how their hearts are being formed, while I am thinking about their safety and well-being. A man's servant role also means that he is a protector and defender of his family, not just of their physical well-being, but their spiritual health as well. In this regard, Saint Joseph is the epitome of fatherhood. He always did what God asked of him. His whole life was a sacrifice of love for Mary and Jesus that serves as the model for fatherhood and holiness. "In giving Joseph the Blessed Virgin as spouse, God appointed him to be not only her life's companion, the witness of her maidenhood, the protector of her honor, but also, by virtue of the conjugal tie, a participator in her sublime dignity. And Joseph shines among all mankind by the most august dignity, since by divine will, he was

---

[90] Matthias Joseph Scheeben, *Mariology: Volume One*, 2nd ed. (New York: B. Herder, 1946), 175.

the guardian of the Son of God and reputed as His father among men."[91]

> Joseph, as quiet servant to God Almighty, is a model for husbands and fathers today. Long before the "Lord's Prayer", Joseph was a living, breathing example of what "Thy will be done" really means. Mary and her child were entrusted to Joseph's care and fatherhood within their home. He was the protector of The Holy Family and provided the foundation for Jesus' early growth and maturity. Joseph was devoted in love and sacrifice to Mary, and took great care in providing a secure setting for their growing Son, Jesus. He understood the importance of placing God in supreme position at the center of his life and in Kingship over his family.[92]

Saint Joseph stands in stark contrast to Adam. Both men have one thing in common: they are both silent, but the implications of that silence will have lasting effects on humanity. In the Garden of Eden, Adam stood by and did nothing while Satan formed his wife's conscience away from God the Father, destroying her heart in the process and unleashing sin into the world. In retrospect, Eve may have looked toward her husband while listening to Satan's lies, expecting Adam to defend and protect her, to place himself in the chasm between life and death, and to battle Satan to defend the purity and dignity of his family. This was not to be. His silence confirmed his complicity. Adam negated his responsibility as "husband", as the man chosen by God to serve, protect, and defend all that was entrusted to him, and mankind has lived with the effects of Original Sin ever since.

Furthermore, when confronted by God about what had occurred, Adam, out of fear, refused to accept responsibility for his actions and, out of shame, blames his wife for his decision not to "man-up". Adam's wife, the woman born from his side as flesh of his flesh, following her husband's poor example of headship and leadership in the family, also refuses to accept responsibility for her actions and blames Satan for her decision to turn away from God: "And he said, 'I heard

[91] Leo XIII, Encyclical Letter *Quamquam Pluries*, April 15, 1889, no. 11, http://www.vatican.va/holy_father/leo_xiii/encyclicals/documents/hf_l-xiii_enc_15081889_quamquam-pluries_en.html.

[92] Rick Sarkisian, *The Mission of the Catholic Family: On the Pathway to Heaven* (San Diego: Basilica Press, 1999), 6–7.

the sound of you in the garden, and I was afraid, because I was naked; and I hid myself.' He said, 'Who told you that you were naked? Have you eaten of the tree of which I commanded you not to eat?' The man said, 'The woman whom you gave to be with me, she gave me fruit of the tree, and I ate.' Then the LORD God said to the woman, 'What is this that you have done?' The woman said, 'The serpent beguiled me, and I ate.' "[93]

This is not the case with Saint Joseph. "When ... Mary had been betrothed to Joseph, before they came together she was found to be with child of the Holy Spirit; and her husband Joseph, being a just man and unwilling to put her to shame, resolved to send her away quietly."[94] At the time of the Incarnation, Joseph was married— not simply engaged—to Mary.[95] Joseph would have understood the importance of covenant relationship under the Mosaic Law, and, as a just man, he would have struggled with Mary's pregnancy since he was not the biological father.

There are two schools of thought on what was in Joseph's mind and heart at this time. One school says that Joseph assumed Mary's pregnancy came about as a result of an adulterous relationship, and because of his deep love for her, he could not subject Mary to the prescriptions of the Law, which required the person (man or woman) found breaking the sixth commandment to receive the death penalty,

[93] Gen 3:10–13.
[94] Mt 1:18–19.
[95] "Mary ... was 'a virgin' who was 'betrothed.' This tells us three important things about Mary. First, since Jewish women were typically betrothed around the age of 13, Mary probably was very young when she received this most weighty message from the angel Gabriel about her call to serve as the mother of the Messiah. Second, as a betrothed woman, Mary would have been legally married to Joseph, but still living with her own family. Here we see how Jewish betrothal was not the same as our modern notion of engagement. Betrothal was the first step in a two-stage marriage process. At their betrothal, Mary and Joseph would have exchanged their consent to marry each other before witnesses, and this would have made them legally married. However, as a betrothed wife, Mary would have remained living with her own family apart from her husband for up to one year until the second step of marriage took place. In this second step, the husband would take his wife to his own home for normal married life to begin. Therefore, when the angel Gabriel appeared to her, Mary would have been living between these two stages of marriage: She would have been Joseph's wife, but not yet dwelling with him. Third, according to Jewish marriage customs, sexual relations would not take place until the second stage of marriage. Thus, since Mary is a betrothed woman and not yet living with her husband, it would come as no surprise that she was a 'virgin' " (Dr. Edward P. Sri, "The Original Mary: Our Lady's Life Before the Annunciation", *Lay Witness* magazine, January/February 2007, p. 25).

so he decided to end the relationship so as not to bring shame to Mary.[96] The other school posits that Joseph knew the child in Mary's womb was conceived by the Holy Spirit (see Mt 1:18), and that he believed himself unworthy to care for God's Son. His decision to "send her away quietly" was a humble attempt to recuse himself from the relationship so as not to interfere with God's plan.[97]

Regardless of which school of thought one subscribes to, the important thing to remember is that when God revealed His plan of salvation to him, Joseph trusted God. "'Joseph, son of David, do not fear to take Mary your wife, for that which is conceived in her is of the Holy Spirit; she will bear a son, and you shall call his name Jesus, for he will save his people from their sins.' All this took place to fulfil what the Lord had spoken by the prophet: 'Behold, a virgin shall conceive and bear a son, and his name shall be called Emmanuel' (which means, God with us). When Joseph woke from sleep, he did as the angel of the Lord commanded him".[98] Unlike Adam, Joseph valiantly served, protected, and defended his wife and adopted son as head of the Holy Family. Joseph is silent (there are no recorded words of Joseph in Scripture),[99] but his actions speak louder than his words. The Gospels give us a glimpse into the challenges faced by Joseph as he lived out his vocation as husband and father, seeking the face of the Lord and finding Him in the pace and rhythm of everyday life.

---

[96] "If a man is found lying with the wife of another man, both of them shall die, the man who lay with the woman, and the woman; so you shall purge the evil from Israel. If there is a betrothed virgin, and a man meets her in the city and lies with her, then you shall bring them both out to the gate of that city, and you shall stone them to death with stones" (Deut 22:22–24); cf. Lev 20:10.

[97] This view is often supported by the teaching of the Church Fathers and other theologians. "He sought to put her away, because he saw in her a great sacrament, to approach which he thought himself unworthy" (Origen, *Catena Aurea*), and "Joseph was minded to put away the Blessed Virgin not as suspected of fornication, but because in reverence for her sanctity, he feared to cohabit with her" (Thomas Aquinas, *Summa Theologica*, III, q. 3, a. 3 ad 2).

[98] Mt 1:20–24.

[99] "The Gospels do not record any word ever spoken by Joseph along that way. But the silence of Joseph has its own special eloquence, for thanks to that silence we can understand the truth of the Gospel's judgment that he was 'a just man' (Matthew 1:19)" John Paul II, Apostolic Exhortation *Redemptoris Custos* (Guardian of the Redeemer), August 15, 1989, 17 (hereafter cited as *RC*).

Joseph raised a family in poverty with great courage and dignity.[100] When I deliver Christmas food boxes to our neighbors in need, I feel somewhat saddened at the conditions I find as I enter their homes. I see families making the best of what little they have. I see that the food I am bringing may be the only full meal they would eat for the entire week. I see the joy on the faces of children who make sure that they say a heartfelt "Thank you!", and all I can do is smile and say, "You're welcome, Merry Christmas", as I leave to go to the next house. I knew that on Christmas Day, I would be warm, well fed, and surrounded by family and friends. Santa would bring lots of presents, and we would "make the rounds" to several Christmas parties, celebrating the season with much joy and happiness. But as I drove home, I thought of the stable where Jesus was born, of the manger that was His bed, of Mary and Joseph's great courage in raising a child in poverty, trusting in God alone, and I smiled thinking that the families I visited were not celebrating Christmas—they were living it! Christ, who as a child was entrusted to the care of his earthly father, Joseph, offers a sign of hope for the whole human family, a sign of peace for those suffering from hardships of every kind, a sign of freedom for the poor and oppressed, a sign of mercy for those caught up in the vicious circle of sin and addiction, a sign of love and consolation for those who feel lonely and abandoned.[101]

---

[100] "And she gave birth to her first-born son and wrapped him in swaddling cloths, and laid him in a manger, because there was no place for them in the inn" (Lk 2:7). "And when the time came for their purification according to the law of Moses, they brought him up to Jerusalem to present him to the Lord (as it is written in the law of the Lord, 'Every male that opens the womb shall be called holy to the Lord') and to offer a sacrifice according to what is said in the law of the Lord, 'a pair of turtledoves, or two young pigeons'" (Lk 2:22–24). Turtle doves were offered by those families who could not afford the normal offering of a lamb or goat: "And when the days of her purifying are completed, whether for a son or for a daughter, she shall bring to the priest at the door of the tent of meeting a lamb a year old for a burnt offering, and a young pigeon or a turtledove for a sin offering, and he shall offer it before the LORD, and make atonement for her; then she shall be clean from the flow of her blood. This is the law for her who bears a child, either male or female. And if she cannot afford a lamb, then she shall take two turtledoves or two young pigeons, one for a burnt offering and the other for a sin offering; and the priest shall make atonement for her, and she shall be clean" (Lev 12:6–8).

[101] Cf. John Paul II, "Midnight Mass: Homily of the Holy Father", December 24, 2002, http://www.vatican.va/holy_father/john_paul_ii/homilies/2002/documents/hf_jp-ii_hom _20021224_christmas-night_en.html.

Joseph was truly guardian of the Redeemer and the Blessed Mother when death threatened to destroy their family. "[A]n angel of the Lord appeared to Joseph in a dream and said, 'Rise, take the child and his mother, and flee to Egypt, and remain there till I tell you; for Herod is about to search for the child, to destroy him.' And he rose and took the child and his mother by night, and departed to Egypt, and remained there until the death of Herod. This was to fulfil what the Lord had spoken by the prophet, 'Out of Egypt have I called my son.' "[102] The plight of Joseph and the Holy Family is no different than that of refugees today who because of war, natural disaster, and corrupt governments are forced to leave their country of origin and immigrate to another country to begin their lives again. Once more, Joseph trusted God and faithfully followed God's command. Joseph never imagined that this would be his life, but he realized that following God's will means sacrifice, and that sometimes God puts you not where you want to be but where He needs you. "And so Jesus' way back to Nazareth from Bethlehem passed through Egypt. Just as Israel had followed the path of the exodus 'from the condition of slavery' in order to begin the Old Covenant, so Joseph, guardian and cooperator in the providential mystery of God, even in exile watched over the one who brings about the New Covenant."[103]

Years later, after the Holy Family's return to Israel and their home in Nazareth, the evangelist Luke records their annual pilgrimage to Jerusalem:

Now his parents went to Jerusalem every year at the feast of the Passover. And when he was twelve years old, they went up according to custom; and when the feast was ended, as they were returning, the boy Jesus stayed behind in Jerusalem. His parents did not know it, but supposing him to be in the company they went a day's journey, and they sought him among their kinsfolk and acquaintances; and when they did not find him, they returned to Jerusalem, seeking him. After three days they found him in the temple ... and his mother said to him, "Son, why have you treated us so? Behold, your father and I have been looking for you anxiously." And he said to them, "How is it that you sought me? Did you not know that I must be in my Father's house?" And they did not understand the saying which he

[102] Mt 2:13–15.
[103] RC 14.

spoke to them. And he went down with them and came to Nazareth, and was obedient to them; and his mother kept all these things in her heart. And Jesus increased in wisdom and in stature, and in favor with God and man.[104]

This part of our Lord's life speaks volumes about Saint Joseph. As the head of his family, Joseph served as the "priest" of the home, ensuring that the entire family honored God by worshipping Him faithfully in their daily home life, with the community at the synagogue, and with all of Israel at the temple in the Holy City. As the spiritual leader, Joseph understood the grave responsibility that came with borrowing God's sacred name "father", and that his primary responsibility was to ensure that, in his home, God was *feared*, that is, reverenced and respected in accord with the Scriptures: "[A]s for me and my house, we will serve the LORD."[105] In exercising his sacred responsibility as husband and father—by his stewardship of love and example of holiness—Joseph created an atmosphere of life-giving communion in the home in which the Holy Family listened to God with the ear of their hearts and responded to His call with loving fidelity. Saint Joseph carried out his duties steadfastly with the law of God firmly in his heart:

> Hear, O Israel: The LORD our God is one LORD; and you shall love the LORD your God with all your heart, and with all your soul, and with all your might. And these words which I command you this day shall be upon your heart; and you shall teach them diligently to your children, and shall talk of them when you sit in your house, and when you walk by the way, and when you lie down, and when you rise. And you shall bind them as a sign upon your hand, and they shall be as frontlets between your eyes. And you shall write them on the doorposts of your house and on your gates.[106]

Another significant aspect is Joseph's "death" experience in losing Jesus for three days. It is important to understand that Joseph was not careless or irresponsible. When journeying to the Passover in Jerusalem, families often travelled in large caravans, intermingling with

---

[104] Lk 2:41–46, 48–52.
[105] Josh 24:15.
[106] Deut 6:4–9.

each other along the way. Furthermore, this would not have been the family's first trip to Jerusalem, since Luke records that the pilgrimage occurred annually. Hence, Joseph and Mary had no reason to be concerned for Jesus' safety since they had returned home safely without incident in prior years. In this context, combined with the fact that Jesus was now well past the age of reason and old enough to comprehend His actions, it was easy to see why they thought their son was with other family members or friends.

There is no doubt that Joseph and Mary, upon discovering that Jesus was missing, were gravely concerned and worried to death about His safety and well-being. Any parent would be. I am sure that Joseph took charge of the search effort and, with Mary at his side, retraced their steps as they combed Jerusalem day and night looking for the child. Joseph turned his anxiety into focused action, perseverance, and diligence all while comforting and reassuring the Blessed Mother every step of the way. Joseph never gave up hope and, upon finding Jesus in the temple, allowed Christ's anxious mother—who had probably already run up to and hugged Jesus with tears of joy in her eyes and a spirit of thankfulness in her heart—to address their son. Mary is clearly upset (like any parent would be), and her question to Jesus is tinged with a subdued frustration experienced by both she and Joseph, as if Jesus' actions were deliberate: "Son, why have you treated us so? Behold, your father and I have been looking for you anxiously." Jesus' matter-of-fact answer gives His parents no relief but, instead, confuses them. I am confident that, on the way back to Nazareth, Joseph used this incident as a teachable moment, lovingly but sternly telling Jesus not to do anything like that again. Jesus respected and listened to His earthly father:

> The growth of Jesus "in wisdom and in stature, and in favor with God and man" (Luke 2:52) took place within the Holy Family under the eyes of Joseph, who had the important task of "raising" Jesus, that is, feeding, clothing and educating him in the Law and in a trade, in keeping with the duties of a father.... For his part, Jesus "was obedient to them" (Luke 2:51), respectfully returning the affection of his "parents." In this way he wished to sanctify the obligations of the family and of work, which he performed at the side of Joseph.[107]

[107] RC 16.

Mary kept all of these things in her heart, but, after the finding in the temple, there are no further mentions of Joseph. It is presumed that Joseph died sometime between finding Jesus in Jerusalem and the start of His public ministry. Joseph is not present at the wedding feast of Cana or the foot of the Cross, where the Lord gives care of His mother to the beloved disciple John, which He would not have done if Joseph was still alive to take care of his wife. Thus, Joseph's vital role in salvation history ends prior to Christ's death. Mary's soul would be pierced by the suffering and death of her Son on the Cross, while Joseph's suffering and "death" would be limited to the events of Christ's childhood: living in poverty, fleeing persecution, providing for his family in a foreign country, losing his son for three days. Joseph's three days without Jesus foreshadowed the world's three days without Christ while He lay in the sleep of death. I believe one of Christ's great joys when He descended to Sheol on Holy Saturday was seeing His earthly father again, looking him in the eyes, grasping his hand, and saying, "Well done, good and faithful servant . . . enter into the joy of your master."[108]

Men need to understand and appreciate the role of Saint Joseph: that the power and authority he exercised was always in service to the Father and to his family. We too can experience this same power of life-giving love in our lives, through the grace of the Holy Spirit, if we open ourselves to the Lord and ask for it. Every decision a father makes cannot be his own; he must always place the best interest of his family first above everything else. We must make ourselves vulnerable before God and allow His Spirit to form and shape us into the men that Christ calls us to be. In the spirit of Saint Joseph, we must tear down the walls of lechery, deceit, and licentiousness constructed within us by the culture and make room in our hearts for the richness and beauty of truth given to us by Christ in our Catholic faith, a truth that frees us to love.

What lessons can Saint Joseph teach men today?

In revealing and in reliving on earth the very fatherhood of God, a man is called upon to ensure the harmonious and united development of all the members of the family: he will perform this task by

---

[108] Mt 25:23.

exercising generous responsibility for the life conceived under the heart of the mother, by a more solicitous commitment to education, a task he shares with his wife, by work which is never a cause of division in the family but promotes its unity and stability, and by means of the witness he gives of an adult Christian life which effectively introduces the children into the living experience of Christ and the Church.[109]

A man plays an active role in his children's prayer life and humbly allows them to participate in his prayer life as well. Most importantly, by being an example of what it means to live and act as a man of God, fathers show their children firsthand what personal relationship with Jesus looks like and how that relationship is lived out daily within the truth, goodness, and beauty of our Catholic faith.

Men must strive to possess the qualities of fatherhood lived in the spirit of Saint Joseph. These include empathetic, careful, and attentive listening. As chief servants of the domestic church, the holy Catholic Church, and the culture, we must develop the skills to become excellent managers of our time and resources that must be exercised "in accord with the knowledge, competence, and preeminence which [we] possess [and] with consideration for the common good and the dignity of persons".[110] We must lead those under our authority and care by Christ's example of service, honed under the tutelage of Joseph, because it is only by imitating the self-sacrificing Christ that we can ever hope to be role models and heroes worthy of gratitude and honor. Before any of this can happen, we fathers must have the courage to take the first big step: we must dethrone the reign of sin so that we can welcome Jesus Christ as Lord of our lives.

In contemporary culture, fatherhood is often a job description instead of a way of life. Fatherhood is reduced to having a good time and satisfying desires instead of a call to holiness and sanctification. We need to recognize this fact and courageously take very deliberate and concrete steps toward truth—to make a conscious decision as men to *make the time and not excuses* to pray every day, to make the Holy Sacrifice of the Mass the center of our lives, to frequent the Sacrament of Reconciliation and Eucharistic Adoration, and to educate

---

[109] FC 25.
[110] CCC 907.

ourselves on what the Church teaches are essential if we are to maintain a true spirit of fatherhood.

> Fathers of families find in Joseph the best personification of paternal solicitude and vigilance.... For Joseph, of royal blood, united by marriage to the greatest and holiest of women, reputed the father of the Son of God, passed his life in labor, and won by the toil of the artisan the needful support of his family.... Joseph, content with his slight possessions, bore the trials consequent on a fortune so slender, with greatness of soul, in imitation of his Son, who having put on the form of a slave, being the Lord of life, subjected himself of his own free-will to the spoliation and loss of everything.[111]

*Father to Son.* My father, a popular singer-songwriter from Barbados, would not have won any "Father of the Year" awards when we were growing up in New Jersey. He had three loves in his life: alcohol, cigarettes, and womanizing. He was not Christian but an agnostic who never went to church. The only time I heard my father use the Lord's name was in vain. He fathered numerous children with other women. My parents were divorced during my junior year in college, and the only home I had ever known was sold. Living in a new home in a new city with a broken family was a heartwrenching experience. When I am asked what it's like being a child of divorce I say that marriage is a wonderful thing but it is also the Cross, and divorce is when the parents put the Cross down and the kids pick it up.

A few years later, when I informed my father that I was joining the Benedictines, our relationship went from bad to nonexistent. He was not just disappointed with my decision—he was downright angry. Our conversation went something like this: "You're going to do what? You are the first person in our family to go to college. I spent all that money sending you to one of the best universities in the country. You studied economics and business, and instead of making something of yourself, you're going to waste your life in that monastery living with a bunch of men? What is wrong with you? What am I supposed to tell my friends?" I told him what he could tell his

---

[111] *Quamquam Pluries* 4.

friends, and on that day my father became like Lazarus in the tomb: he was dead to me.

Many years later when my Eternal Word Television Network series *Behold the Man: Spirituality for Men* debuted, my father received lots of phone calls: "Isn't that your son on TV?" My father, who as far as I knew only set foot in a Catholic church on his wedding day, began watching the program. Then he began watching the Mass. Then he started watching reruns of Mother Angelica. Then he started praying. My father, a professional entertainer, decided to stop singing Caribbean music and started singing and recording Gospel music exclusively. Then, like Lazarus coming out of the tomb, he called me and we spoke for thirty-one minutes and twelve seconds, which is the longest conversation we'd had in almost twenty years. He spent most of the call talking to me about his relationship with Jesus Christ.

Soon after, I was shown the awesome power of prayer, forgiveness, and divine mercy. After years of not having a meaningful relationship with the man who destroyed our family, I met face-to-face with my father. I did not hear the words of repentance that I so longed to hear from him. Instead, this talented and gifted musician, who was lost and who only now after seventy-four years was coming to faith in Jesus Christ, showed me the meaning of fatherhood by his example when he sang this song:

> O Lord, sweet Jesus, have mercy on me. My eyes were wide open, yet I failed to see. Dear Lord, I beg you have mercy; please, have mercy on me. I am so sorry. Lord, forgive me. Please show me the way. I can't go on living this life without you. Sweet Jesus, please tell me what to do. Lord, I'm depending on you. I want to live a life that's honest and true. I will let nothing stand in my way. Sweet Jesus, please hear my prayer. O Lord, teach me how to pray, I beg you, because at times I know not what to say but when I think of Calvary I know my Jesus loves me. Dear Lord, I beg you have mercy.[112]

I listened to him sing. Afterward, I stood in my father's face, filled with bitterness and indignation, and said, "I'm going to ask you a

---

[112] Harold D. Sivers, lyrics to "Mercy" on *Thank You, Lord*, music CD (East Orange, N.J.: DML Productions, 2008).

question right now. If you've ever loved me even once as your son, don't lie to me. If you're going to lie, then say nothing. What happened to you?" My father looked me straight in the eye and, in a state of complete vulnerability, said, "The Blessed Mother and Divine Mercy." I was shocked, awed, and stunned. My father had become a man who learned to embrace the Cross in his life—to open himself deeply to the love, peace, and true joy of discipleship in Christ—and began to live this reality every day of his life. My father discovered what all fathers must learn: it is only when we begin to understand the gift of vulnerability and humility lived from the Cross that we will know what spiritual fatherhood is all about.

Any man can be a daddy, but it takes a real man to be a father. When men live the Catholic faith with fidelity and joy, then we can be sure that our actions will be worth more than a thousand words and have confidence that our love for Christ will be written into the hearts of our sons and daughters, our parishioners, and society. When men live the faith with passion and conviction, Catholicism will no longer become a fond memory that fades from our hearts over time. A father's living witness to covenant communion and intimacy will become his enduring legacy, a precious gift for his children, and a sure sign of hope in God's endless mercy and love.

# Chapter Seven

# Work

Work is for man, not man for work.

— *Catechism of the Catholic Church*, no. 2428

God created man and put him in the Garden of Eden to till (serve) and to keep (protect and defend) it. God entrusts man with caring for His creation and allows him to name the animals.[1] These acts are not simply to keep man busy or provide him with something to do to pass the time. Man is imbued with preternatural gifts and human dignity.[2] Thus, work is a participation in God's productive activity through which man exercises authority in God's name as stewards of His creation and, in doing so, man "perfects" himself; he becomes more of the person who God created him to be. In serving, protecting, and defending God's creative work, a man maintains his dignity and honors the Lord by his life. Work is a union of wills where man "fills", "subdues", and has "dominion" over the earth, ruling in the image of God—with holiness, and in uprightness and truth:

---

[1] " 'Be fruitful and multiply, and fill the earth and subdue it; and have dominion over the fish of the sea and over the birds of the air and over every living thing that moves upon the earth.' And God said, 'Behold, I have given you every plant yielding seed which is upon the face of all the earth, and every tree with seed in its fruit; you shall have them for food. And to every beast of the earth, and to every bird of the air, and to everything that creeps on the earth, everything that has the breath of life, I have given every green plant for food' " (Gen 1:28–30). Cf. Gen 2:19–20.

[2] Preternatural gifts are "favors granted by God above and beyond the powers or capacities of the nature that receives them but not beyond those of all created nature. Such gifts perfect nature but do not carry it beyond the limits of created nature. They include three great privileges to which human beings have no title—infused knowledge, absence of concupiscence, and bodily immortality. Adam and Eve possessed these gifts before the Fall" (John A. Hardon, S.J., *Modern Catholic Dictionary* [New York: Doubleday, 1979], 437).

For man, created to God's image, received a mandate to subject to himself the earth and all it contains, and to govern the world with justice and holiness; a mandate to relate himself and the totality of things to Him Who was to be acknowledged as the Lord and Creator of all. Thus, by the subjection of all things to man, the name of God would be wonderful in all the earth. This mandate concerns the whole of everyday activities. For while providing the substance of life for themselves and their families, men and women are performing their activities in a way which appropriately benefits society. They can justly consider that by their labor they are unfolding the Creator's work, consulting the advantages of their brother men, and are contributing by their personal industry to the realization in history of the divine plan.[3]

After the Fall, work takes on a different character and meaning:

And to Adam he said, "Because you have listened to the voice of your wife, and have eaten of the tree of which I commanded you, 'You shall not eat of it,' cursed is the ground because of you; in toil you shall eat of it all the days of your life; thorns and thistles it shall bring forth to you; and you shall eat the plants of the field. In the sweat of your face you shall eat bread till you return to the ground, for out of it you were taken; you are dust, and to dust you shall return."[4]

The man's decision to listen to the voice of his wife, manifested in his failing to serve, protect, and defend her from Satan's mendacity—and in direct defiance of God's command—made him equally culpable for the genesis of Original Sin. Now cut off from the life of God, work becomes arduous; sin has not only separated man from God but also ruptured the relationship between man and all of creation. Consequently, the soil from which he was taken does not yield its fruit easily. The plants of the field are now mixed with briar that needs to be cut back and removed to access the food within. The work is tedious and laborious, requiring physical exertion that makes muscles

---

[3] GS 34. Cf. Wis 9:1–3: "O God of my fathers and Lord of mercy, who have made all things by your word, and by your wisdom have formed man, to have dominion over the creatures you have made, and rule the world in holiness and righteousness, and pronounce judgment in uprightness of soul".

[4] Gen 3:17–19.

ache and sweat flow. Work, tinged with a sense of anxiety, fills man with tension and trepidation. This pattern of work will be repeated day after day for the rest of his life until man once again becomes one with the earth in his grave.

In the parable of the sower, Jesus speaks about seeds that are sown among thorns, saying, "As for what was sown among thorns, this is he who hears the word, but the cares of the world and the delight in riches choke the word, and it proves unfruitful."[5] Looking back to the Fall, we see that Adam heard and understood God's command—His call to communion—but freely chose to turn away from Love: to cut himself off from God's life and embrace emptiness. Man's wounded and fallen nature is in need of redemption and salvation. Work, as an extension of man, is now turned in on itself and is also in need of redemption. All of this would be accomplished through the Word becoming flesh, the second Person of the Trinity assuming a human nature in the hypostatic union and, in the Paschal Mystery—in His glorious work of salvation on the Cross—restoring what was lost.[6] Christ heals, elevates, and perfects our human nature and transforms work—still difficult and demanding—into a participation in His saving work for humanity.

An authentic Catholic male spirituality sees work in light of the Cross. "By enduring the hardship of work in union with Jesus, the carpenter of Nazareth and the one crucified on Calvary, man collaborates in a certain fashion with the Son of God in his redemptive work. He shows himself to be a disciple of Christ by carrying the cross, daily, in the work he is called to accomplish. Work can be a means of sanctification and a way of animating earthly realities with the Spirit of Christ."[7] A Catholic man must conduct his affairs in light of God's original purpose for work (to serve, protect, and defend), and in solidarity with Christ's work on the Cross and in His Church.

> O blessed are those who fear the LORD
> and walk in his ways!
> By the labor of your hands you shall eat.

---

[5] Mt 13:22.

[6] The hypostatic union is when, in the Incarnation, the Word of God in His divine nature as the second Person of the Trinity was perfectly united to a human nature without confusion, change, separation, or division. Jesus is true God and true man. Cf. CCC 456–78.

[7] CCC 2427.

You will be happy and prosper;
Your wife like a fruitful vine in the heart of your house;
Your children like shoots of the olive,
around your table.
Indeed thus shall be blessed
the man who fears the Lord. (Ps 128:1–4)

*The Suffering Servant.*

> For he grew up before him like a young plant, and like a root
> out of dry ground; he had no form or comeliness that we should
> look at him, and no beauty that we should desire him. He was
> despised and rejected by men; a man of sorrows, and acquainted
> with grief; and as one from whom men hide their faces he was
> despised, and we esteemed him not. Surely he has borne our griefs
> and carried our sorrows; yet we esteemed him stricken, struck down
> by God, and afflicted. But he was wounded for our transgressions, he
> was bruised for our iniquities; upon him was the chastisement that
> made us whole, and with his stripes we are healed.[8]

Principally through his work, industry, and engagement in secular
affairs imbued with an authentic spirituality rooted in Christ crucified, a man places the Church in a position to influence the culture
in profound and meaningful ways. We must "be present as signs of
courage and intellectual creativity in the privileged places of culture,
that is, the world of education—school and university—in places of
scientific and technological research, the areas of artistic creativity,
and works in the humanities".[9] Therefore, "there cannot be two parallel lives in their existence: on the one hand, the so-called 'spiritual'
life, with its values and demands, and on the other, the so-called
'secular' life, that is, life in a family, at work, in social relationships, in
the responsibilities of public life and in culture."[10]

"To be able to discover the actual will of the Lord in our lives
always involves the following: a receptive listening to the Word of
God and the Church, fervent and constant prayer, recourse to a wise
and loving spiritual guide, and a faithful discernment of the gifts and

[8] Is 53:2–5.
[9] CL 44.
[10] CL 59.

talents given by God, as well as the diverse social and historical situation in which we live."[11] Men "should also hold in high esteem professional skill ... and the virtues related to social behavior, namely, honesty, a spirit of justice, sincerity, courtesy, moral courage; without them, there is not true Christian life."[12] Work is a means to an end, not an end in itself. Therefore, absent a holistic and comprehensive moral, spiritual, and intellectual formational program integrated into his work ethic and rooted in serving, protecting, and defending his family, Church, and society, the putting into practice of male spirituality would be sterile.

An authentic male spirituality for the workplace is deeply spiritual, "based on a commitment to holiness ... fed by prayer and the sacraments".[13] Male spirituality "is completely integrated and indeed completed in family and professional life. This unity of life inevitably leads to an evangelization not only of individuals through friendship but also extends to entire societies and cultures. All of this necessitates being of one heart, mind and will with the Church, along with a readiness to seek out the spiritual and intellectual formation necessary to reach the goal of personal holiness."[14] This union reaches concrete expression in the Mass and in the Eucharist:

> *The Eucharist is also the sacrifice of the Church.* The Church, which is the Body of Christ, participates in the offering of her Head. With him, she herself is offered whole and entire. She unites herself to his intercession with the Father for all men. In the Eucharist the sacrifice of Christ becomes also the sacrifice of the members of his Body. The lives of the faithful, their praise, sufferings, prayer, and work, are united with those of Christ and with his total offering, and so acquire a new value. Christ's sacrifice present on the altar makes it possible for all generations of Christians to be united with his offering.[15]

The word "liturgy" (*leitourgia* in Greek) means "a work for or on behalf of the people". The Holy Sacrifice of the Mass and the

[11] *CL* 58.

[12] *CL* 60.

[13] C. John McCloskey III, "Spirituality in the Professions and Workplace", EWTN.com, accessed January 17, 2015, www.ewtn.com/library/BUSINESS/FR90206.HTM; article was taken from *Faith and Reason*, Summer 1990.

[14] Ibid.

[15] *CCC* 1368 (emphasis in original).

Eucharist, as the fruit of Christ's redemptive work on the Cross, is the primary work of the Church—it is the start of our work week as Catholic men. All of the sacraments empower us to work diligently and faithfully to build up treasure in heaven so as not to get caught up in the thorns and weeds of this life. Therefore, in order to serve effectively our families, the Church, and society, our faith life must be integrated into our work life. In this way, the world will see the good work that we do and give glory to God:

> The faithful ... must assist one another to live holier lives even in their daily occupations. In this way the world is permeated by the spirit of Christ and more effectively achieves its purpose in justice, charity and peace. [Men] have the principal role in the universal fulfillment of this purpose. Therefore, by their competence in secular fields and by their personal activity, elevated from within by the grace of Christ, let them labor vigorously so that by human labor, technical skill and civic culture created goods may be perfected for the benefit of every last man, according to the design of the Creator and the light of His Word.... In this manner, through the members of the Church, will Christ progressively illumine the whole of human society with His saving light.[16]

The successful integration of prayer and work is epitomized in the Rule of Saint Benedict. Saint Benedict taught that "idleness is the enemy of the soul. Therefore, the brethren ought to be occupied at certain times in manual labor, and again at fixed hours in sacred reading" and prayer.[17] He envisioned his rule as a "school of the Lord's service", an interrelated and harmonious balance between the two important duties of monks, that is, *ora et labora* (prayer and work) with the primary work being prayer (the Divine Office and *lectio divina*) followed by the work of manual labor, which is itself a prayerful and active participation in Christ's sufferings. Saint Paul says, "Now I rejoice in my sufferings for your sake, and in my flesh I complete what is lacking in Christ's afflictions for the sake of his body, that is, the Church"[18]. Christ's one sacrifice on the Cross was complete and perfect, lacking

---

[16] *LG* 36.

[17] Saint Benedict, *St. Benedict's Rule for Monasteries*, trans. Leonard J. Doyle (Collegeville, Minn.: Liturgical Press, 1948), 67.

[18] Col 1:24.

in nothing. The only thing missing from the equation of salvation is, as Saint Paul indicates, our participation through "the flesh". It is in and through our trials, tribulations, and hardships—the thorns, thistles, and briers that are inevitable in this life—that Catholic men unite our-selves to, and find purpose and meaning in, the crucified Christ. This participation in the work of suffering is not just for ourselves but for the sake of the Church, which is one body in Christ. It is critically import-ant for Catholic men who are striving to imitate Christ, as we attempt to make sense of the world around us, to understand the symbiotic relationship between serving and suffering well.

There is a profound and indissoluble link between sharing in the Cross of Christ and sharing in the kingdom of Christ. Work means suffering with the Lord, and through his work—for the sake of his own redemption—a man is brought closer to Christ and the redemp-tion of others. The "glory" involved in man's redemption is that the redeemed Christ is active in him, and the power of the Risen Lord enables him to suffer and to share in His Crucifixion, Passion, and death. When he suffers with Christ now, man knows that he will one day share in His Resurrection. Suffering with and in Christ is suffer-ing for the sake of manifesting God's kingdom:

> To the prospect of the Kingdom of God is linked hope in that glory which has its beginning in the Cross of Christ. The Resurrection revealed this glory—eschatological glory—which, in the Cross of Christ, was completely obscured by the immensity of suffering. Those who share in the sufferings of Christ are also called, through their own sufferings, to share in *glory*. Paul expresses this in various places. To the Romans he writes: "We are ... fellow heirs with Christ, provided we suffer with him in order that we may also be glorified with him. I con-sider that the sufferings of this present time are not worth comparing with the glory that is to be revealed in us". In the Second Letter to the Corinthians we read: "For this slight momentary affliction is preparing for us an eternal weight of glory beyond all comparison, because we look not to the things that are seen but to things that are unseen". The Apostle Peter will express this truth in the following words of his First Letter: "But rejoice in so far as you share Christ's sufferings, that you may also rejoice and be glad when his glory is revealed."[19]

---

[19] John Paul II, Apostolic Letter *Salvifici Doloris*, On the Christian Meaning of Human Suffering, February 11, 1984, no. 22.

God has allowed man to suffer, and He has graced man with the ability to suffer through Jesus. By man's free cooperation with this suffering through his work, united to the work of Christ, man, in a certain qualified sense, becomes "worthy" of the kingdom. Through the Passion and death of Christ, a man is made a son of God in Baptism. There is a cooperation that occurs and can only be truly realized in a loving relationship of communion to which God calls him through the suffering he experiences in and through his work. This cooperation happens by grace, which is a gift of God, and the only thing that man contributes is his free-willed fiat in submission to God's holy will. The work of salvation belongs to God, but, nevertheless, man has a role through cooperation, which is why he can talk about being made worthy of the dignity of the kingdom. By enduring the suffering inherent in his work, man is made worthy of the kingdom of God: Christ's redemption is worked in him. Thus, the Catholic man

> finds in human work a small part of the Cross of Christ and accepts it in the same spirit of redemption in which Christ accepted his Cross for us. In work, thanks to the light that penetrates us from the Resurrection of Christ, we always find a *glimmer* of new life, of the *new good*, as if it were an announcement of "the new heavens and the new earth" in which man and the world participate precisely through the toil that goes with work.... On the one hand this confirms the indispensability of the Cross in the spirituality of human work; on the other hand the Cross which this toil constitutes reveals a new good springing from work itself, from work understood in depth and in all its aspects and never apart from work.[20]

The ordeal of man's work can, in some way, be related to the Cross of Christ and be used as a way of deepening the experience of God's merciful love. Redemption is not a pure substitution. Christ did not suffer so that man would not have to; Jesus suffered to enable us to love as He loves. Through the work of the Cross a man can, by his work on earth, participate in Christ's suffering. Jesus suffered to make more fully ours what He has accomplished in the Paschal Mystery— union with the Father. Christ surrendered Himself wholly over to

---

[20]John Paul II, Encyclical Letter *Laborem Exercens* (On Human Work), September 14, 1981, no. 27 (hereafter cited as *LE*).

the Father and carried out God's plan of salvation. What Christ has objectively accomplished has to be subjectively appropriated by man, and his free embrace of suffering acts as one of the vehicles for this appropriation. Man can take the suffering that he experiences in his work, and by uniting himself with Christ the Suffering Servant, he is brought back to the Father. Thus, man can share in Jesus' own communion with the Father in a way that he could not before.

> As a result of Christ's salvific work, man exists on earth *with the hope* of eternal life and holiness. And even though the victory over sin and death achieved by Christ in his Cross and Resurrection does not abolish temporal suffering from human life, nor free from suffering the whole historical dimension of human existence, it nevertheless *throws a new light* upon this dimension and upon every suffering: the light of salvation. This is the light of the Gospel, that is, of the Good News. At the heart of this light is the truth expounded in the conversation with Nicodemus: "For God so loved the world that he gave his only Son." This truth radically changes the picture of man's history and his earthly situation: in spite of the sin that took root in this history both as an original inheritance and as the "sin of the world" and as the sum of personal sins, God the Father has loved the only-begotten Son, that is, he loves him in a lasting way; and then in time, precisely through this all-surpassing love, he "gives" this Son, that he may strike at the very roots of human evil and thus draw close in a salvific way to the whole world of suffering in which man shares.[21]

The difficulties and struggles of work create the possibility of rebuilding goodness in the one who suffers. The complete answer to the question of suffering will be found only in Christ because it is only in the full Revelation of Divine Love that man finds the truth. Redemptive suffering through work is an expression, ultimately, of God's love. This is difficult to see since His love is made manifest in pain, yet men must trust that God is able to work good out of evil and bring about a greater good. Faith, then, is required of the one who labors, and, as men of faith, we must learn to embrace the truth of suffering and see the Cross as God's instrument of merciful love. In His infinite wisdom, God knows that by allowing individuals

---

[21] John Paul II, *Salvifici Doloris*, no. 15 (emphasis in original).

to abuse their freedom and, as a consequence, to bring suffering into the world, He is able to bring a greater good out of it. Hence, the greater good is not only an expression of God's merciful love for those who suffer but the conduit that brings men into that merciful love. When Catholic men share this love with others through suffering well in our daily work, we become agents of God's merciful love in the alleviation of suffering in our fellow workers. By embracing suffering ourselves and alleviating it in others, man is made in the image of the Suffering Servant; he grows closer to the Father and is able to participate more fully in the Father's own life. "For it was fitting that he, for whom and by whom all things exist, in bringing many sons to glory, should make the pioneer of their salvation perfect through suffering."[22]

All work, and the suffering inherent in it, has been redeemed by Christ on the Cross. Suffering, then, is capable of being used as the means of encountering and experiencing God's gracious, compassionate love. No man's work, no matter how pedestrian it may appear, is unimportant in the building of God's kingdom on earth. Consequently, no personal suffering remains utterly pointless or meaningless.

> In order to discover the profound meaning of suffering, following the revealed word of God, we must open ourselves wide to the human subject in his manifold potentiality. We must above all accept the light of Revelation not only insofar as it expresses the transcendent order of justice but also insofar as it illuminates this order with Love, as the definitive source of everything that exists. Love is also the fullest source of the answer to the question of the meaning of suffering. This answer has been given by God to man in the Cross of Jesus Christ.[23]

> > If any one will not work, let him not eat.
> > For we hear that some of you are walking in idleness,
> > mere busybodies, not doing any work.
> > Now such persons we command and exhort
> > in the Lord Jesus Christ to do their work
> > in quietness and to earn their own living.
> > Brethren, do not be weary in well-doing. (2 Thess 3:10–13)

[22] Heb 2:10.
[23] John Paul II, *Salvifici Doloris*, no. 13.

*The Protector of Work's Integrity: Professional Competency.* In order for a man to be successful at his work, he must undoubtedly possess a certain level of professional competency. This is true both in man's ecclesial and secular endeavors. The Second Vatican Council, in emphasizing communion and unity within the Church, provided "a structure and path in which each member's unique individuality, talent, and gifts can be respected, esteemed, and creatively developed for service".[24] Likewise, the revised Code of Canon Law, promulgated in 1983, provides an excellent example of *communio et unitas* in contemporary ecclesiology and is a superb template for Catholic men to establish and promote within their hearts, minds, and souls professional competency standards that can be integrated into their daily work life.

Part 2 of Canon 228, for example, details the specific competencies that lay persons must possess in order to hold ecclesiastical offices as experts and advisors, either individually or in a council,[25] that can be readily applied to all Catholic men (lay and ordained) who strive to integrate their faith and their work. These include (1) a keen awareness of and an essential familiarity with what the work entails as well as, by implication, proficient knowledge of the teachings of the Catholic faith, (2) the ability to exercise good judgment and discretion, and (3) probity (honesty) and rectitude (moral integrity).[26] It should be noted that the Canon is quite clear in stating that these persons must not simply embody these competencies, but *excel* at them, which indicates that the capacity to hold ecclesiastical office is not a right

---

[24] Kevin E. McKenna, *The Ministry of Law in the Church Today* (Notre Dame, Ind.: University of Notre Dame Press, 1998), 4.

[25] The Canon Law Society of Great Britain and Ireland notes that "since no further specification is made in the text, this may be understood as referring to councils or synods at all levels, from the parish finance committee (see Can. 537) to an ecumenical council (see Can. 339 §2)" (*The Canon Law Letter and Spirit: A Practical Guide to the Code of Canon Law*, prepared by The Canon Law Society of Great Britain and Ireland in association with The Canadian Canon Law Society [Collegeville, Minn.: Liturgical Press, 1995], 129).

[26] I would also add that the individual should be a practicing Catholic, as prescribed in Canons 205 and 209, and should adhere to the dictates of Canons 210–12. See Canons 149 and 483 §2 as well. (See James A. Coriden, Thomas J. Green, and Donald E. Heintschel, eds., *The Code of Canon Law: A Text and Commentary* [New York: Paulist Press, 1985]; however, the foregoing work is weak on this point. In discussing the competence of laypersons, they give very little attention to the virtues and focus primarily on academic and professional competencies.)

freely exercised by the faithful, but is rooted in their qualification and suitability.[27] This is no different in the temporal setting where a worker's performance is evaluated against a set of performance objectives and criteria that are used to determine competency and identify areas for improvement.

Canon 145 recognizes the diversity of gifts and talents bestowed by the Spirit upon the entire *koinonia* of the Body of Christ. It respects the professional competency of the laity, whose duty it is "to extend the divine plan of salvation ever increasingly to all men ... *according to their abilities* ... that they may zealously participate in the saving work of the Church."[28]

These Church laws (and others) manifestly demonstrate the seriousness of the Church's efforts to promote and develop competence in ministry. Canon Law, in fulfillment of the mandates of Vatican II, establishes professional, competent norms for the participation of lay persons in the ministerial life of the Church but also gives valuable insight into the relationship between "faith" and "work" in the secular world. In this way, the Church, through her transcendent and temporal dimensions, fervently executes her mission to evangelize

---

[27] In my opinion, this only applies to ecclesiastical offices and does not infringe upon the normative rights of the faithful, as in Canon 212, §2–§3; cf. n. 25–26, on p. 192. Coriden, Green, and Heintschel note that "lay persons may 'cooperate' in the exercise of the power of governance, but only clergy have the capacity for this power", which is attributed to the lack of "consensus on the theoretical basis for lay persons to exercise power in the Church" and must be contextualized within a "satisfactory theoretical framework" (*Code of Canon Law*, 164). I would argue that this framework has already been established by the Second Vatican Council in *Gaudium et Spes*. The commentators overemphasize power distribution within ecclesiastical offices and do not fully appreciate or understand the distinct role of the laity within the autonomy of the temporal order: "Laymen should also know that it is generally the function of their well-informed Christian conscience to see that the divine law is inscribed in the life of the *earthly* city. Let the layman not imagine that his pastors are always such experts, that to every problem which arises, [the layman] can readily give [pastors] a concrete solution, or even that such is their mission. Rather, enlightened by Christian wisdom and giving close attention to the teaching authority of the Church, *let the layman take on his own distinctive role*" (*GS* 43 [emphasis added]). The distinct roles of the laity (cooperation) and the clergy (administration) within ecclesiastical offices are rooted in Vatican II ecclesiology, that is, in the distinction between (and not the separation of) the transcendent and temporal orders. See *GS* 30; cf. Canon 227.

[28] *LG* 33 (emphasis added). "Therefore, by their competence in secular fields and by their personal activity, elevated from within by the grace of Christ, let them work vigorously so that by human labor, technical skill, and civil culture created goods may be perfected according to the design of the Creator and the light of his Word" (*LE* 25).

and, in a meaningful and loving way, continues to fulfill her responsibilities and obligations for the spiritual, physical, and emotional wellbeing of the entire Body of Christ.

Canon Law shows that the Catholic Church, in her postconciliar commitment and authentic witness to greater plurality and depth in Christian life, incorporates the dynamic of ecclesial diversity in unity with respect to ministry and, by implication, to all dimensions of man's work. The Church's teaching reflects the fact that "Jesus wanted his community to be structured and joined in unity, and to be not only a hierarchical structure but also a spiritual and visible social organism."[29] The Church does this by incorporating and promoting the ecclesiology of Vatican II throughout her official documents, recognizing the universal call to holiness of all the faithful in opening ecclesiastical offices to lay persons, and establishing standards that engender and promote professional competence in the ministerial life of the Church that can also apply to the secular work environment. In this way, the Church, in an intrinsically pastoral nature, promotes both ecclesial and secular work for the good of souls.

*Keeping Ministry in Perspective: The Autonomy of the Temporal Order.* In light of the above examination of man's work with respect to the professional competency perspectives outlined in Canon Law— and their implications for the secular work environment—a brief examination of the sometimes tension-filled relationship between the work of ordained and lay ministers *within* the Church is warranted. This issue is particularly relevant given the fact that Catholic men serving as lay ministers at the parish level are a clear minority,[30] and

---

[29] McKenna, *Ministry of Law*, 18.

[30] According to the now defunct National Pastoral Life Center (NPLC), 30,632 lay ecclesial ministers work at least twenty hours per week in paid positions in parishes. An additional 2,163 volunteers work at least twenty hours per week in parishes. Two-thirds of all parishes (66 percent) have paid lay ministers working at least twenty hours per week, up from 53 percent in 1990 and 60 percent in 1997. The report also states that 80 percent of lay administrative positions in parishes are held by women and only 20 percent by men (see David DeLambo, *Lay Parish Ministers: A Study of Emerging Leadership* [New York: National Pastoral Life Center, 2005], 45, 88). An earlier NPLC report noted that "parishes have become 'feminized' not only because many lay ministers are women, but also because middle class parishes have become more concerned with nurturing members" (see National Pastoral Life Center, *Lay and Religious Parish Ministry: A Study Conducted for the National Conference of Catholic Bishops*, 1991, http://www.resourcingchristianity.org/grant-product/lay-and-religious-parish -ministry-a-study-conducted-for-the-national-conference-of-catholic-bishops-1991,andhttp:// www.usccb.org/about/laity-marriage-family-life-and-youth/lay-ecclesial-ministry/lay -ecclesial-ministry-faqs.cfm#q7).

that any serious movement toward involving more men in parish life and ministry needs a fruitful discussion of the inherent obstacles and challenges to success, as well as a theological framework and context from which to approach ecclesial service.

The division between lay and ordained ministry, though different in both substance and degree, is not a separation, since within the People of God "they share a common dignity from their rebirth in Christ. They have the same filial grace and the same vocation to perfection", and "a true equality with regard to the dignity and to the activity common to all the faithful for the building up of the Body of Christ."[31]

In the distinction of ministerial roles, ordained ministry exercises prominence within the transcendent order and "is rooted in the Apostolic Succession, and vested with 'potestas sacra' consisting of the faculty and the responsibility of acting in the person of Christ the Head and the Shepherd. It is a priesthood which renders its sacred ministers servants of Christ and of the Church by means of authoritative proclamation of the Word of God, the administration of the sacraments, and the pastoral direction of the faithful".[32] Lay ministry, on the other hand, exercises prominence within the temporal order. "In the exercise of all their earthly activities, [the laity] can gather their humane, domestic, professional, social, and technical enterprises into one vital synthesis with religious values, under whose supreme direction all things are harmonized unto God's glory."[33] It must be remembered that ordained ministry is always at the service of the priesthood of all believers since ministerial priesthood "is a means by which Christ unceasingly builds up and leads his Church".[34]

The sex abuse scandal has caused many Catholics to question the Church's authority, and some have advocated for the implementation of secular models of authority in order to "improve" and "democratize" the Church's hierarchical structure. This idea is doomed to failure. Despite the fact that a few priests and bishops have sinned

[31] LG 32.

[32] Congregation for the Clergy et al., *Instruction on Certain Questions Regarding the Collaboration of the Non-Ordained Faithful in the Sacred Ministry of Priest*, Theological Principles, "The Common Priesthood of the Faithful and the Ministerial Priesthood", August 15, 1997, www.vatican.va/roman_curia/pontifical_councils/laity/documents/rc_con_interdic_doc_15081997_en.html.

[33] GS 43.

[34] CCC 1547.

and have chosen not to live in accord with the faith they are bound to protect and serve, the doctrines and teaching contained in Holy Scripture and Sacred Tradition still hold true. Personal sin is not greater or more powerful than the strength of God's law, for Christ has promised that, in His Church, the gates of hell will not prevail against it (see Mt 16:18). Adopting secular authority models will do nothing except undermine and erode the foundational truths of our Catholic faith.

The unique functions and characteristics of the temporal and transcendent orders can be maintained and respected through a collaborative approach to Church ministry. Such an approach promotes and encourages participation in the Church's life and mission, while achieving balance within and recognizing the autonomy of both orders of creation. Moreover, in regard to the theology of ministry developed at the Second Vatican Council, it is clear that the Council promotes "collaboration of all the faithful ... whether it is in the spiritual order, bringing the message of Christ and his grace to men, or in the temporal one, permeating and perfecting secular reality with an evangelical spirit. This is especially true in the primary areas of evangelization and sanctification—'it is in this sphere most of all that the lay apostolate and the pastoral ministry complete each other.'"[35]

Notwithstanding what has been stated above, laity simultaneously belong to the City of God (the transcendent or heavenly order) and the City of Man (the temporal or earthly order), yet each order, as we have seen, has its own proper autonomy. "Autonomy" here does not have the sense of "individualism". Rather, "autonomy" means that laity should have a deep appreciation of the principles that govern every aspect of the temporal order without having a reference point in divine revelation. The laity have to ensure that the values of the transcendent order, which encompasses them, penetrate the temporal order while acknowledging that the temporal order has its own inherent law.

God has built an order into creation (cf. Gen 1) and has formed our minds so as to be commensurate with that order. Therefore, without necessarily appealing to divine revelation and grace, we can grasp

---

[35] Congregation for the Clergy et al., *Instruction on Certain Questions*, Preface, quoting the Second Vatican Council decree *Apostolicam Actuositatem*, nos. 5 and 6.

and properly live within the temporal order and apply the Church's expertise about man to that order. The laity have a special obligation not to divorce the transcendent and temporal orders but to ensure that the two interpenetrate one another. Again, there is a *distinction* between the two orders, but this distinction should not become a *separation*. On this point, the Second Vatican Council states that "earthly progress must be carefully distinguished from the growth of Christ's kingdom. Nevertheless, to the extent that the former can contribute to the better ordering of human society, it is of vital concern to the kingdom of God."[36]

As previously stated, secular duties and activities belong properly (although not exclusively) to lay people, while the clergy are the caretakers and guardians of the transcendent, sacramental order. Lay Catholic men, with assistance and support of the clergy, are to become as competent as possible in their individual disciplines and professions, bringing the truth of the Gospel and the natural law to bear on the temporal order. It is the layman's proper duty to take that expertise in humanity and apply it to whatever area of the temporal order he is called to. The autonomy of the temporal order was given significant emphasis at Vatican II, which underscored the concept in this way: "Let there be no false opposition between professional and social activities on the one part, and religious life on the other. The Christian who neglects his temporal duties neglects his duties toward his neighbor and even God, and jeopardizes his eternal salvation."[37]

The role of the clergy is to safeguard and disseminate the truths of the transcendent realm to laity who are in the midst of concrete political, economic, and cultural situations.[38] The clergy are to inform the laity of the key principles that govern the Church's expertise in humanity so that laypersons can properly judge each aspect of the temporal order in light of its compatibility with the Catholic truth about man. "In effect, a collaboration of all the faithful exists in both orders of the Church's mission; whether it is in the spiritual order, bringing the message of Christ and his grace to men, or, in the temporal one, permeating and perfecting secular reality with the

[36] GS 39.
[37] GS 43.
[38] Cf. GS 42.

evangelical spirit."[39] It is within the Church's evangelization mission to which all ministers are called that "the lay apostolate and pastoral ministry complete each other."[40]

However, contemporary philosophical and cultural trends, such as secular humanism, moral relativism, and political correctness, along with the imposition of secular models of leadership and authority into the Church's ecclesial model (which also undermines and diminishes the role of men as lay leaders in the parish), lead to a dualism within the temporal order where the exercise of ministry is turned into a means to a political end instead of an end in itself. As a result, ecclesial ministry becomes subordered to a sociopolitical or temporal end "where there is only one history, one in which the distinction between the history of salvation and profane history is no longer necessary."[41]

If, therefore, the ecclesial ministry becomes a mere means to a worldly end and if the Church becomes a mere means to a political end, then the essential dignity of the Church is lost—faith becomes politicized, and the autonomy of the temporal order is rejected. This politicization of the faith ultimately leads to the laicization of the clergy and the clericalization of the laity within ecclesial ministry. The clergy, who are supposed to be the guardians of the sacramental order, instead derive their relevance and effectiveness from engagement in temporal affairs. Likewise, the authentic vocation of the lay faithful is devalued, and the laity come to believe that their dignity within the Church derives primarily from participation in clerical tasks.

If the distinction between clergy and laity is not made, which shows that the temporal order is something unique to the laity and expresses the high dignity of the role of the lay faithful, the laity will believe that they have a "right" to participate in tasks that are proper to the sacramental order. The obliteration of the distinction between clergy and laity devalues the authentic vocation of the laity and gives rise to confusion and abuse within the Church's ministerial life. Father C. John McCloskey summarizes the dilemma this way:

[39] Congregation for the Clergy et al., *Instruction on Certain Questions*, Preface.
[40] Ibid.
[41] Congregation for the Doctrine of the Faith, *Instruction on Certain Aspects of the "Theology of Liberation"*, August 6, 1984, no. IX.3, www.vatican.va/roman_curia/congregations/cfaith/documents/rc_con_cfaith_doc_19840806_theology-liberation_en.html.

The Second Vatican Council makes clear that the laity "have the capacity to assume from the hierarchy certain ecclesiastical functions, which are to be performed for a spiritual purpose" (*Lumen Gentium*, no. 33). This involvement is good and necessary. However, the idea, unfortunately, is indeed widespread in our country, due to a faulty interpretation of the Conciliar documents, that the laity manifests its involvement in the Church chiefly through participation in liturgical functions, parish councils, church positions, etc., rather than in family, work, political, social, and cultural life. In short, in some circles there is an emphasis on sharing "power" rather than service and a concept that somehow the laity become more integrated in the life of the Church the more clericalized their function. Apart from the danger of this clericalization for the identity of the laity itself, this train of thought leads inevitably to a shirking of responsibility for the state of the world by Catholic laymen; at the same time the enemies of God and the Church will not find any determined opposition to their machinations by committed Catholic laymen. However, totally committed Catholics are needed on the sports field, on Broadway, in the university, in the media, and indeed in all legitimate activities, as well as being involved in liturgical and parochial activities.[42]

> If the LORD does not build the house,
> in vain do its builders labor;
> If the LORD does not watch over the city,
> in vain does the watchman keep vigil.
> In vain is your earlier rising,
> your going later to rest,
> You who toil for the bread you eat:
> when he pours gifts on his beloved
> while they slumber. (Ps 127:1–2)

*Leadership Aspects of Work:* Abad *and* Shamar. Philosopher Donald DeMarco once remarked that "a leadership vacuum exists in our culture. This is not a matter for mere casual observation, but one that elicits a strong sense of deprivation. We need leaders; and they are as cherished as they are rare."[43] Modern philosophical trends and the

---

[42] McCloskey, "Spirituality in the Professions and Workplace". Cf. *GS* 36.

[43] Donald DeMarco, "The Virtue of Leadership", Catholic Educator's Resource Center, http://www.catholiceducation.org/en/controversy/politics-and-the-church/the-virtue-of-leadership.html.

influence of secular thought and culture, with its disordered values, ideologies, and disintegrated view of the person, cloud the vision of a civil society and infect the minds and hearts of Christ-centered servant-leaders. This crisis in contemporary leadership is fueled by subjective and relativistic ideologies that form the foundation of societal norms, and place man at the center of all reality and truth.

This view is in direct contrast to what is objectively true, good, and beautiful, and, therefore, the relativistic perspective is the antithesis to authentic leadership that serves (*abad*) and protects and defends (*shamar*) both family and culture, not the self. The leaders of the twenty-first century must not be "self"-centered, but must freely give of themselves so that they can be gifts to others. Catholic men in positions of authority and leadership should strive to exemplify and epitomize the characteristics of the Good Shepherd by embodying the archetype of *abad* and *shamar* for the edification of the whole world. Effective leaders should personify and exude virtue,[44] and foster ongoing growth in personal formation so that the seeds of *abad* and *shamar* are firmly rooted in the rich soil of the Catholic faith.

What are the qualities of such a leader? "For Aristotle there were three: ethos, pathos, and logos. The ethos is his moral character and the source of his ability to convince others [of what is true]; the pathos is his ability to touch feelings and move people emotionally; the logos is his ability to give solid reasons for particular actions and, therefore, to move people intellectually."[45]

This is especially important within today's society, where our leaders must be present "in the world, that is, in each and in all of the secular professions and occupations.... They are called there by God [and] by exercising their proper function and being led by the spirit of the gospel they can work for the sanctification of the world from within, in the manner of leaven. In this way they may make Christ known to others, especially by the testimony of a life resplendent in faith, hope and charity. [They are] closely involved in temporal affairs

---

[44] "Human virtues are firm attitudes, stable dispositions, habitual perfections of intellect and will that govern our actions, order our passions, and guide our conduct according to reason and faith. They make possible ease, self-mastery, and joy in leading a morally good life. The virtuous man is he who freely practices the good" (*CCC* 1804).

[45] DeMarco, "Virtue of Leadership".

of every sort. It is therefore his special task to illumine and organize these affairs in such a way that they may always start out, develop, and persist according to Christ's mind, to the praise of the Creator and the Redeemer."[46] Hence, it is within the context of leadership develop-ment in the Catholic tradition where ethos, pathos, and logos merge with the temporal and transcendent orders to cast the foundation for *abad* and *shamar*. As such, men in leadership roles must embrace a holistic leadership development model that educates the soul and heart as well as the mind. This is accomplished through moral, spiritual, and intellectual formation rooted in the natural law, sound doctrine, and the principles of Catholic social thought and justice that educate for character as well as career. This all-encompassing approach to forma-tion is essential on-the-job training that flows from and is informed by the theological and cardinal virtues.

The theological or supernatural virtues are faith, hope, and love. "The theological virtues are the foundation of Christian moral activ-ity; they animate it and give it its special character. They inform and give life to all the moral virtues. They are infused by God into the souls of the faithful to make them capable of acting as his children and of meriting eternal life."[47]

Faith is the theological virtue by which we believe in God, in all that God has said and disclosed to us in divine revelation, and in all that the Church proposes for our belief in matters of faith and morals. Faith allows us to discover God's providence and loving pres-ence in all the events and circumstances of our lives. Any man who truly believes in God and in His infinite love gives his life over to the Father without hesitation or reservation. In that complete self-giving, a man finds the gift of faith—the peace and certainty for which his heart longs. "In God's gift of faith, a supernatural infused virtue, we realize that a great love has been offered us, a good word has been spoken to us, and that when we welcome that word, Jesus Christ the Word made flesh, the Holy Spirit transforms us, lights up our way to the future and enables us joyfully to advance along that way on wings of hope."[48]

---

[46] *LG* 31.

[47] *CCC* 1813.

[48] Francis, Encyclical Letter *Lumen Fidei* (The Light of Faith), June 29, 2013, no. 7.

Hope is the theological virtue by which we desire the kingdom of heaven and eternal life as our ultimate goal, placing all of our trust in Christ's promises and relying not on our own strength but on the grace of the Holy Spirit:

> Anyone who does not know God, even though he may entertain all kinds of hopes, is ultimately without hope, without the great hope that sustains the whole of life (cf. *Ephesians* 2:12). Man's great, true hope which holds firm in spite of all disappointments can only be God—God who has loved us and who continues to love us "to the end," until all "is accomplished" (cf. *John* 13:1 and 19:30). Whoever is moved by love begins to perceive what "life" really is.... "This is eternal life, that they know you the only true God, and Jesus Christ whom you have sent" (*John* 17:3). Life in its true sense is ... a relationship. And life in its totality is a relationship with him who is the source of life. If we are in relation with him who does not die, who is Life itself and Love itself, then we are in life. Then we "live."[49]

Charity (love) is the theological virtue by which we love God above all things for His own sake, and our neighbor as ourselves for the love of God. Love should always lead to mutual respect, understanding, patience, unselfishness, and all else that allows us to see the face of God in others. Exercising charity in humble service is central to our ability to lead effectively.

> This proper way of serving others also leads to humility. The one who serves does not consider himself superior to the one served.... Christ took the lowest place in the world—the Cross—and by this radical humility he redeemed us and constantly comes to our aid.... The more we do for others, the more we understand and can appropriate the words of Christ: "We are useless servants" (Luke 17:10). We recognize that we are not acting on the basis of any superiority or greater personal efficiency, but because the Lord has graciously enabled us to do so.... We are only instruments in the Lord's hands; and this knowledge frees us from the presumption of thinking that we alone are personally responsible for building a better world. In all humility we will do what we can, and in all humility we will entrust the rest

---

[49] Benedict XVI, Encyclical Letter *Spe Salvi* (Saved in Hope), November 30, 2007, no. 27.

to the Lord. It is God who governs the world, not we. We offer him our service only to the extent that we can, and for as long as he grants us the strength.[50]

The cardinal or superlative virtues include prudence, justice, temperance, and fortitude. "Prudence is the virtue that disposes practical reason to discern our true good in every circumstance and to choose the right means of achieving it.... It is prudence that immediately guides the judgment of conscience. The prudent man determines and directs his conduct in accordance with this judgment."[51] For example, when a time arises for fraternal correction or discipline, it would not be prudent to speak to the individual openly and in public for all to hear. The virtue of prudence demands that such action take place in private and with charity.

"Justice is the moral virtue that consists in the constant and firm will to give their due to God and neighbor.... The just man ... is distinguished by habitual right thinking and the uprightness of his conduct toward his neighbor."[52] The company where you work has objective criteria for merit raises based on job performance. Two of your employees have worked equally hard all year and have met the criteria. It would be unjust to give one employee a higher percentage wage increase over the other simply because he has a more pleasant demeanor. The virtue of justice dictates that, since both men met the criteria, they both should receive an equal percentage raise. Justice also includes giving our due to God, which means honoring and keeping His commandments. God is our Creator and Redeemer, and it is fitting, just, and right to praise, bless, adore, and glorify Him by attending the Holy Sacrifice of the Mass every Sunday and Holy Day of Obligation with our families.

"Temperance is the moral virtue that moderates the attraction of pleasures and provides balance in the use of created goods. It ensures the will's mastery over instincts and keeps desires within the limits of what is honorable."[53] Temperance draws a line between legitimate pleasure (having a drink with friends) and decadence (becoming

[50] DCE 35.
[51] CCC 1806.
[52] CCC 1807.
[53] CCC 1809.

severely intoxicated), laziness and overwork, true sportsmanship (congratulating the other team that beat you) and obsession with winning (rubbing it in the other team's face when you win).

"Fortitude is the moral virtue that ensures firmness in difficulties and constancy in the pursuit of the good. It strengthens the resolve to resist temptations and to overcome obstacles in the moral life."[54] When your so-called friends want you to go to a strip club after work, you stand firm in your faith and resolve not to participate, even if it means you will be mocked and ridiculed. A man who lives the virtue of fortitude is not afraid to lead by example.

The qualities of contemporary leadership should include practical aspects as well. Effective leaders should be empathetic, careful, and attentive listeners, excellent managers of time and resources, and skilled coordinators. These qualities must be exercised "in accord with the knowledge, competence, and preeminence which they possess [and] with consideration for the common good and the dignity of persons".[55] In this way, the leader not only works toward personal growth and enrichment but goes out of his way to develop the gifts, skills, and talents of those whom he leads.

Without a comprehensive leadership model rooted in virtue, the putting into practice of *abad* and *shamar* would be sterile. "Because the very plan of salvation requires it, the faithful should learn how to distinguish carefully between those rights and duties which are theirs as members of the Church, and those which they have as members of human society. Let them strive to harmonize the two, remembering that in every temporal affair they must be guided by a Christian conscience. For even in secular affairs there is no human activity which can be withdrawn from God's dominion."[56] The faith life of a leader should be completely integrated and, indeed, completed in family and professional life. This "unity of life" inevitably leads to a transformation, not only of individuals as a response to dynamic, faith-based leadership, but also of entire societies and cultures.

We must be ever vigilant that this leadership model does not become dissociated from genuine authority rooted in truth. If the

[54] *CCC* 1808.
[55] *CCC* 907.
[56] *LG* 36.

leader has no involvement with truth, then he has little substance to offer those who follow him. Our inspiration, zeal, fervor, and charismatic appeal as leaders must not derive from mere desperation and superstition, but must be anchored in a source that is solid, authoritative, and realistic;[57] it must be entrenched in the Catholic faith. "This is what saves leadership from demagoguery and dictatorship. It is what distinguishes the leader from the false prophet or the self-serving manipulator."[58] Professional competence, strength of character, and a strong faith qualify a leader for a position of authority from which flows our mission to *abad* and *shamar*. Ultimately, all authority is derived from God; hence, a leader has true authority if his sense of moral, intellectual, and spiritual values are consonant with the good of all persons.[59]

> A true leader, the one for whom a culture has such great need, is neither an opportunistic follower or an ambitious front-runner. If he is truly to lead people to some fulfilling destiny, as did Moses, he must lead them without separating himself from them. He must be uncommon enough to inspire people to struggle to achieve a good end [building confidence, respect, and trust in the process]. At the same time, he must be common enough so that the common man can emulate him. The paradox of the common-uncommon man is also the paradox of the servant-leader.... A father's leadership follows the same form.[60]

In Luke's Last Supper narrative, for example, the apostles argue about who among them is the greatest. Jesus replies, "[L]et the greatest among you become as the youngest, and the leader as one who serves.... I am among you as one who serves."[61] The apostle John also quotes Jesus at the Last Supper, saying, "Truly, truly, I say to you, a servant is not greater than his master; nor is he who is sent greater than he who sent him. If you know these things, blessed are you if you do them."[62] This style of leadership is in direct contradiction to a

[57] See DeMarco, "Virtue of Leadership".
[58] Ibid.
[59] See ibid.
[60] Ibid.
[61] Lk 22:26–27.
[62] Jn 13:16–17.

culture that provides us with a leadership model based on power used to control, authority used to dominate, and "truth" that cannot discern objective reality. Being a leader is not "all about the Benjamins". Rather, it is all about the Beatitudes (see Mt 5:1–12).

There is an inherent link between leadership and the unity of life. The unity of life of the leader "is of the greatest importance: indeed they must be sanctified in professional and social life. Therefore, [in response to the call to leadership, Catholic men] must see their daily activities as an occasion to join themselves to God, fulfill his will, and to serve other people."[63] Awareness that a leader's work "is a participation in God's activity ought to permeate ... even 'the most ordinary, everyday activities. They can justly consider that by their labor they are unfolding the Creator's work ... and contributing by their personal industry, to the realization in history of the divine plan.' "[64]

The Catholic man as leader must see clearly with the eyes of faith, through the lenses of *abad* and *shamar*. This vision, in turn, must give strength to those who follow, give concreteness to leadership goals, and extend charitably to the broader community. Leaders "need a life in harmony with their faith, so they can become the light of the world. They need that undeviating honesty which can attract all to the love of truth and goodness."[65] As faith-filled leaders, men must not be afraid to respond to God's call. As servants of truth, we must respond out of a faith, hope, and love that conquers fear, that conquers death, and that gives us the courage to say, "Speak, Lord, for your servant is listening."[66]

*The Apostolate and Evangelization.* In embodying a Catholic spirituality through work in the apostolate, men become the evangelizing Church in the world and play a crucial role in the reconciliation and conversion of mankind by living out the call to holiness in union with the crucified Christ. Our mission in the world is to seek the kingdom of God by engaging in temporal affairs and ordering them according to the plan of God. Through Baptism and our commitment to give our lives in loving sacrifice for our wives, the Church,

[63] *CL* 17.

[64] *LE* 115; cf. *GS* 34.

[65] Vatican Council II, Decree on the Apostolate of the Laity, *Apostolicam Actuositatem*, November 18, 1965, no. 13.

[66] Cf. 1 Sam 3:10.

and the culture, men are "made one body with Christ and are established among the People of God. They are, in their own way, made sharers in the priestly, prophetic, and kingly functions of Christ."[67]

The essence of Catholic male spirituality in the apostolate lies within his participation in this threefold *munera*. Men are united to Christ and share in His priestly mission through "the offering they make of themselves and their daily activities" united to Christ's offering in the Eucharist at Mass and on the Cross.[68] Men share in the prophetic mission of Christ through "their ability and responsibility to accept the Gospel in faith and proclaim it in word and deed without hesitating to courageously identify and denounce evil".[69] Men also exercise their kingship "above all in the spiritual combat in which they seek to overcome in themselves the kingdom of sin, and then to make a gift of themselves so as to serve in justice and charity".[70]

The proper role and vocation of men is found in the universal call to holiness, their state in life, and their vocation within the temporal order. "This is especially true in the primary areas of evangelization and sanctification" where men provide a "consistent witness in their personal, family, and social lives by proclaiming and sharing the gospel of Christ in every situation they find themselves, and by their involvement with the task of explaining, defending, and correctly applying Christian principles to the problems of today's world."[71]

"The prayer and sacramental life" of the Catholic man, "while prior to the active life, has to be intimately connected with it. Therefore, professional and family life, lived in the presence of God, should be the overflow of the interior life."[72] Noted cultural historian Christopher Dawson makes the following observation:

---

[67] *LG* 31. Furthermore, "the importance of work in human life demands that its meaning be known and assimilated in order to 'help all people to come closer to God, the Creator and Redeemer, to participate in his salvific plan for man and the world, and to deepen ... friendship with Christ in their lives, by accepting, through faith, a living participation in his threefold mission as Priest, Prophet and King'" (*RC* 23).

[68] *CL* 14.

[69] Ibid.

[70] Ibid. Saint Paul elaborates on this point in his "armor of God" discourse in Ephesians 6:10–19.

[71] Congregation for the Clergy et al., *Instruction on Certain Questions*, Preface.

[72] McCloskey, "Spirituality in the Professions and Workplace".

A Christian has only to *be* in order to change the world, for in that
act of being there is contained all the mystery of the supernatural life.
It is the function of the Church to sow this divine seed, to produce
not merely good men, but *spiritual* men. Insofar as the Church fulfills
this function it transmits to the world a continuous stream of spiritual energy.... A despiritualized Christianity is powerless to change
anything; it is the most abject of failures, since it serves neither [the]
natural nor the spiritual order.[73]

The apostolate has an important role to play in developing an
authentic man's spirituality. The apostolate, primarily exercised by
the individual, flows from a truly Christian life.[74] It is "a personal
call and commitment to sanctify others starting with the family, and
spreading out in ever widening concentric circles to colleagues, [co-
workers,] friends, and acquaintances. The apostolate is only limited
by the lack of interior life or apostolic zeal of the individual: 'Such
an individual form of apostolate can contribute greatly to a more
extensive spreading of the Gospel, indeed, it can reach as many places
as there are daily lives of individual members of the lay faithful.' "[75]
Hence, wherever the Catholic man "finds himself, there the Church
will be exercising her evangelical mission to preach to the very ends
of the earth the gospel of Christ."[76]

The characteristics of an effective, fruitful, and faith-building
apostolate include (a) a primacy of the vocation of each Christian
man to holiness, favoring the connection between faith and real life;
(b) a profession of the Catholic faith, following faithfully the teaching
authority of the Church; (c) a firm and convinced communion with
the pope and bishops and a mutual respect among all the forms of
apostolate in the Church; (d) a participation in the apostolic end
of the Church; and (e) a commitment of service to society by the
light of the social doctrine of the Church.[77]

*Work in Light of Family, Church, and Society.* A Catholic man's
approach to work must incorporate all aspects of his life: personal,

[73] Christopher Dawson, *Christianity and the New Order* (London: Sheed and Ward, 1931),
103 (emphasis added).
[74] Cf. *CL* 28.
[75] McCloskey, "Spirituality in the Professions and Workplace". Cf. ibid.
[76] Ibid.
[77] See *CL* 30.

familial, and societal, while labor itself involves the whole person: body, mind, and spirit. "As a person he works, he performs various actions belonging to the work process; independently of their objective content, these actions must all serve to realize his humanity, to fulfill the calling to be a person that is his by reason of his very humanity."[78] Work is sharing in the activity of the Creator where man perfects God's work in creation and redemption, and brings it to fruition.[79] Each man "must stand before the world as a witness to the resurrection and life of the Lord Jesus and as a sign that God lives.... [Men] must do their part to nourish the world with spiritual fruits.... In a word, 'what the soul is to the body let Christians be to the world.' "[80]

Man is the subject of work, and is matured and made more fully human by his labor. "In fact there is no doubt that human work has an ethical value of its own, which clearly and directly remain linked to the fact that the one who carries it out is a person, a conscious and free subject, that is to say a subject that decides about himself."[81] When he works, a man desires the fruit of his labor to be utilized by himself and others. He wishes to be part of the work process, sharing in the responsibility and creativity of the enterprise. As such, in accord with his dignity as a person, he should be as involved as possible in decision making, profit sharing, and all appropriate dimensions of the work to which he is called.

> By his labor a man supports himself and his family, is joined to his fellow men and serves them, and is enabled to exercise genuine charity and be a partner in the work of bringing divine creation to perfection. Indeed, we hold that by offering his labor to God man becomes associated with the redemptive work itself of Jesus Christ,

---

[78] *LE* 6. Pope John Paul II continues, "Work is a good thing for man—a good thing for his humanity—because through work man *not only transforms nature*, adapting it to his own needs, but he also *achieves fulfillment* as a human being and indeed, in a sense, becomes 'more a human being' " (no. 9; emphasis in original).

[79] "The word of God's revelation is profoundly marked by the fundamental truth that *man*, created in the image of God, *shares by his work in the activity of the Creator* and that, within the limits of his own human capabilities, man in a sense continues to develop that activity, and perfects it as he advances further and further in the discovery of the resources and values contained in the whole of creation" (*LE* 25; emphasis in original).

[80] *LG* 38.

[81] *LE* 6.

who conferred an eminent dignity on labor when at Nazareth He worked with His own hands. From all these considerations there arise every man's duty to labor faithfully and also his right to work. It is the duty of society, moreover, according to the circumstances prevailing in it, and in keeping with its proper role, to help its citizens find opportunities for adequate employment. Finally, payment for labor must be such as to furnish a man with the means to cultivate his own material, social, cultural, and spiritual life worthily, and that of his dependents.[82]

Work is also a pillar of family life both in the domestic church and in the parish, which must be supported financially. The home is the first school where children come to learn the meaning of work. The most important aspect of work in the home or parish, however, is the moral, spiritual, and intellectual formation of children and parishioners in the Catholic faith. Through this formation, nourished by the sacraments of initiation (Baptism, Confirmation, and the Eucharist), "there is communicated and nourished that charity toward God and man which is the soul of the entire apostolate. [They] are called in a special way to make the Church present and operative in those places and circumstances where only through them can she become the salt of the earth. Thus every layman, in virtue of the very gifts bestowed upon him, is at the same time a witness and a living instrument of the mission of the Church herself 'according to the measure of Christ's bestowal.' "[83]

God also reveals that periods of rest and leisure are inherent in work. Men have a tendency to equate "rest" with "nonproductivity". We do not make relaxation and rest a priority, often rationalizing this behavior with the excuse "I don't have time", when the truth is we make time for those things that are important to us. Leaving time for physical activity, recreation, retreats, and time with family and friends is critical because these are essential elements of a man's physical, emotional, and spiritual well-being. We have a responsibility to our family,

---

[82] GS 67. Furthermore, "those *responsible for business enterprises* are responsible to society for the economic and ecological effects of their operations. They have an obligation to consider the good of persons and not only the increase of *profits*. Profits are necessary, however. They make possible the investments that ensure the future of a business and they guarantee employment" (*CCC* 2432; emphasis in original).

[83] LG 33.

the Church, and to God to ensure we remain as mentally, physically, and spiritually healthy as possible in order to live our vocations to the fullest. As Saint John Paul II stated so beautifully,

> This description of creation, which we find in the very first chapter of the Book of Genesis, is also *in a sense the first "gospel of work."* For it shows what the dignity of work consists of: it teaches that man ought to imitate God, his Creator, in working, because man alone has the unique characteristic of likeness to God. Man ought to imitate God both in working and also in resting, since God himself wished to present his own creative activity under the form of *work and rest.* This activity by God in the world always continues, as the words of Christ attest: "My Father is working still ...": he works with creative power by sustaining in existence the world that he called into being from nothing, and he works with salvific power in the hearts of those whom from the beginning he has destined for "rest" in union with himself in his "Father's house." Therefore man's work too not only requires a rest every "seventh day," but also cannot consist in the mere exercise of human strength in external action; it must leave room for man to prepare himself, by becoming more and more what in the will of God he ought to be, for the *"rest" that the Lord reserves for his servants and friends.*[84]

Work also identifies a man with his culture; hence, his work in society benefits the common good of all its citizens. This is where the moral virtues, particularly fortitude, courage, and hope, play a significant role. Work after the Fall is an inspired toil—an arduous good.[85] The molding and shaping of a man's moral character and conscience by the truth, goodness, and beauty of Catholicism—that extends to his work—and the discipline that the labor of work requires are a participation in the Cross of Christ. Toil is also good because of

---

[84] *LE* 25 (emphasis in original).

[85] "All *work*, whether manual or intellectual, is inevitably linked with *toil*. The Book of Genesis expresses it in a truly penetrating manner: the original *blessing* of work contained in the very mystery of creation and connected with man's elevation as the image of God is contrasted with the *curse* that *sin* brought with it: 'Cursed is the ground because of you; in toil you shall eat of it all the days of your life.' This toil connected with work marks the way of human life on earth and constitutes *an announcement of death*: 'In the sweat of your, face you shall eat bread till you return to the ground, for out of it you were taken'" (*LE* 27; emphasis in original).

its sacrificial aspects: it can be joined to the sufferings of Christ and offered up. Suffering is a means to follow and imitate Christ:

> Sweat and toil, which work necessarily involves the present condition of the human race, present the Christian and everyone who is called to follow Christ with the possibility of sharing lovingly in the work that Christ came to do. This work of salvation came about through suffering and death on a Cross. By enduring the toil of work in union with Christ crucified for us, man in a way collaborates with the Son of God for the redemption of humanity. He shows himself a true disciple of Christ by carrying the cross in his turn every day in the activity that he is called upon to perform.[86]

Suffering has the power to convert people from sin and bring them to a higher degree of holiness and sanctity. It is precisely through work—especially when it is the most demanding and painful—that a man's labor is the most noble and capable of being part of the redemptive sacrifice. Saint Joseph the Worker knew this better than anyone, and he serves as a model for all Catholic men to follow:

> Work was the daily expression of love in the life of the Family of Nazareth. The Gospel specifies the kind of work Joseph did in order to support his family: he was a carpenter. This simple word sums up Joseph's entire life.... Human work, and especially manual labor, receive special prominence in the Gospel. Along with the humanity of the Son of God, work too has been taken up in the mystery of the Incarnation, and has also been redeemed in a special way. At the workbench where he plied his trade together with Jesus, Joseph brought human work closer to the mystery of the Redemption.... What is crucially important here is the sanctification of daily life, a sanctification which each person must acquire according to his or her own state, and one which can be promoted according to a model accessible to all people: "St. Joseph is the model of those humble ones that Christianity raises up to great destinies;... he is the proof that in order to be a good and genuine follower of Christ, there is no need of great things—it is enough to have the common, simple and human virtues, but they need to be true and authentic."[87]

[86] Ibid.
[87] RC 22, 24.

*Chapter Eight*

# The Armor of God

Christ, the final Adam, by the revelation of the mystery of the Father and His love, fully reveals man to himself and makes his supreme calling clear.

*— Gaudium et Spes*, no. 22

If you were on your deathbed and your son was standing before you, what would your last words be to him? David, the greatest king in the history of Israel, faced this very scenario: "When David's time to die drew near, he charged Solomon his son, saying, 'I am about to go the way of all the earth. Be strong, and show yourself a man'."[1] In his last moments on earth, David does not tell his son how to defeat his enemies, how to be popular and loved by the people, or how to accumulate wealth. Instead, David tells Solomon that he must be a man. But he doesn't stop there. He goes on to tell his son how he must be a *man of God*:

> [K]eep the charge of the LORD your God, walking in his ways and keeping his statutes, his commandments, his ordinances, and his testimonies, as it is written in the law of Moses, that you may prosper in all that you do and wherever you turn; that the Lord may establish his word which he spoke concerning me, saying, "If your sons take heed to their way, to walk before me in faithfulness with all their heart and with all their soul, there shall not fail you a man on the throne of Israel."[2]

The great warrior-king David personifies what every father, every priest, and every man who mentors the next generation of men can

[1] 1 Kings 2:1–2.
[2] 1 Kings 2:3–4.

and must do: prepare our sons for spiritual battle! David tells Solomon that if he follows the law of the Lord and puts the Lord first in his life, he will prosper, and if he becomes a living example of fidelity and holiness to his children, future generations of kings will not fail in their mission to serve, protect, and defend God's chosen people. If Catholic men are to thrive in today's society, and become beacons of hope, strength, and light in a culture of despair, darkness, and death, we must be armed and equipped to face Satan head-on as if our lives and eternal salvation depend on it.

If someone were to enter my home and try to kill my wife and children, they would have to step over my dead body to get to them. To serve, protect, and defend must be every man's attitude regarding his family, the Church, and the culture. This is our mission lived from the heart of the crucified Christ. *Abad* and *shamar* are not simply *what* we do as men but define *who* we are.

In his Letter to the Ephesians, Saint Paul describes the armor of God that every Catholic man must don in order to accomplish his mission on earth.

> Put on the whole armor of God, that you may be able to stand against the wiles of the devil. For we are not contending against flesh and blood, but against the principalities, against the powers, against the world rulers of this present darkness, against the spiritual hosts of wickedness in the heavenly places. Therefore take the whole armor of God that you may be able to withstand in the evil day, and having done all, to stand. Stand therefore, having fastened the belt of truth around your waist, and having put on the breastplate of righteousness, and having shod your feet with the equipment of the gospel of peace; besides all these, taking the shield of faith, with which you can quench all the flaming darts of the Evil One. And take the helmet of salvation, and the sword of the Spirit, which is the word of God. Pray at all times in the Spirit, with all prayer and supplication. To that end keep alert with all perseverance, making supplication for all the saints.[3]

*"The Whole Armor of God"*. When Jesus tell us that "foxes have holes, and birds of the air have nests; but the Son of man has nowhere to lay his head",[4] He is saying that the work of evangelization—of

---

[3] Eph 6:11–18.
[4] Lk 9:58.

sharing the Good News of our faith in love with conviction and authority—is never finished. Catholic men cannot rest while the storms of spiritual poverty and economic instability shake us violently, and the tempest of sexual immorality and unspeakable sins against a culture of life rage all around us. How should we respond? Should we be frightened and unsettled? Should we panic as we listen to political pundits, business analysts, and self-assured politicians who sound like prophets of doom? Or should we instead take up the challenge of Jesus: "If any man would come after me, let him deny himself and take up his cross daily and follow me" to glory.[5] Men who live in the presence of God have nothing to fear! When we become overwhelmed by the trials and tribulations of life, we must have unwavering trust in God the Father so that He can pour out on us a spirit of freedom: a spirit of love that casts out all fear, removes all doubt, and eliminates all obstacles that hinder us from being true followers of Christ.

There is a great lesson in this for all of us who are called to be men of God and warriors for Christ: the importance of sharing the gift of vulnerability. With absolute trust and confidence, we must not be afraid to place our hearts and lives in the hands of Christ. The Lord made Himself totally vulnerable on the Cross in a complete and perfect act of love and sacrifice. In order to evangelize effectively, we too must not be afraid to break ourselves open and pour ourselves out in love, because it is in our weakness that Christ is the strongest.

"Manning-up" can only begin when the desire and longing for intimate communion with God is reawakened within us, leading us from the slavery of sin to life in Jesus Christ. When we recognize and respond to the voice of the Lord calling us, then we will have the courage to speak out against the evils of abortion, euthanasia, human cloning, and embryonic stem cell research, and to defend the basic right to life from the moment of conception to natural death. When we set our hand on the plow, we will safeguard and promote family life by supporting monogamous marriage between one man and one woman, and denouncing contraception and cohabitation. When we boldly proclaim the kingdom of God, we will protect the freedom of parents regarding the education of their children and the right to exercise a well-formed conscience. We will protect our youth from

[5] Lk 9:23.

substance abuse, fornication, child sex trafficking, and other modern forms of slavery, and reestablish the Holy Family as *the* model of family life.

Saint Paul says to the Galatians, "For freedom Christ has set us free; stand fast therefore, and do not submit again to a yolk of slavery."[6] As long as men choose to remain slaves to sin and conduits for moral relativism, the family, the Church, and society will suffer. But the Lord encourages us to "[l]eave the dead to bury their own dead; but as for you, go and proclaim the kingdom of God."[7] Men can no longer live their lives in fear, ashamed and afraid to share their faith with others. When we do this we allow fear to empty us of love, leaving a deep void that needs to be filled. The culture has convinced us that being a real man means filling this emptiness with pleasure or power or prestige, and we fool ourselves into believing that it is easier to live a lie than to seek the truth.

This is exactly the point Pope Benedict XVI makes in *Caritas in Veritate*. "Love", the Holy Father says, "is an extraordinary force which leads people to opt for courageous and generous engagement.... It is a force that has its origin in God [who is] Eternal Love and Absolute Truth. Each person finds his good by adherence to God's plan for him in order to realize it fully: in this plan, he finds his truth, and through adherence to this truth he becomes free (cf. John 8:22)."[8] If men are to lead the way in helping this culture rediscover its freedom—which is what evangelization is all about—we first must be free ourselves.

Why are we called to evangelize? By our Baptism into Christ's death, we are called to be disciples. A disciple is one who hears, who accepts, and who carries out the teaching of Jesus in his life. A disciple follows and imitates Jesus. Each man who has been baptized has this mission and calling: to actively share his experience of knowing Jesus Christ personally and then inviting others to share in His life.

For far too long, we Catholic men have been filled with a spirit of apathy and embarrassment about sharing our faith. We keep the faith to ourselves and contain it within the walls of the church. When

---

[6] Gal 5:1.

[7] Lk 9:60. See also Mt 8:22.

[8] Benedict XVI, Encyclical Letter *Caritas in Veritate*, Charity in Truth, June 29, 2009, Vatican translation (Boston: Pauline Books and Media, 2009), no. 1.

we are challenged by our friends and loved ones about why we are Catholic, we cower. When the culture tries to shove subjective truth down our throats, we worry about being politically correct. When unborn children are slaughtered and marriage is redefined, we remain silent or turn the other way. We *must* pray, of course, but we must also act and speak the truth in love. We must go forward with the Holy Spirit at our side and meet people where they are and witness to them. We should evangelize with confidence knowing that we have the fullness of truth in the Catholic Church rooted in the transcendent principles of faith, hope, and love that allow us to give ourselves completely to the Living God, Jesus Christ, who is the Truth that sets us free.

"Blessed are you when men revile you and persecute you and utter all kinds of evil against you falsely on my account."[9] We are called to preach the Gospel in its fullness, and not just the parts that we like. This means that when we live our faith every day through the witness of our life we will be persecuted, mocked, ridiculed, and scorned just as Christ was as He made His way to Calvary. Life is too short to worry about what other people think. We are called by God to be saints: to live our faith with courage and conviction in this time and in this place, and to put all our trust in God. The Scriptures encourage each man to "keep the LORD ever in my sight: since he is at my right hand, I shall stand firm."[10] We must live the faith that we profess with great joy, passion, and enthusiasm! We are to rejoice and be glad, for our reward will be great in heaven.

"*Stand therefore, having girded your loins with truth.*" One of the most tangible signs of crisis among men in the culture today is the fashion trend known as "sagging", where young men wear beltless pants significantly below the waist, often exposing their underwear and, in some cases, their buttocks. Sagging was adopted from the United States prison system, where belts are sometimes prohibited to prevent prisoners from using them as weapons or committing suicide by hanging themselves. After hip-hop artists popularized the style in the 1990s, sagging later became a symbol of cultural awareness, freedom from authority, and the rejection of societal values.

[9] Mt 5:11.
[10] Ps 16:8.

Sagging is the antithesis of biblical teaching that describes the secur-
ing of the pants around the waist (also known as "girding your loins")
as the way men prepare for battle.[11] The concept of "girding your
loins" is also used in a spiritual sense to describe how God prepares
men to carry out His holy will, as evidenced in Ephesians: "Stand
therefore, having girded your loins with truth".[12] Girding ourselves
with the truth of the Catholic faith—in preparation for spiritual battle against sin—is an essential element of becoming an authentically
Catholic man of God. Girding the loins of our hearts, minds, and
souls in solidarity with the crucified Christ (often depicted with his
loins girt on the Cross) leads a man to repentance, reconciliation, and
spiritual renewal as he sincerely seeks to deepen his relationship with
our Father in heaven.

The invitation to participate in the mystery of Christ's Passion,
death, and Resurrection always calls us to new life. A new life
requires us to relinquish the old, just as faith requires that we surrender everything to God. Surrendering and 'letting go' is never easy,
and we must look to Jesus as our example of what it means to make
a gift of our life. Through prayer, we ask God to lower the walls that
we've erected between Him and ourselves, so that, by the power of
the Holy Spirit, Jesus enters into our most guarded places, willing to
set us free to love. Christ allows us to see and understand that by the
power of God and none other, we can be transformed by prayer. We
must die to the ways of this world so that Christ can live in us.

Know and understand this: Satan is trying to kill us. He is out
to destroy covenant relationship with God. The devil is the one

---

[11] When preparing for battle, the lengthy robes that men wore would get in the way. The
garment would be secured ("girded") by pulling up the fabric of the tunic so that the length
in front stopped at the upper thigh. The man would then pull the material forward so the
back of the tunic was snug against the backside. Next, he tucked the extra front material
down between his legs and gathered it behind his back. At this point, he collected half of the
material behind him evenly on each side of his back. The final step involved wrapping each
side of the material around his waist and tying it together in front.

[12] Eph 6:14; also the following:, "But you, gird up your loins; arise, and say to them
everything that I command you" (Jer 1:17); "The LORD is king, with majesty enrobed;
the LORD has robed himself with might, he has girded himself with power" (Ps 93:1);
"Let your loins be girded and your lamps burning, and be like men who are waiting for
their master to come home from the marriage feast, so that they may open to him at once
when he comes and knocks" (Lk 12:35–36); "Therefore gird up your minds, be sober, set
your hope fully upon the grace that is coming to you at the revelation of Jesus Christ"
(1 Pet 1:13).

who "'throws himself across' God's plan and His work of salvation accomplished in Christ.... When we ask to be delivered from the Evil One, we pray as well to be freed from all evils, present, past and future, of which Satan is the author and instigator."[13] But we live in a culture that finds it easier to believe a lie than to live the truth, that embraces the thirty-second sound bite as if it were divine revelation and rarely accepts the obligations and responsibilities of faith—lived in the light of truth, goodness, and beauty—with all that Jesus demands and expects of us.

"See to it that no one makes a prey of you by philosophy and empty deceit, according to human tradition, according to the elemental spirits of the universe, and not according to Christ."[14] We cannot acquiesce to "pop" psychology and New Age spirituality, which lead us away from a faith rooted in Christ and centered in the Eucharist, and toward beliefs based on little more than sophisticated nonsense. There are some men, for example, who try various kinds of "spiritual healing" that implies that faith in Christ is unnecessary; we simply have to get in touch with our inner healing power. Moreover, certain schools of philosophy and psychology actually play a role in the Church, as evidenced by the use of the Enneagram along with its cousins Reiki, the labyrinth, and astrology. "The New Age Movement is very harmful in that it encourages its members to feel free to pursue their own type of spirituality, thus leading them away from the Catholic Church. This movement teaches its followers that everyone is their own God and that they have powers within themselves to control the supernatural. The very attractive lure of the New Age Movement is that one will see instant changes in their life. There is not a need for prayer or discipline within the New Age Movement. There is no God in this movement, it is all about self."[15]

Even faithful Catholic men who at times struggle with certain aspects of their faith look for "new" ways to bring themselves closer to the Lord. Occasionally, they come in contact with certain methods and ideologies that have nothing to do with Catholic teaching and add to the confusion that helps fuel further misconceptions about

[13] CCC 2851, 2854.
[14] Col 2:8. See also Lev 19:26ff.
[15] "New Age Movement", ConcernedCatholics.org, accessed May 15, 1999, www.concernedcatholics.org/newage.htm.

the faith that ultimately undermine and destroy the very fabric of these men's Catholic identity.

> The New Age concept of God is rather diffuse, whereas the Christian concept is a very clear one. The New Age god is an impersonal energy, really a particular extension or component of the cosmos; god in this sense is the life-force or soul of the world. Divinity is to be found in every being, in a gradation "from the lowest crystal of the mineral world up to and beyond the Galactic God himself, about Whom we can say nothing at all. This is not a man but a Great Consciousness." In some "classic" New Age writings, it is clear that human beings are meant to think of themselves as gods.... God is no longer to be sought beyond the world, but deep within myself. This is very different from the Christian understanding of God as the maker of heaven and earth and the source of all personal life. God is in himself personal, the Father, Son and Holy Spirit, who created the universe in order to share the communion of his life with creaturely persons. "God, who 'dwells in unapproachable light', wants to communicate his own divine life to the men he freely created, in order to adopt them as his sons in his only-begotten Son. By revealing himself God wishes to make them capable of responding to him, and of knowing him, and of loving him far beyond their own natural capacity." God is not identified with the Life-principle understood as the "Spirit" or "basic energy" of the cosmos, but is that love which is absolutely different from the world, and yet creatively present in everything, and leading human beings to salvation.[16]

Here is the truth: we cannot save ourselves! Salvation comes from only one Source: the One True God—the God of Abraham, Isaac, and Jacob; the God of Peter, James, and John; the God of Muslims, Jews, and atheists—and He is none other than our Lord Jesus Christ. He is the God of Isaiah, who foretold His coming and who tells us that the Savior gave His back to those who beat Him, His cheeks to those who plucked His beard, His face to buffets and spitting. He is the God of Saint Paul, who tells us that His name is above every

---

[16] Pontifical Council for Culture and Pontifical Council for Interreligious Dialogue, *Jesus Christ, the Bearer of the Water of Life: A Christian Reflection on the "New Age"*, February 3, 2003, Section 4 (*New Age* and Christian Faith in Contrast), www.vatican.va/roman_curia /pontifical_councils/interelg/documents/rc_pc_interelg_doc_20030203_new-age_en.html.

other name, and that at the name of Jesus every knee must bend in heaven, on earth, and under the earth, and that every tongue proclaim to the glory of God the Father that Jesus Christ is Lord.[17] He is the God of Luke the Evangelist who says that the greatest is the one who serves: the one who makes a gift of himself, who breaks himself open and pours himself out in love just as Jesus did on the Cross.

When we compromise our Catholic faith, we join our voices to an anemic culture that shouts, "Crucify Him!" When we start believing that we are our own gods and shut our hearts to the voice of the Lord speaking through His Church, we join the culture of death in driving the nails deeper into the flesh of Christ. When we would rather watch sports than receive the Holy Eucharist at Mass every week, we look up at the crucified Christ and say with the crowd, "Save yourself."

The truth and beauty of Sacred Scripture cries out to us loud and clear that the idols of men are merely silver and gold, the work of human hands. The psalmist describes the fruits of this culture of cohabitation, contraception, euthanasia, and so-called alternative lifestyles: "[T]hey have mouths but they cannot speak; they have eyes but they cannot see; they have ears but they cannot hear; they have nostrils but they cannot smell; with their hands they cannot feel; with their feet they cannot walk. No sound comes from their throats. Their makers will come to be like them and so will all who trust in them."[18]

Let us not settle for spirituality-lite, where we seek "feel good" spirituality that kills the life of God within us. When this happens, we will use the labyrinth instead of the Stations of the Cross, astrology instead of the Rosary, and tarot cards instead of Eucharistic Adoration. It is the Blood of the Lamb that redeems us! The truth that Jesus has revealed remains throughout eternity, taught and defended by the Church, who has been appointed Mother and Teacher of truth. Christ asks us to pick up our Crosses and follow Him to eternal life—to turn away from the world's ways and keep our eyes fixed on Him. This means sacrifice; it means that people will hate us because we are not afraid to defend the sanctity of life and marriage—for Jesus tells us, "You will be delivered up even by parents and brothers and

---

[17] See Phil 2:5–11.
[18] Ps 115:4–8.

kinsmen and friends, and some of you they will put to death; you will be hated by all for my name's sake. But not a hair of your head will perish. By your endurance you will gain your lives."[19]

The truth of our salvation comes only in and through Jesus Christ, who gave His life so that we might live. The truth of our salvation will come when we lovingly lay down our lives at His feet. The truth of our salvation will come when we stand up for our Catholic faith, even when that means we will be rejected, mocked, and scorned. The truth of our salvation will come when we are able to say with Jesus, "Father, into Your hands I commend my spirit."[20]

*"Having put on the breastplate of righteousness."* A Protestant minister once challenged me on the Sacrament of Reconciliation, asking why Catholics go to a priest to confess their sins. During our discussion, he said, "You Catholics and your sacraments! You don't have to go to a priest in some dark box to have your sins forgiven. All you have to do is pray to Jesus! We are covered by the Blood of the Lamb, and when we confess our sins to Him we are forgiven." So I asked him, "How do you know *for sure* that your sins are forgiven? What is the sign from God—the guarantee—that when you pray to Jesus your sins are actually forgiven?" Somewhat perplexed he replied, "You just pray to Jesus, and the Holy Spirit gives you a feeling in your heart that you've been cleansed by the Blood of the Lamb." I responded, "A feeling? You're basing the forgiveness of sins on how you feel? How do you know that's not acid reflux?"

I continued, "Let's say, for example, that you and I are friends. We get into a horrible fight one day that ruins our friendship and we are no longer speaking to each other. A year from now my wife asks me if the issue between you and me has been healed. I tell her that I know in my heart you have forgiven me. But how do I know for sure? The fact is I don't. Unless I call or e-mail or visit you—unless I have a personal encounter with you—I have no idea if our friendship has been healed." I then asked the pastor to show me in the Bible where Jesus, who is God, says out of His own mouth, "Pray to Me and your sins will be forgiven." He looked through his Bible and the closest verse he could find was in the First Letter of John: "[T]he blood of Jesus his Son cleanses us from all sin. If we say we have no sin, we deceive ourselves, and the truth is not in us. If we confess our sins, he is faithful and just, and will forgive our sins and cleanse us from all unrighteousness."[21]

I expressed two issues with this verse. First, while I wholeheartedly agree that "the blood of Jesus his Son cleanses us from all sin", the verse does *not* say to confess your sins directly to Jesus. Later on in the same letter, John says, "If *any one* sees his brother committing what is not a deadly sin, *he will ask,* and God will give him life for those whose sin is not deadly."[22] The apostle James adds: "Is any among you sick? Let him call for the elders of the Church, and *let them pray over him,* anointing him with oil in the name of the Lord; and *the prayer of faith will save the sick man,* and the Lord will raise him up; *and if he has committed sins, he will be forgiven. Therefore confess your sins to one another, and pray for one another, that you may be healed.* The prayer of a righteous man has great power in its effects.... My brethren, if any one among you wanders from the truth and some one brings him back, let him know that *whoever brings back a sinner from the error of his way will save his soul from death and will cover a multitude of sins.*"[23] Clearly, these passages show that intercessory prayer is an efficacious means that God uses to forgive sins. Second, I asked him to show me the verse where Jesus Himself says "pray directly to me" for the forgiveness of sins. He could not find such a verse, because it does not exist.

I went on to make my point. Christ gives us the guarantee of forgiveness in Scripture. In Matthew 16, after calling Simon the "rock" upon which the Church would be built,[24] Jesus goes on to say, "I will

---

[21] 1 Jn 1:7–9. "John envisions, not a general admission of weakness or even sinfulness, but the confession of specific acts of wrongdoing (Psalm 32:3–5). God, for his part, is eager to show mercy to the contrite spirit (Psalm 51:17). Contrary to the teaching of some, the need for repentance, confession, and forgiveness is ongoing throughout the Christian life; otherwise, the Lord would not urge believers to seek forgiveness on a continuing basis (Matthew 6:12; Luke 11:4). Note that in biblical terms 'confession' (Greek *homologeo*) is something you do with your lips and not simply in the silence of your heart (Mark 1:5; Romans 10:10; James 5:16)" (*Ignatius Catholic Study Bible: The New Testament*, RSV, Second Catholic Edition [San Francisco: Ignatius Press, 2010], 469).

[22] 1 Jn 5:16 (emphasis added).

[23] Jas 5:14–16; 19–20 (emphasis added).

[24] Jesus said in Aramaic, "You are *Kepha* and on this *Kepha* I will build my Church." In Aramaic, *kepha* means a massive stone, and *evna* means a little pebble. Some argue that, because the Greek word for rock is *petra*, "Petros" actually means "a small rock" and therefore Jesus was attempting to diminish Peter. However, Jesus was speaking Aramaic and used *Kepha*, not *evna*. Using "Petros" to translate "Kepha" was done simply to reflect the masculine

give *you* the keys of the kingdom of heaven, and whatever *you* bind on earth shall be bound in heaven, and whatever *you* loose on earth shall be loosed in heaven."[25] This same commission is later given to all the apostles in Matthew 18: "Truly, I say to you, whatever *you* bind on earth shall be bound in heaven, and whatever *you* loose on earth shall be loosed in heaven."[26] In John 20, "[H]e breathed on them, and said to them, 'Receive the Holy Spirit. If *you* forgive the sins of any, they are forgiven; if *you* retain the sins of any, they are retained."[27] Jesus' own words clearly give specific and direct authority to forgive sins in His name to His apostles. So the question becomes, why did Jesus establish the forgiveness of sins in this way?

In Christ Jesus, God the Father no longer wanted to speak to us though prophets, leaders, and kings. The Word becoming flesh and dwelling among us shows that God wanted to—literally—reach out and touch us with His own hands, and love us with His own heart. He wanted to know us personally.

The forgiveness of sins is something only God can do, which was implicit in Jewish theology. Jesus Himself was a Jew, so in order to appreciate the Jewish understanding of the forgiveness of sins and the importance of a personal encounter with the Lord, we need to look at the Pentateuch, specifically, the Book of Leviticus.

---

noun of Peter. If the translator wanted to identify Peter as the "small rock", he would have used *lithos*, which means a little pebble in Greek. Jesus called Peter the massive rock, not the little pebble, on which He would build the Church. Moreover, Jesus renames Simon *Kepha* in Mark 3:16 and John 1:42.

[25] Mt 16:19–20 (emphasis added). The verses are clear that Jesus, after acknowledging Peter's receipt of divine revelation, turns the whole discourse to the person of Peter: Blessed are "you" Simon, for flesh and blood has not revealed this to "you", and I tell "you", "you" are Peter, and on this rock I will build My Church. I will give "you" the keys to the kingdom, and whatever "you" bind and loose on earth will be bound and loosed in heaven. Jesus' whole discourse relates to the person of Peter, not his confession of faith. In Isaiah 22:20–22, we read: "In that day I will call my servant Eliakim the son of Hilkiah, and I will clothe him with your robe, and will bind your belt on him, and will commit your authority to his hand; and he shall be a father to the inhabitants of Jerusalem and to the house of Judah. And I will place on his shoulder the key of the house of David; he shall open, and none shall shut; and he shall shut, and none shall open." In the Davidic kingdom, there were royal ministers who conducted the liturgical worship and bound the people in teaching and doctrine. There was also a prime minister or chief steward of the kingdom who held the keys. Jesus gives Peter these keys to His earthly kingdom, the Church. This representative has decision-making authority over the people: when he shuts, no one opens. See also Rev 1:18; 3:7; 9:1; 20:1.

[26] Mt 18:18 (emphasis added).

[27] Jn 20:22–23 (emphasis added).

Leviticus 5:1–4, for example, lists a number of sins. It then says in verse 5, "When a man is guilty in any of these, he shall confess the sin he has committed, and he shall bring his guilt offering to the LORD for the sin which he has committed ... and *the priest* shall make atonement for him for his sin" (emphasis added). A few verses later, we read: "Thus the priest shall make atonement for him for the sin which he has committed in any one of these things, and he shall be forgiven" (v. 13).

> And again, "He shall also make restitution for what he has done amiss in the holy thing, and shall add a fifth to it and give it to the priest; and the priest shall make atonement for him with the ram of the guilt offering, and he shall be forgiven. If any one sins, doing any of the things which the LORD has commanded not to be done, though he does not know it, yet he is guilty and shall bear his iniquity. He shall bring to the priest a ram without blemish out of the flock, valued by you at the price for a guilt offering, and the priest shall make atonement for him for the error which he committed unwittingly, and he shall be forgiven" (vv. 16–18). Over and over again, we see that when the Jews needed their sins forgiven, they went to the priest.[28]

Jesus said, "Do not think that I have come to abolish the law and the prophets; I have come not to abolish them but to fulfil them."[29] Precisely because Jesus Christ is the *Agnus Dei qui tollit peccata mundi*, the true High Priest and the sacrificial victim who offered Himself for our sins, we no longer have to bring a lamb, a goat, bread, or any other sin offering. We only need to bring ourselves and our sins before the Lord. Jesus wants us to experience Him in a truly personal way and fulfills the Old Testament law in John 20 by giving authority to forgive sins in His name to His earthly priests. The priest acts in persona Christi, and when we hear the words of absolution from the priest ("I absolve you"), we are hearing the words of Jesus, who Himself said, "He who hears you hears me, and he who rejects you rejects me, and he who rejects me rejects him who sent me" (Lk 10:16). This is the guarantee; this is how we know for sure that our sins are forgiven, that the slate is wiped clean.

"*Shod your feet with the equipment of the gospel of peace.*" When we hear the word "peace" our minds are immediately drawn to the end

---

[28] Cf. Lev 4:13–20; 4:22–26; 4:27–31; 4:32–35; 5:5–13; 5:15–18; 12:6–8; 14:15–20; 16:20–24, 32–34; 19:20–22.

[29] Mt 5:17.

of war and conflict both in the world and in ourselves. In the face of "the evils and injustices that accompany" all hostilities, we Christians are called "to prayer and to action so that the [Lord God] may free us from the ancient bondage of war."[30] Hence, we should always seek and strive after peace. If, however, we desire a true and lasting peace, we must look beyond what can be accomplished solely by human effort; we must look to the Cross: "For in him all the fulness of God was pleased to dwell, and through him to reconcile to himself all things, whether on earth or in heaven, making peace by the blood of his cross."[31]

The Lord challenges men to seek a deeper peace with hearts that denounce all anger and hatred, which leads to sin and death.[32] Peace, then, is not merely the absence of war, and it is not limited to maintaining a balance of powers between adversaries. "Peace cannot be attained on earth without [these essential elements]: safeguarding the goods of persons, free communication among men, respect for the dignity of persons and peoples, and the assiduous practice of fraternity. [In short, true] peace is the work of justice and the effect of charity."[33]

Jesus Christ is peace personified. Our Lord is not a symbol for peace; He is peace itself. He is the peace that was prophesied by Isaiah: "For to us a child is born, to us a son is given; and the government will be upon his shoulder, and his name will be called 'Wonderful Counselor, Mighty God, Everlasting Father, Prince of Peace.' Of the increase of his government and of peace there will be no end, upon the throne of David and over his kingdom, to establish it, and to uphold it with justice and with righteousness from this time forth and for evermore."[34] This peace is the subject of Zechariah's *Benedictus*, where he proclaims, "[T]hrough the tender mercy of our God, when the day shall dawn upon us from on high to give light to those who sit in darkness and in the shadow of death, to guide our feet into the way of peace."[35] He is the peace

---

[30] *CCC* 2307.
[31] Col 1:19–20.
[32] Cf. *CCC* 2302.
[33] *CCC* 2304.
[34] Is 9:6–7.
[35] Lk 1:78–79.

given to us in the Word-made-flesh, who allows us to share in His divine life, as Saint Paul reminds us: "For he is our peace, who has made us both one, and has broken down the dividing wall of hostility ... making peace", and reconciling us "to God in one body through the cross, thereby bringing the hostility to an end."[36] This is the peace that calmed the apostle's fears and empowered them on the day of the Resurrection: "Jesus came and stood among them and said to them, 'Peace be with you.' When he had said this, he showed them his hands and his side. Then the disciples were glad when they saw the Lord. Jesus said to them again, 'Peace be with you. As the Father has sent me, even so I send you.' "[37]

"Blessed are the peacemakers, for they shall be called sons of God."[38] Peacemakers are those who help to break down the many barriers that divide people from their Catholic faith. The Father sent His Son to break down the walls between God and His people, and sometimes even between the people themselves. If we truly are to be God's adopted sons, we must strive for peace not only in the world but also in our own lives, and in our families and parishes. We must learn to recognize those people, situations, or conditions that cause us to worry—to be anxious and afraid—and that prevent us from having true peace. We must then pray deeply and fervently to our Lord and Savior Jesus Christ in Eucharistic Adoration so that, like Mary, we may give birth to peace by the witness of our faith. As Saint Paul says, "Have no anxiety about anything, but in everything by prayer and supplication with thanksgiving let your requests be made known to God. And the peace of God, which passes all understanding, will keep your hearts and your minds in Christ Jesus."[39]

Let us "hear what the LORD God has to say, a voice that speaks of peace; peace for his people and his friends and those who turn to him in their hearts.... [For the] LORD will make us prosper and our earth shall yield its fruit. Justice shall march before him and peace shall follow his steps."[40] With unwavering faith and trust in God's mercy, love, and gift of salvation, let us be confident in Christ's words of

36 Eph 2:14–16.
37 Jn 20:19–21.
38 Mt 5:9.
39 Phil 4:6–7.
40 Ps 85:9, 13–14.

blessing: "Peace I leave with you; my peace I give to you; not as the world gives do I give to you. Let not your hearts be troubled, neither let them be afraid."[41]

"[*Take*] *the shield of faith, with which you can quench all the flaming darts of the Evil one.*"

[P]reach the word, be urgent in season and out of season, convince, rebuke, and exhort, be unfailing in patience and in teaching. For the time is coming when people will not endure sound teaching, but having itching ears they will accumulate for themselves teachers to suit their own likings, and will turn away from listening to the truth and wander into myths. As for you, always be steady, endure suffering, do the work of an evangelist, fulfil your ministry.[42]

Not unlike the Church of the twenty-first century, Saint Leo the Great faced great moral challenges in his day. During his papacy, barbarian armies actively persecuted Christian communities, while heretics from within the Church spread errors about the Person and nature of Jesus. With steadfast conviction and brilliance, Pope Leo boldly proclaimed the truth of the Catholic faith regarding the divine and human natures of Jesus, healing the festering wound of disunity that tarnished the Church.

When a large army of barbarians came to attack Rome, Saint Leo courageously rode out to meet the pagan leader Attila the Hun, armed only with his great trust in God. Attila admired the pope's fearlessness. Leo's humility and charity earned him great respect among the barbarians. Rome was saved because the pope was willing to give his life to protect and defend the faith.

With the fervor of Saint Leo the Great, we must protect and defend the Catholic faith against an ever-advancing culture of death. We live in a world of eclipse, in a world consumed by a darkness whose far-reaching shadows of abortion, contraception, pornography, and the redefinition of marriage are cast across the threshold of family life. This is not a time for spineless cowards! Our Blessed Mother assures us that if we dedicate ourselves to prayer and make a serious effort to live the truth of our faith, then, strengthened by Christ's Body

[41] Jn 14:27.
[42] 2 Tim 4:2–5.

and Blood in the Holy Eucharist, we can overcome the power of sin that weakens us, and overcome the lies of Satan that both entice and preclude us from being the men who God created and calls us to be.

Let us heed the words of her Son, our Lord Jesus Christ, by being vigilant at all times and pray that we have the strength to escape the tribulations that are imminent.[43] We can only be battle ready if we are truly free of serious sin, and this freedom can be found in its full-ness in the image of the crucified Christ. If we valiantly follow Him with confidence and conviction, He will lead us out of the heart of darkness and into His own wonderful light.

Our Lord told Saint Faustina of the mercy He wants to give to the world, if only we will believe in His love. If we are honest with ourselves, we realize that we are often lukewarm at best. Sunday after Sunday we hear the Word of God and receive our Lord in the Most Blessed Sacrament of the Eucharist, and yet we walk away, for the most part unchanged, knowing full well that Christ is calling us to change our lives, to become one with Him, which means we must reject popular opinion and the ways of the world. We allow ourselves just enough faith to be comfortable until that faith calls us to stand up for the truth that makes us uncomfortable, trembling in the fear of being rejected and unpopular.

Each one of us has been set apart when we were consecrated to the Most Holy Trinity on the day of our Baptism. We have been set aside for a holy purpose. To do God's work, we cannot think or act like everyone else; we are to follow in the footsteps of Jesus Christ. We are called to be foot soldiers in the army of God led by Christ our King and the Blessed Virgin Mary as Queen. Our hope for salva-tion lies within the light of Christ, who "shines down even into the deepest darkness"[44] of our hearts to restore our sense of sin and find comfort in the brightness of God's presence.

We need God's light in our world, now more than ever. One of the greatest weapons in our spiritual arsenal in this battle against the seed of Satan is total consecration to the Blessed Virgin Mary. At Fatima, she exhorts us to "sacrifice yourselves for sinners, and say many times, especially whenever you make some sacrifice: O

---

[43] See Lk 21:36.

[44] Hans Urs von Balthasar, *Light of the Word: Brief Reflections on the Sunday Readings* (San Francisco: Ignatius Press, 1993), 179.

Jesus, it is for love of You, for the conversion of sinners, and for reparation for the sins committed against the Immaculate Heart of Mary."[45] Our Blessed Mother—the icon of the Church who always leads us to her Son—is a beacon of hope that pierces the dense fog of anxiety and trepidation, and illuminates our path to the solid rock of our faith who is Christ crucified. All that remains is our choice to either "accept God's love so that it can prove effective and fruitful in us, or cower in our darkness in order to evade the light of this love".[46]

The triumph of God's love through Mary's Immaculate Heart frees us for participation in works of mercy, thereby bringing God's light into the world. To evangelize means to bear witness in a convincing manner to the victory of God's love over the power of sin and death. This means, first and foremost, standing up for and defending the truth.

What does a soldier in the army of Mary look like?

> We know that they shall be true disciples of Jesus Christ, walking in the footsteps of His poverty, humility, contempt of the world, charity; teaching the narrow way of God in pure truth according to the holy Gospel, and not according to the maxims of the world; troubling themselves about nothing;... fearing and listening to no mortal, however influential he may be. They shall have in their mouths the two-edged sword of the Word of God. They shall carry on their shoulders the bloody standard of the Cross, the Crucifix in their right hand and the Rosary in their left, the sacred Names of Jesus and Mary in their hearts, and the modesty and mortification of Jesus in their own behaviour. These are the great men who are to come, but Mary is the one who, by order of the Most High, shall fashion them for the purpose of extending His empire over that of the impious [and] the idolaters.[47]

*"Take the helmet of salvation."* "Lord, how I love your law! It is ever in my mind.... You have imposed your will with justice and with

---

[45]John Hauf, ed., *The Message of Fatima: Lucia Speaks* (Washington, N.J.: AMI Press, 1997), 17.

[46]Von Balthasar, *Light of the Word*, 178.

[47]Louis de Monfort, *True Devotion to Mary*, trans. Fr. Frederick Faber (Rockford, Ill.: Tan Books, 1985), 35.

absolute truth.... Your word is founded on truth; your decrees are eternal".[48]

The first thing that comes to mind when most people think of the word "law" is "rules and regulations", defined as the system of rules that a particular country, community, or organization recognizes as regulating the actions of its members and that is enforced by the imposition of penalties. Or maybe you have a more scientific mind, where "law" would be a statement of fact, deduced from observation, to the effect that a particular natural or scientific phenomenon always occurs if certain conditions are present. If you look beyond the temporal or earthly realm and toward the spiritual, then "law" is a body of divine commandments expressed in the Bible or other religious texts. When the Catholic Church thinks of "law", she articulates four basic types: eternal law, divine law, natural law, and positive law.

The eternal law is the mind of God through which He providentially governs all of reality. In other words, the eternal law is God's inner intelligibility from which he generates all things visible and invisible.[49] These would include, in part, the laws of physics, cosmology, chemistry, molecular biology, etc.

The divine law is that part of the eternal law that has been revealed to us by God. The fullness of this revelation is Jesus Christ, the Word that became flesh, true God from true God. "Now they know that everything that you have given me is from you; for I have given them the words which you gave me, and they have received them and know in truth that I came from you; and they have believed that you sent me"[50]

The natural, moral law is human participation in that portion of the eternal law that can be known rationally.[51] In other words, natural law is that portion of the eternal law (transcendent truth) placed

[48] Ps 119:97, 138, 160.
[49] "Law is a rule of conduct enacted by competent authority for the sake of the common good. The moral law presupposes the rational order, established among creatures for their good and to serve their final end, by the power, wisdom, and goodness of the Creator. All law finds its first and ultimate truth in the eternal law" (CCC 1951).
[50] Jn 17:7-8.
[51] "The moral law is the work of divine Wisdom. Its biblical meaning can be defined as fatherly instruction, God's pedagogy. It prescribes for man the ways, the rules of conduct that lead to the promised beatitude; it proscribes the ways of evil which turn him away from God and his love. It is at once firm in its precepts and, in its promises, worthy of love" (CCC 1950).

within us by God—by virtue of His creating human nature—where we can come to know the reality of God by reason alone. Saint Paul describes the basic tenets of natural law in the opening chapters of his Letter to the Romans:

> For what can be known about God is plain to them, because God has shown it to them. Ever since the creation of the world his invisible nature, namely, his eternal power and deity, has been clearly perceived in the things that have been made.[52]

> When Gentiles who have not the law do by nature what the law requires, they are a law to themselves, even though they do not have the law. They show that what the law requires is written on their hearts, while their conscience also bears witness and their conflicting thoughts accuse or perhaps excuse them on that day when, according to my gospel, God judges the secrets of men by Christ Jesus.[53]

Positive or human law is that part of the natural law that man uses to govern society and serve the common good. Human laws ought to be compatible with the natural law but not encompass all of the natural law. Any civil law that is incompatible with the natural law is, in its very essence, not a genuine law. Examples would include abortion, physician-assisted suicide, and so-called homosexual "marriage".

A Catholic man living an authentically male spirituality dons the helmet of salvation that protects his mind, forms his conscience in accord with the natural law, and helps direct his moral life. The natural law "hinges upon the desire for God and submission to him, who is the source and judge of all that is good, as well as upon the sense that the other is one's equal. Its principal precepts are expressed in the Decalogue"[54] or Ten Commandments, which are summarized by Jesus in the greatest commandments: love God and your neighbor as yourself.[55] Natural law, then, consists in first principles of morality

---

[52] Rom 1:19–20.

[53] Rom 2:14–16.

[54] CCC 1955.

[55] "Teacher, which is the great commandment in the law?" And he said to him, "You shall love the Lord your God with all your heart, and with all your soul, and with all your mind. This is the great and first commandment. And a second is like it, You shall love your neighbor as yourself. On these two commandments depend all the law and the prophets" (Mt 22:36–40).

that can be known intuitively by practical reason. These core principles (known as synderesis) form the heart of the natural law, that is, to do good and avoid evil. "This law is called 'natural' ... because reason, which decrees it, properly belongs to human nature.... The natural law is nothing other than the light of understanding placed in us by God; through it we know what we must do and what we must avoid."[56]

Conscience, then, is taking synderesis and applying it to the particular case; it is the specific application of the general principles of natural law. The natural law is intrinsically designed to make us free since "human freedom finds its authentic and complete fulfillment precisely in the acceptance of the moral law given by God".[57] Man, then, is truly free and genuinely happy when he uses his free will to align his conscience with the transcendent truths of the moral life "as the response due to the many gratuitous initiatives taken by God out of love for man".[58] The formation of conscience in accord with the natural law and, additionally, with the teachings of the Catholic Church is not "brainwashing" but authentic freedom, because it is the Person and truth of Jesus Christ that sets us free.[59] "The natural law, present in the heart of each man and established by reason, is *universal* in its precepts and its *authority extends to all men*. It expresses the dignity of the person and determines the basis for his fundamental rights and duties; for there is a true law: right reason. It is in

[56] CCC 1955.
[57] VS 35.
[58] VS 10.
[59] See Jn 8:31–32. "Further light is shed on the subject if one considers that the highest norm of human life is the divine law—eternal, objective and universal—whereby God orders, directs and governs the entire universe and all the ways of the human community by a plan conceived in wisdom and love. Man has been made by God to participate in this law, with the result that, under the gentle disposition of divine Providence, he can come to perceive ever increasingly the unchanging truth. Hence every man has the duty, and therefore the right, to seek the truth in matters religious in order that he may with prudence form for himself right and true judgments of conscience.... Moreover, as the truth is discovered, it is by a personal assent that men are to adhere to it. On his part, man perceives and acknowledges the imperatives of the divine law through the mediation of conscience. In all his activity a man is bound to follow his conscience faithfully in order that he may come to God, for whom he was created. It follows that he is not to be forced to act in a manner contrary to his conscience. Nor, on the other hand, is he to be restrained from acting in accordance with his conscience, especially in matters religious" (Vatican Council II, Declaration on Religious Freedom, *Dignitatis Humanae*, December 7, 1965, no. 3).

conformity with nature, is diffused among all men, and is immutable and eternal; ... no one can abrogate it entirely."[60]

This abrogation of the natural law has become ubiquitous in our society, particularly in the judicial system that routinely dismisses natural law and the common good, replacing them with subjective human laws that favor individual lifestyle choices. The redefinition of marriage is a good example of this. The Catholic Church is often accused of attempting to legislate morality by "imposing" her teaching on others. The fact is that every human law legislates someone's morality. There is no such thing as a law that does not have some kind of moral code behind it. The laws allowing abortion and physician-assisted suicide support someone's particular moral stance, as distorted as it may be.[61] Although the natural law cannot be removed from man's heart, its practical application in specific circumstances (the

---

[60] *CCC* 1956 (emphasis added). "In the depths of his conscience, man detects a law which he does not impose upon himself, but which holds him to obedience. Always summoning him to love good and avoid evil, the voice of conscience can when necessary speak to his heart more specifically: do this, shun that. For man has in his heart a law written by God; to obey it is the very dignity of man; according to it he will be judged. Conscience is the most secret core and sanctuary of man. There he is alone with God, whose voice echoes in his depths. In a wonderful manner conscience reveals that law which is fulfilled by love of God and neighbor. In fidelity to conscience, Christians are joined with the rest of men in the search for truth, and for the genuine solution to the numerous problems which arise in the life of individuals from social relationships. Hence the more right conscience holds sway, the more persons and groups turn aside from blind choice and strive to be guided by the objective norms of morality. Conscience frequently errs from invincible ignorance without losing its dignity. The same cannot be said for a man who cares but little for truth and goodness, or for a conscience which by degrees grows practically sightless as a result of habitual sin" (*GS* 16).

[61] "The natural law, in the abstract, can nowise be blotted out from men's hearts. But it is blotted out in the case of a particular action, in so far as reason is hindered from applying the general principle to a particular point of practice, on account of concupiscence or some other passion" (Thomas Aquinas, *Summa Theologica*, I-II, 94, VI). "Some people, however, disregarding the dependence of human reason on Divine Wisdom and the need, given the present state of fallen nature, for Divine Revelation as an effective means for knowing moral truths, even those of the natural order, have actually posited a *complete sovereignty of reason* in the domain of moral norms regarding the right ordering of life in this world. Such norms would constitute the boundaries for a merely 'human' morality; they would be the expression of a law which man in an autonomous manner lays down for himself and which has its source exclusively in human reason. In no way could God be considered the Author of this law, except in the sense that human reason exercises its autonomy in setting down laws by virtue of a primordial and total mandate given to man by God. These trends of thought have led to a denial, in opposition to Sacred Scripture (cf. Matthew 15:3–6) and the Church's constant teaching, of the fact that the natural moral law has God as its author, and that man, by the use of reason, participates in the eternal law, which it is not for him to establish" (*VS* 36).

conscience) can be affected by moral relativism, immoral habits, and unnatural vices such as pornography, contraception, and masturbation.[62] The further a man moves away from exemplifying the natural law by the way he lives, the more he severs the connection between the natural law and the virtues that build character, deepen our love for the faith, and engender heroic courage.

Saint Paul boldly wears the helmet of salvation when he says to the Romans, "I appeal to you therefore, brethren, by the mercies of God, to present your bodies as a living sacrifice, holy and acceptable to God, which is your spiritual worship. Do not be conformed to this world but be transformed by the renewal of your mind, that you may prove what is the will of God, what is good and acceptable and perfect"[63]. The Church teaches that the "conscience must be informed and moral judgment enlightened. A well-formed conscience is upright and truthful. It formulates its judgments according to reason, in conformity with the true good willed by the wisdom of the Creator. The education of conscience is indispensable for human beings who are subjected to negative influences and tempted by sin to prefer their own judgment and to reject authoritative teachings".[64]

---

[62] "The judgment of conscience is a *practical judgment*, a judgment which makes known what man must do or not do, or which assesses an act already performed by him. It is a judgment which applies to a concrete situation the rational conviction that one must love and do good and avoid evil. This first principle of practical reason is part of the natural law; indeed it constitutes the very foundation of the natural law, inasmuch as it expresses that primordial insight about good and evil, that reflection of God's creative wisdom which, like an imperishable spark (*scintilla animae*), shines in the heart of every man. But whereas the natural law discloses the objective and universal demands of the moral good, conscience is the application of the law to a particular case; this application of the law thus becomes an inner dictate for the individual, a summons to do what is good in this particular situation. Conscience thus formulates *moral obligation* in the light of the natural law: it is the obligation to do what the individual, through the workings of his conscience, *knows* to be a good he is called to do *here and now*. The universality of the law and its obligation are acknowledged, not suppressed, once reason has established the law's application in concrete present circumstances. The judgment of conscience states 'in an ultimate way' whether a certain particular kind of behaviour is in conformity with the law; it formulates the proximate norm of the morality of a voluntary act, 'applying the objective law to a particular case'" (*VS* 59; emphasis in original).

[63] Rom 12:1–2.

[64] CCC 1783. "The Church thus appears before us as the social subject of responsibility for divine truth.... Therefore it is required, when the Church professes and teaches the faith, that she should adhere strictly to divine truth and should translate it into living attitudes of 'obedience

We cannot continue to allow secular culture and ideology—
with its promulgation of subjective, relativistic truth—to displace
the objective, absolute truth of Catholic doctrine and principles.
"We must ... examine our conscience before the Lord's Cross."[65]
The process of conscience formation takes a lifetime, which is why
it is imperative that men come together as a band of brothers in
groups—whether it be in a parish setting or within a fraternal organization like Men of Christ or the Knights of Columbus—to work
together to defeat the enemy, "take the hill" of our culture, and
replace the flag of moral debauchery with the stanchion of the Cross.

> His death on the Cross speaks—that is to say the inscrutable depth of
> his suffering and abandonment. The Church never ceases to relive his
> death on the Cross and his Resurrection, which constitute the content
> of the Church's daily life. Indeed, it is by the command of Christ him-
> self, her Master, that the Church unceasingly celebrates the Eucharist,
> finding in it the "fountain of life and holiness", the efficacious sign of
> grace and reconciliation with God, and the pledge of eternal life. The
> Church lives his mystery, draws unwearyingly from it and continually
> seeks ways of bringing this mystery of her Master and Lord to human-
> ity ... as the Apostle did: "For I decided to know nothing among
> you except Jesus Christ and him crucified." The Church stays within
> the sphere of the mystery of the Redemption, which has become the
> fundamental principle of her life and mission.[66]

"*The sword of the Spirit, which is the word of God.*" I have personally
spoken to many former Catholics who left the Catholic faith because
they believed they were not nourished spiritually by the Word of

---

in harmony with reason.' Christ himself, concerned for this fidelity to divine truth, promised the
Church the special assistance of the Spirit of truth, gave the gift of infallibility to those whom he
entrusted with the mandate of transmitting and teaching that truth.... Consequently, we have
become sharers in this mission of the prophet Christ, and in virtue of that mission we together
with him are serving divine truth in the Church. Being responsible for that truth also means loving
it and seeking the most exact understanding of it, in order to bring it closer to ourselves and others in all its saving power, its splendour and its profundity joined with simplicity" (John Paul II,
Encyclical Letter *Redemptor Hominis* [The Redeemer of Man], March 4, 1979, no. 19).

[65] *CCC* 1785.
[66] John Paul II, *Redemptor Hominis*, no. 7.

God—that a disconnect existed between Scripture, the sacraments, and their daily life. After hearing their stories, I still cannot understand why they left the Church. After all, the Second Vatican Council teaches that Sacred Scripture provides spiritual nourishment to the People of God in order to enlighten our minds, strengthen our wills, and set our hearts on fire with the love of God.[67] But why isn't this the experience of many Catholics, especially those who are leaving the Church or who come to church for the sacraments but watch the Trinity Broadcast Network to hear the Word of God?

When we come together at the Holy Sacrifice of the Mass, we should not sit back like mere spectators while the readings pass us by and our minds wander off to the nether region of our imaginations. We need to walk more closely with Jesus on the road to Emmaus. When the Word of God is proclaimed, we should praise the Lord and exclaim with joy, "Did not our hearts burn within us while he talked to us on the road, while he opened to us the Scriptures?"[68] We need to recapture a sense of awe and wonder in listening to and appreciating the depth of Sacred Scripture.[69]

Saint John in his Gospel says that "[i]n the beginning was the Word, and the Word was with God, and the Word was God.... And the Word became flesh and dwelt among us, full of grace and truth."[70] Truly immersing ourselves in God's Word is much more than reading pages in a holy book; it is a personal, life-changing, Spirit-filled encounter with the Lord Jesus Christ. In the Word, we don't just hear about Jesus; we listen to Him. In the Word, we don't just become friends with Jesus; we fall in love with Him. In the Word, we don't simply say we are good people; we give our lives to Him. In His goodness and wisdom, God chose to reveal Himself and to make known to us the purpose of His will through Christ, through whom we have access to the Father in the Holy Spirit, and in whom we come to share in the love and life of God.[71]

---

[67] See *DV* 23.
[68] Lk 24:32.
[69] Cf. Neh 8:8–10.
[70] Jn 1:1, 14.
[71] Cf. *DV* 2.

I sincerely admire and respect the Protestant's deep love and passion for the Bible. However, some Protestants contend that Catholics do not share a similar hunger and thirst for God's Word in Sacred Scripture, or place far too much emphasis on teachings not rooted in or based upon biblical principles. A God-fearing Protestant minister once challenged me on this very point saying, "You can't show me from the Word of God where your Mass comes from!" I then said I will use his Bible to show from Scripture alone, verse by verse, exactly where every line of the Mass and the language we use at Mass could be found. Our process was simple: using a missal, I would show him what we say at Mass and tell him the passage of Scripture where the line could be found, which he would confirm by checking the verse in his Bible. I asked him to stop me if he found a line of the Mass that was not biblically based.

What follows is a replication of our encounter.[72]

**Priest**: In the name of the Father, + and of the Son, and of the Holy Spirit [*Go therefore and make disciples of all nations, baptizing them in the name of the Father and of the Son and of the Holy Spirit ... (Matthew 28:19)*]

**People**: Amen. [*Blessed be the* LORD, *the God of Israel, from everlasting to everlasting!" Then all the people said "Amen!" and praised the* LORD. *(1 Chronicles 16:36)*]

**A Priest**: The grace of our Lord Jesus Christ and the love of God, and the communion of the Holy Spirit be with you all. [*The grace of the Lord Jesus Christ and the love of God and the fellowship of the Holy Spirit be with you all. (2 Corinthians 13:13)*]

–OR–

**B Priest**: Grace to you and peace from God Our Father and the Lord Jesus Christ. [*Grace and peace to you from God our Father and the Lord Jesus Christ. (2 Corinthians 1:2)*]

–OR–

**C Priest**: The Lord be with you. [*The* LORD *be with you! (Ruth 2:4)*]

---

[72] The following is an excerpt from my book *The Mass in Sacred Scripture* (Portland, Ore.: Aurem Cordis Publications, 2012), 23–34.

People: And with your spirit. [*The Lord be with your spirit (2 Timothy 4:22)*] and [*The grace of our Lord Jesus Christ be with your spirit (Galatians 6:18)*]

Priest and People:

I confess to almighty God and to you, my brothers and sisters, that I have greatly sinned [*Therefore, confess your sins to one another and pray for one another, that you may be healed. (James 5:16)*] and [*My offenses truly I know them; my sin is always before me. Against you, you alone, have I sinned; what is evil in your sight I have done. (Psalm 51:5–6)*] and [*If we confess our sins, he is faithful and just, and will forgive our sins and cleanse us from all unrighteousness (1 John 1:9)*] and [*But David's heart smote him after he had numbered the people. And David said to the LORD, "I have sinned greatly in what I have done" (2 Samuel 24:10)*]

in my thoughts and in my words, [. . . *do not be haughty . . . wise in your own estimation. (Romans 12:16)*] and [*The tongue . . . exists among our members as a world of malice, defiling the whole body . . . (James 3:6)*]

in what I have done and in what I have failed to do; [*So for one who knows the right thing to do and does not do it, it is a sin. (James 4:17)*]

through my fault, through my fault, through my most grievous fault; [*But the tax collector, standing far off, would not even lift up his eyes to heaven, but beat his breast, saying, "God, be merciful to me a sinner!" (Luke 18:13)*]

therefore I ask Blessed Mary [*Yes, from this day forward all generations shall call me blessed. (Luke 1:48)*]

ever-Virgin, [*Therefore the Lord himself will give you this sign: the virgin shall be with child, and bear a son, and shall name him Immanuel. (Isaiah 7:14)*]

all the Angels and Saints, [*And another angel came and stood at the altar with a golden censer; and he was given much incense to mingle with the prayers of all the saints upon the golden altar before the throne; and the smoke of the incense rose with the prayers of the saints from the hand of the angel before God. (Revelation 8:3–4)*]

and you, my brothers and sisters, to pray for me to the Lord our God. [*If any one sees his brother committing what is not a mortal sin, he will ask, and God will give him life for those whose sin is not mortal (Baruch 1:13)*] and [*Brothers, pray for us (1 Thessalonians 5:25)*] and [*If any one sees his brother committing what is not a mortal sin, he will ask, and God will give him life for those whose sin is not mortal. (1 John 5:16)]*

**Priest**: May almighty God have mercy on us, forgive us our sins, and bring us to everlasting life. [*If we confess our sins, he is faithful and just, and will forgive our sins and cleanse us from all unrighteousness. (1 John 1:9)]*

**People**: Amen. [*Let all the people say, Amen! (1 Chronicles 16:36)]*

## Kyrie

Lord, have mercy. [*Let us pray and beg our LORD to have mercy on us and to grant us deliverance. (Tobit 8:4)]*

Christ, have mercy. [*Grace, mercy, and peace from God the Father and Christ Jesus our Lord. (1 Timothy 1:2)]* and [*wait for the mercy of our Lord Jesus Christ. (Jude 1:21)]*

Lord, have mercy. [*The crowd rebuked them, telling them to be silent; but they cried out the more, "Lord, have mercy on us, Son of David!" (Matthew 20:31)]*

### -OR-

Have mercy on us, Lord, for we have sinned against you. [*My sin is always before me. Against you only have I sinned, and done what is evil in your sight . . . (Psalm 51:6)]* and [*Hear, O Lord, and have mercy, for we have sinned before thee. (Baruch 3:2)]*

### -OR-

Show us, O Lord, your mercy. [*Do not let us be put to shame, but deal with us in your kindness and great mercy. (Daniel 3:42)]*

And grant us your salvation. [*Show us, O LORD, your kindness, and grant us your salvation. (Psalm 85:8)]*

## Gloria

**Glory to God in the highest, and on earth peace to people of good will** [*Glory to God in the highest, and on earth peace among men of goodwill. (Luke 2:14)]*

**We praise you,** [*Praise the LORD! Praise the LORD from the heavens, praise him in the heights! Praise him, all his angels, praise him, all his host! Praise him, sun and moon, praise him, all you shining stars! Praise him, you highest heavens, and you waters above the heavens! Let them praise the name of the LORD! (Psalm 105:1–5)]*

we bless you, [*We bless you from the house of the LORD. (Psalm 118:26)*]

we adore you, [*Adore the LORD in his holy court. (Psalm 29:2)*]

we glorify you, [*Glorify the LORD with me. (Psalm 34:4)*] and [*To him be glory forever. Amen. (Romans 11:36)*]

we give you thanks for your great glory. [*Amen. Blessing and glory, wisdom and thanksgiving, honor, power and might be to our God forever and ever. Amen. (Revelation 7:12)*]

Lord God, heavenly King, O God, almighty Father [*The Lord has established his reign, [our] God, the almighty. (Revelation 19:6)*]

Lord Jesus Christ, Only Begotten Son, [*Grace, mercy, and peace will be with us from God the Father and from Jesus Christ, the Father's Son in truth and love. (2 John 3)*]

Lord God, Lamb of God, Son of the Father, you take away the sins of the world, have mercy on us; [*Behold, the Lamb of God, who takes away the sin of the world. (John 1:29)*]

you take away the sins of the world, receive our prayer; [*The LORD has heard my plea; the LORD will accept my prayer. (Psalm 6:10)*]

you are seated at the right hand of the Father, have mercy on us. [*It is Christ (Jesus) who died, rather, was raised, who also is at the right hand of God, who indeed intercedes for us. (Romans 8:34)*] and [*we have such a high priest, one who is seated at the right hand of the throne of the Majesty in heaven (Hebrews 8:1)*]

For you alone are the Holy One, [*I know who you are—the Holy One of God! (Luke 4:34)*]

you alone are the Lord, [*Who will not fear you, Lord, or glorify your name? For you alone are holy. All the nations will come and worship before you, ... (Revelation 15:4)*] and [*O LORD our God, save us from his hand, that all the kingdoms of the earth may know that thou alone art the LORD. (Isaiah 37:20)*]

you are the Most High, Jesus Christ, [*He will be great and will be called Son of the Most High, ... (Luke 1:32)*]

with the Holy Spirit, in the glory of God the Father. Amen. [*The Advocate, the Holy Spirit that the Father will send in my name ... (John 14:26)*] and [*... and every tongue confess that Jesus Christ is Lord, to the glory of God the Father. (Philippians 2:11)*]

[The Liturgy of the Word consists of four readings from Scripture: the first is typically from the Old Testament, the second a
psalm, followed by a reading from one of the epistles. Finally,
the Gospel is proclaimed during which the people stand out of
respect for the Word of God.]

A homily on the readings follows. [*I charge you in the presence of
God and of Christ Jesus ... preach the word, be urgent in season and out
of season, convince, rebuke, and exhort, be unfailing in patience and in teaching. (2 Timothy 4:1–2)*]

## Profession of Faith

**Priest and People:** I believe in one God, the Father almighty, maker
of heaven and earth, [*... God most High, maker of heaven and earth.
(Genesis 14:19)*] and [*The* LORD *appeared to Abram, and said to him, "I
am God Almighty" (Genesis 17:1)*] and [*For he created all things that they
might exist (Wisdom 1:14)*]

of all things visible and invisible. [*For in him all things were created, in
heaven and on earth, visible and invisible ... (Colossians 1:16)*]

I believe in one Lord Jesus Christ, the Only Begotten Son of God,
[*Therefore the child to be born will be called holy, the Son of God. (Luke
1:35)*] and [*He said to me, "You are my son, today I have begotten you."
(Psalm 2:7)*]

born of the Father before all ages. [*Jesus said to them, "Truly, truly, I
say to you, before Abraham was, I am." (John 8:58)*] and [*... all things were
created through him and for him. He is before all things, and in him all things
hold together. (Colossians 1:16–17)*]

God from God, Light from Light, true God from true God, [*He reflects
the glory of God and bears the very stamp of his nature, upholding the universe
by his word of power (Hebrews 1:3)*] and [*And the city has no need of sun or
moon to shine upon it, for the glory of God is its light, and its lamp is the Lamb
(Revelation 21:23)*] and [*Jesus said to them, "The light is with you for a little
longer. Walk while you have the light, lest the darkness overtake you; he who
walks in the darkness does not know where he goes. While you have the light,
believe in the light, that you may become sons of light." (John 12:35–36)*]

begotten, not made, consubstantial with the Father; [*"I and the Father
are one." (John 10:30)*]

through him all things were made. [*In the beginning was the Word, and
the Word was with God, and the Word was God. He was in the beginning*

*with God. All things were made through him, and without him was not any-*
*thing made that was made. In him was life, and the life was the light of men.*
*(John 1:1–4)]*

For us men and for our salvation he came down from heaven, [*No one*
*was ascended into heaven but he who descended from heaven, the Son of man.*
*(John 3:13)]* and [*For I have come down from heaven, not to do my own will,*
*but the will of him who sent me (John 6:38)]* and [*I came from the Father and*
*have come into the world (John 16:28)]*

and by the Holy Spirit was incarnate of the Virgin Mary, and became
man. [*When his mother Mary had been betrothed to Joseph, before they came*
*together she was found to be with child of the Holy Spirit. (Matthew 1:18)]*

For our sake he was crucified under Pontius Pilate, [*Then he handed*
*him over to them to be crucified. (John 19:16)]* and [*Let all the house of Israel*
*therefore know assuredly that God has made him both Lord and Christ, this*
*Jesus whom you crucified (Acts 2:36)]*

he suffered death and was buried, and rose again on the third day in
accordance with the Scriptures. [*For I delivered to you as of first impor-*
*tance what I also received, that Christ died for our sins in accordance with the*
*scriptures, that he was buried, that he was raised on the third day in accordance*
*with the scriptures. [1 Corinthians 15:3–4)]*

He ascended into heaven [*While he blessed them, he parted from them, and*
*was carried up to heaven. (Luke 24:51)]*

and is seated at the right hand of the Father. [*. . . seek the things that are*
*above, where Christ is, seated at the right hand of God. (Colossians 3:1)]* and
[*Is it Christ Jesus, who died, yes, who was raised from the dead, who is at the*
*right hand of God, who indeed intercedes for us? (Romans 8:34)]*

He will come again in glory to judge the living and the dead [*I charge*
*you in the presence of God and of Christ Jesus who is to judge the living and*
*the dead (2 Timothy 4:1)]*

and his kingdom will have no end. [*. . . and of his kingdom there will be*
*no end. (Luke 1:33)]*

I believe in the Holy Spirit, the Lord, the giver of life, [*"And in the last*
*days it shall be, God declares, that I will pour out my Spirit upon all flesh."*
*(Acts 2:17)]* and [*Then the* LORD *God formed man of dust from the ground,*
*and breathed into his nostrils the breath of life; and man became a living being.*
*(Genesis 2:7)]* and [*And when he had said this, he breathed on them, and*
*said to them, "Receive the Holy Spirit." (John 20:22)]*

who proceeds from the Father and the Son, [... *for if I do not go away,
the Counselor will not come to you; but if I go, I will send him to you ...
(John 16:7)*] and [*And I will pray the Father, and he will give you another
Counselor, to be with you forever. (John 14:16)*]

who with the Father and the Son is adored and glorified, [*Then God
said, "Let us make man in our image, after our likeness." (Genesis 1:26)*]
and [*God has sent the Spirit of his Son into our hearts (Galatians 4:6)*]

who has spoken through the prophets. [*The prophets who prophesied of
the grace that was to be yours searched and inquired about this salvation, they
inquired what person or time was indicated by the Spirit of Christ within them
when predicting the sufferings of Christ and the subsequent glory. (1 Peter
1:10–11)*] and [*"The Spirit of the LORD speaks by me, his word is upon my
tongue." (2 Samuel 23:2)*]

I believe in the one, holy, catholic and apostolic Church. [... *so we,
though many, are one body in Christ, and individually members one of
another. (Romans 12:5)*] and [*There is one body and one Spirit, just as you
were called to the one hope that belongs to your call, one Lord, one faith, one
baptism, one God and Father of us all, who is above all and through all and
in all. (Ephesians 4:4–6)*]

I confess one Baptism for the forgiveness of sins [... *Repent and be
baptized every one of you in the name of Jesus Christ for the forgiveness of
your sins; ... (Acts 2:38)*] and [*There is one body and one Spirit, just as you
were called to the one hope that belongs to your call, one Lord, one faith, one
baptism, one God and Father of us all, who is above all and through all and
in all. (Ephesians 4:4–6)*]

and I look forward to the resurrection of the dead and the life of the
world to come. Amen. [*For if we have been united with him in a death like
his, we shall certainly be united with him in the resurrection like his (Romans
6:5)*] and [*He also took up a collection, man by man, to the amount of two
thousand drachmas of silver, and sent it to Jerusalem to provide for a sin
offering. In doing this he acted very well and honorably, taking account of the
resurrection. (2 Maccabees 12:43)*]

Intercessions. [*I thank God in all my remembrance of you, always in every
prayer of mine for you all making my prayer with joy. (Philippians 1:3–4)*]

Gifts brought to the altar [*So if you are offering your gift at the altar,
and there remember that your brother has something against you, leave your
gift there before the altar and go; first be reconciled to your brother, and then
come and offer your gift (Matthew 5:23–24)*] and [*Bring the full tithes into

*the storehouse, that there may be food in my house; and thereby put me to the test, says the LORD of hosts, if I will not open the windows of heaven for you and pour down for you an overflowing blessing. (Malachi 3:10)]*

Priest: Blessed are you, Lord God of all creation, for through your goodness we have received the bread we offer you: fruit of the earth and work of human hands, [*For everyman, moreover, to eat and drink and enjoy the fruit of all his labor is a gift of God. (Ecclesiastes 3:13)]* and [*"Blessed art thou, O LORD, the God of Israel our father, forever and ever. Thine, O LORD, is the greatness, and the power, and the glory, and the victory, and the majesty; for all that is in the heavens and in the earth is thine; thine is the kingdom, O LORD, and thou art exalted as head above all ..."* (1 Chronicles 29:10–11)]

it will become for us the bread of life. [*I am the bread of life ... (John 6:35)]*

People: Blessed be God for ever. [*Blessed be God! (Psalm 68:36)]*

At this point, the holy and faith-filled minister stopped me and said, "Okay." I explained that I was not finished and that we were only halfway through the Mass. He was satisfied and did not wish to continue.

The Holy Sacrifice of the Mass is deeply rooted in Scripture, and Catholic men, in opening the ears of our hearts to Christ who is feeding us with the gift of His life in word and sacrament, should strive to embrace this relationship with minds and hearts open to God's grace at every Sunday liturgy, just as Jesus embraced His Cross on the way to Calvary. Memorizing the responses at Mass is a good thing, but, ultimately, God does not care how many verses of Scripture we memorize; what matters is how we live out and put into practice in our everyday lives what is in God's Word.

Let us be on fire for the Lord! Let the fire of His love burn away everything that turns our hearts away from Him. When we encounter the Living God in this way, the paralyzing grip of sin will give way to the peace of blessed assurance: "Did our hearts not burn within us when we heard the Word proclaimed and when we received our Lord in the Eucharist?" When we have the courage to live the truth and beauty of our Catholic faith, the fire of the Spirit will consume us. As Catholics, we know that there is no Resurrection without Crucifixion; and knowing that for the sake of the joy that lay before Him

Christ endured His Cross, let us not grow weary and lose heart.[73] Let us always choose to follow Jesus, who through the fire of His love will lead us from sorrow to joy, from despair to hope, from death to everlasting life.

"*Pray at all times in the Spirit, with all prayer and supplication.*" During my monthly visit to my spiritual director, as we talked about how things were going, I excitedly told him about the new direction I was taking with my apostolate, the people I was working with, and my plans for the future. As I was speaking, I noticed that my spiritual director was not smiling; he did not even seem the least bit happy for me. When I finished, he said, "God will never allow any of that to happen unless He is confident that you are ready to carry out His work and honor Him with your whole being. You are ready spiritually and mentally, but not physically. Lose weight."

I was shocked and—quite honestly—hurt and disappointed by his comment. It was only later that I realized he was neither being malicious nor was he trying to motivate me. He gave me a rebuke for a purpose. He realized that in order for God's will to be done, I must be completely open and vulnerable before Him. This is the lesson for us as Catholic men: we must humble ourselves so that God can work in and through us.

The key lies in developing a daily, active prayer life. Prayer is both a gift of grace initiated by God and a response that takes effort on our part. In order for Catholic men to walk humbly before our God in the obedience of faith, we must appreciate the fact that we cannot do this all on our own—that we need God's help every step of the way, especially during those times in our lives when we all feel that God is not hearing or answering our prayers.

It is precisely during those periods when we feel that the Lord is chastising us or allowing us to experience a Cross in our lives— whether it be the loss of a job, caring for an elderly parent, depression, addiction, suffering from a chronic illness—that we are led into the very heart of Christ's own suffering and death. *The real Cross is to believe that Jesus is Lord of every single situation in our lives.* Life is not about avoiding suffering—none of us can do that. Life is about finding meaning in the suffering that is unavoidable. We must remember

---

[73] Cf. Heb 12:3.

that nothing can separate us from the love of God, and if we want His will to become a part of who we are, we must wait on God and have complete confidence in His mercy and love.

One of the toughest challenges in life is to have faith in very difficult moments. My best friend whom I had known since we were nine years old—who stood next to me when I married my wife—died of cancer at age thirty-eight. He left behind a wife and two small children. The same five of us who were groomsmen at his wedding—including me as the best man—were now pallbearers at his funeral.

There was so much sadness that weekend. I will never forget the stoic image of his mother, and the look of utter anguish and despair on his wife's face when the casket was closed for the last time. It was one of the most difficult and painful experiences of my life. I kept thinking, "How are they going to get past this? How is his wife going to manage a full-time career while raising her sons alone? How do you give praise and thanks to God—how do you even trust God—at a time like this?"

There are many times since then when I feel that God is not listening, when He feels very distant from me and my prayers, when I think He is not paying attention. Our Lord Himself experienced this on Calvary when, in His human nature, He was allowed to endure the emptiness and darkness that we have all felt: "My God, my God, why have you forsaken me?".[74] But His cry from the Cross is not an act of desolation but one of hope and redemption. The fact is that no matter who we are, all of us experience the darkness of struggle, and it is from that darkness that we grow in our faith. Those of us who walk in the darkness of divine abandonment have a childlike sense of trust that God will act in His time, which in turn cultivates an intense closeness to the Holy Spirit, who leads us to the light of truth.

How do we respond when God tells us it is not time for Him to act? Should we be angry? Should we turn away from Him with hatred and disgust in our hearts? Should our faith be shaken? In the moment of divine abandonment, we must put all our cards on the table (go all in) and with humble, trusting faith conquer God's heart. Jesus, completely won over by our faith, perseverance, and complete trust and confidence in Him, will acknowledge our faith before the

[74] Mt 27:46.

Father and grant our request.[75] God will alter His plan in salvation history because of our faith in Him.

We all need to be persistent in our life of prayer, realizing that God will not always give us what we *want*, but He will always give us what we *need*, in His time and in accord with His will. God is a Loving Father who wants what is best for us and is willing to open His heart wide to bring us closer to Him. What we need most is the peace and security that can only come from living in total harmony with God's will. The house of the Lord shall be called a house of prayer for all peoples to experience the healing power of God's mercy.[76]

The Holy Spirit allows the seed of faith to take root and grow in us, and if we freely and lovingly cooperate with what God wants to do in us, our lives will bear much fruit. We must make a connection between the faith that we learn and the lived experience of that faith. Sometimes this means picking up our Crosses and following Christ with the understanding that living the truth means being countercultural.

We must stop making excuses for not making prayer the center of our daily lives and make a serious effort to attend weekly Eucharistic Adoration. God speaks to us in the ear of our hearts, and it is within the context of silent contemplation before the Lord that we discern how our lives can be a blessing to Christ and the Church. By spending personal, one-on-one time with Jesus in Adoration, a man can get to know Christ more intimately, come to understand the teachings of the Lord and His Church more deeply, and, along with frequent use of the Sacrament of Reconciliation, overcome the power of sin in his life.

The fruits of Adoration will overflow into his daily life and create an atmosphere of "praying always", that is, of being continually aware that he is in the presence of God. The Catholic man will now spend time every day reading his Bible instead of playing video games. He will use the travel time in his car and on the plane or train listening to podcasts of Catholic programming that will feed his faith instead of talk radio. He will lead his domestic and parish family in praying the Rosary instead of watching prime-time television. He will employ the weapons of fasting and abstinence to overcome sin instead of indulging in fast food.

[75] Cf. Mt 15:21–28.
[76] Cf. Mt 21:13.

He will promote and foster vocations, encouraging his children to consider vocations to the priesthood and religious life. The most important question we can ask as fathers (both at home and in the parish) is not, "What do you want to be when you grow up?" By creating a prayerful atmosphere where we display holy objects and pictures, and pray with our youth and young adults, Catholic men actively draw from the grace of the Holy Spirit we received in Baptism, Confirmation, and the Eucharist, which impels us be the men God created us to be and compels us to discern with our children the truly significant question of life: "How is God speaking to you and using you for His glory?"

The Virgin Mary serves as the quintessential example of obedience to God's will, allowing herself to be used as an instrument for God's glory. The Blessed Mother is

> the woman through whom was born the Son who acquired divine sonship for us by His suffering. But because we are God's sons, "God sent the Spirit of His Son into our hearts, the Spirit who calls Abba! (Father!)". If we did not have the Spirit and the attitude of the Son, we would not be children of the Father. It is this Spirit who permits us to shout to the Father gratefully [and] enthusiastically: "Yes, you really are our Father." But let us not forget that this Spirit was first sent to the Mother as the Spirit that brought her the Son, and thus as "Spirit of the Son" he is also the Spirit of the Father.[77]

*"To that end keep alert with all perseverance, making supplication for all the saints."* Looking at a Roman soldier in full armor, notice that there is one part of the body that is not protected: the back. It was expected that his fellow soldiers—his brothers in the battle—would guard his back, hence the origin of the expression, "I have your back!" Just as we ask the Blessed Virgin Mary and the saints for their prayers to assist us, Catholic men must rely on and support each other in the battle for our souls.

This is a battle we cannot fight alone. We need the fellowship and affirmation of other godly Catholic men to strengthen, encourage, and hold each other accountable. Many opportunities exist today

---

[77] Von Balthasar, *Light of the Word*, 32.

to attend a men's conference, retreat, Bible study, or prayer group, and there is absolutely no excuse why a man—whether he is single, married, or ordained—cannot commit to becoming a vibrant, active member of a men's group at or near his parish. We make time for those things in life that are important to us, and doing everything possible to cultivate and enrich our relationship with God should be first above all else.

*Ready for Battle: The Story of David.* "The LORD said to Samuel ... 'Fill your horn with oil, and go; I will send you to Jesse the Bethlehemite, for I have provided for myself a king among his sons.' "[78] Samuel does as the Lord commands, and when Jesse's sons Eliab, Abinadab, Shammah, and four others come before him, the prophet assumes that the one to be anointed is among them. Samuel attempts to know and understand God's will by judging the outward appearance of Jesse's sons, but the Lord is quick to point out, "Do not look on his appearance or on the height of his stature, because I have rejected him; for the LORD sees not as man sees; man looks on the outward appearance, but the LORD looks on the heart."[79] David is a man after God's own heart (see Acts 13:22) precisely because he is "a man of valor, a man of war, prudent in speech, and a man of good presence".[80] Catholic men must learn to see as God sees and to love as God loves—to see with His eyes, listen with His ears, love with His heart, understand with His mind, and serve with His will. God does not care about the color of our skin, how tall we are, or how much money we have in the bank. God looks beyond what could be observed with the senses and looks to the place where His will resides in us. What does God see when He looks into our hearts? Can God see His reflection, His image, in us?[81]

Sometime later, David hears that the Philistine warrior Goliath the Goth has issued a challenge to the soldiers of Israel. Goliath has mocked

---

[78] 1 Sam 16:1.
[79] 1 Sam 16:7.
[80] 1 Sam 16:18.
[81] See Gen 1:26–27. The word for "image" in Hebrew is the masculine noun *tselem*, which means a shadow that is the outline or representation of the original. Our physical bodies cast a shadow that, although not us, outlines our body and moves as we move. God the Father has no physical nature, so He casts His shadow on our souls. Our interior life as men is the outline of God's Spirit and life in us and represents the depth of our relationship with God: when we speak, God speaks; when we think, God thinks; when we act, God acts.

and defied the Israelite army for forty consecutive days, but Saul's men are too afraid to confront such a formidable opponent.[82] It is easy to see why. Goliath was truly an intimidating figure standing approximately nine feet, nine inches in height.[83] "He had a helmet of bronze on his head, and he was armed with a coat of mail, and the weight of the coat was five thousand shekels of bronze."[84] He wore bronze boots and had a spear that weighed just over nine pounds.[85] In the presence of Goliath, the Israelites "were dismayed and greatly afraid".[86]

Goliath represents today's secular culture, a culture that threatens and intimidates us with violations of religious liberty; that calls contraception "health care"; that commits egregious sins against children, the elderly, and a civilization of love and life; that attempts to force people of good conscience to violate the natural law by redefining marriage and penalizing everyone who does not accept this personal lifestyle-choice decision. Many Catholic men are so intimidated by the size, scope, and depth of this onslaught that we choose not to fight. Instead we tremble with fear; we say and do nothing.

Maybe your battle against Goliath is more personal. What is the "Goliath" in your life that is preventing you from being the man that God, the Church, your family, and this society needs you to be? Is it pornography? Alcohol? Drugs? Contraception? Fear and anxiety? Depression? What is it that has you so scared that you are more comfortable living as a slave to sin rather than living free as a son of God?

Goliath makes the following statement in 1 Sam 17:8: "Why have you come out to draw up for battle? Am I not a Philistine, and are you not servants of Saul?" Goliath picks up on the fact that Israel had

---

[82] In the Scriptures, the number "forty" is derived from the number of gestational weeks in a pregnancy, and symbolically represents periods of trial, testing, and waiting. The biblical use of the number forty has one underlying focus: it is a journey that always leads to a spiritual time of growth and change.

[83] "And there came out from the camp of the Philistines a champion named Goliath, of Gath, whose height was six cubits and a span" (1 Sam 17:4). Six cubits was approximately eighteen inches, and a span was about nine inches, making Goliath approximately 2.97 meters, which equates to nine feet, nine inches tall.

[84] 1 Sam 17:5. A "coat of mail" was a type of armor consisting of small metal rings linked together in a pattern to form a mesh, akin to fish scales. The common shekel weighed approximately .25 ounces, so five thousand shekels equals approximately 1,250 ounces or about seventy-eight pounds.

[85] See 1 Sam 17:7. Six hundred shekels equals approximately 150 ounces or nine pounds.

[86] 1 Sam 17:11.

abandoned God as their king and replaced the Lord of Hosts with Saul. Moses' teaching in the Torah was clear: "You shall fear the LORD your God; you shall serve him, and swear by his name",[87] but the men of Israel rejected God for an earthy king in order to be like everyone else around them.[88] Man of God, who is the king of your life? Are you willing to pick up your Cross and follow Jesus, or are you more concerned about what people will say or how they will perceive you if you start truly living your Catholic faith?

If we are to be men after God's own heart, then we must worship the Lord in spirit and truth by giving ourselves as a gift, as a holy offering, back to God. Sacred Scripture is quite clear on this point: "For I am the LORD your God; consecrate yourselves therefore, and be holy, for I am holy."[89] "[D]o not be conformed to the passions of your former ignorance, but as he who called you is holy, be holy yourselves in all your conduct; since it is written, 'You shall be holy, for I am holy.' "[90] "You, therefore, must be perfect, as your heavenly Father is perfect."[91]

The Goliaths in our lives cause us to fear, and empty us of God's love. The flow of grace through daily prayer and the sacraments fills us with love so that we can truly be "perfect" ("whole" and "complete") in the eyes of God. "There is no fear in love, but perfect love casts out fear. For fear has to do with punishment, and he who fears is not perfected in love. We love, because he first loved us."[92] Filled with confidence in God's love, we can now face Goliath with confidence: "The LORD is my light and my help; whom shall I fear? The LORD is the stronghold of my life; before whom shall I shrink? When evildoers draw near to devour my flesh, it is they, my enemies and foes, who stumble and fall. Though an army encamp against me my heart would not fear. Though war break out against me even then would I trust."[93]

---

[87] Deut 6:13. Cf. Deut 10:20.

[88] " '[N]ow appoint for us a king to govern us like all the nations.' But the thing displeased Samuel when they said, 'Give us a king to govern us.' And Samuel prayed to the LORD. And the LORD said to Samuel, 'Listen to the voice of the people in all that they say to you; for they have not rejected you, but they have rejected me from being king over them' " (1 Sam 8:5–7).

[89] Lev 11:44.

[90] 1 Pet 1:14–16.

[91] Mt 5:48. The word "perfect" in Greek is *teleios*, which means "mature; full grown" and in the Hebrew *tamin*, which means "whole, complete".

[92] 1 Jn 4:18–19.

[93] Ps 27:1–3.

David goes to Saul and offers to fight Goliath. Saul initially dis-
courages him, but David reminds Saul that he has been a faithful
and fearless shepherd: "Your servant used to keep sheep for his
father [Jesse]; and when there came a lion, or a bear, and took a
lamb from the flock, I went after him and struck him and delivered
it out of his mouth; and if he arose against me, I caught him by
his beard, and struck him and killed him. Your servant has killed
both lions and bears; and this uncircumcised Philistine shall be like
one of them, seeing he has defied the armies of the living God."[94]
The Son of David would also be a Good Shepherd who would lay
down His life on the Cross for His sheep.[95] By Baptism, we share in
Christ's death and Resurrection; we are His brothers and, therefore,
are called to be faith-filled, courageous shepherds. Like David the
shepherd, we must run toward danger and stand ready to defend
our families, the Church, and society against any threat in order to
fulfill our mission of sacrifice and service lived in the love that flows
from the wounds of the crucified Christ.

"Then Saul clothed David with his armor; he put a helmet of
bronze on his head, and clothed him with a coat of mail. And David
belted on his sword over his armor, and he tried in vain to go, for
he was not used to them. Then David said to Saul, 'I cannot go with
these; for I am not used to them.' And David put them off."[96] At
first, David tries to put on the armor of man so he could look like
Goliath, but he is unsuccessful. He realizes that, for this battle, he
needs to don the armor of God and fight with the weapons of faith.
Men of God, it is useless for us to fight in this culture war using only
the conventional weapons of logic, reason, sound apologetics, and
impassioned debate. There must also be a profound and overarching
spiritual dimension that we bring into battle. By forming our minds

---

[94] I Sam 17:34–36.

[95] "I am the good shepherd. The good shepherd lays down his life for the sheep. He who is
a hireling and not a shepherd, whose own the sheep are not, sees the wolf coming and leaves
the sheep and flees; and the wolf snatches them and scatters them. He flees because he is a
hireling and cares nothing for the sheep. I am the good shepherd; I know my own and my
own know me, as the Father knows me and I know the Father; and I lay down my life for the
sheep" (Jn 10:11–15). Also, "If a man has a hundred sheep, and one of them has gone astray,
does he not leave the ninety-nine on the hills and go in search of the one that went astray? . . .
So it is not the will of my Father who is in heaven that one of these little ones should perish"
(Mt 18:12, 14).

[96] I Sam 17:38–39.

and hearts in accord with the tenets of the Catholic faith, we become battle ready, putting our faith into action daily by living the Beatitudes, forming our consciences in accord with natural law, and loving God and our neighbor. "You see that a man is justified by works and not by faith alone.... For as the body apart from the spirit is dead, so faith apart from works is dead."[97]

David "took his staff in his hand, and chose five smooth stones from the brook, and put them in his shepherd's bag or wallet; his sling was in his hand, and he drew near to the Philistine."[98] Looking at the literal sense of the passage, David had five stones in the event that Goliath's brothers sought retaliation against him over Goliath's death.[99] In the spiritual sense, the sling and stones are a type of rosary, each stone representing the Our Father bead and reflecting one of the mysteries of our salvation. They also represent the five wounds of Christ, our Lord's battle scars in His victory over sin and death. In our battle against the Goliath of the culture and within ourselves, the rosary is most certainly the weapon of choice. Satan cannot stand to hear the names "Jesus" and "Mary", which are repeated throughout the Rosary. The devil will flee from any man who devoutly prays the Rosary every day.

At this point we must also mention a method which Padre Pio used uninterruptedly and with holy persistence in order to defeat Satan always, everywhere and efficaciously; and it was one which he also placed in the hands of his spiritual children with singular determination: the Rosary. The seraphim of Mary [St. Pio] called the Rosary his "weapon." ... "Always hold Mary's weapon tightly in your hands, and you will always be victorious over the infernal enemies." ... With this weapon the Padre defeated the immense multitude of devils which he had seen raging with anger.... With this "weapon of Mary" he always defeated Satan and all his satellites throughout the entire span

---

[97] Jas 2:24, 26.

[98] 1 Sam 17:40.

[99] "And there was again war with the Philistines at Gob; and Elhanan the son of Jaareoregim, the Bethlehemite, slew Goliath the Gittite, the shaft of whose spear was like a weaver's beam. And there was again war at Gath, where there was a man of great stature, who had six fingers on each hand, and six toes on each foot, twenty-four in number; and he also was descended from the giants. And when he taunted Israel, Jonathan the son of Shime-i, David's brother, slew him. These four were descended from the giants in Gath; and they fell by the hand of David and by the hand of his servants" (2 Sam 21:19–22). See also 1 Chronicles 20:5–8.

of his life.... Fully understanding the power of Mary and the most potent efficacy of her "weapon" against Lucifer, padre Pio gave his last wishes to his spiritual children before he died, as follows: "Love Our Lady and make her loved! Always recite the holy rosary!"[100]

David now confronts Goliath. Unwavering in his faith and armed with a simple weapon, David embarks on what his kinsmen would surely have considered a "suicide mission". They believed that David had no chance of defeating such a colossal enemy. After Goliath mocks David and threatens his life, David says,

> You come to me with a sword and with a spear and with a javelin; but I come to you in the name of the LORD of hosts, the God of the armies of Israel, whom you have defied. This day the LORD will deliver you into my hand, and I will strike you down, and cut off your head; and I will give the dead bodies of the host of the Philistines this day to the birds of the air and to the wild beasts of the earth; that all the earth may know that there is a God in Israel, and that all this assembly may know that the LORD saves not with sword and spear; for the battle is the LORD's and he will give you into our hand.[101]

Men of God, there will be people in your life, possibly members of your own family, who will try to discourage and deter you from taking your faith to the next level. You may have even convinced yourself that the vices and addictions that control and enslave you are too powerful. When we think like that, Satan wins. Pray for a spirit of boldness! "Pray at all times in the Spirit ... that utterance may be given me in opening my mouth boldly to proclaim the mystery of the gospel ... that I may declare it boldly, as I ought to speak."[102] Be prepared to excise from your life anything and anyone that causes, tempts, or leads you to sin, including friends, family, television, alcohol, and the Internet; whatever or whoever it is that is leading you to hell must leave your life—now. Our decisions and actions in this life have eternal consequences.

> And if your hand causes you to sin, cut it off; it is better for you to enter life maimed than with two hands to go to hell, to the unquenchable

---

[100] Fr. Tarcisio of Cervinara, *The Devil in the Life of Padre Pio*, 3rd ed. (2008; repr., San Giovanni Rotondo, Italy: Edizioni Padre Pio da Pietrelcina, 2012), 151, 153–55.

[101] 1 Sam 17:45–47.

[102] Eph 6:18–20.

fire. And if your foot causes you to sin, cut it off; it is better for you
to enter life lame than with two feet to be thrown into hell. And if
your eye causes you to sin, pluck it out; it is better for you to enter the
kingdom of God with one eye than with two eyes to be thrown into
hell, where their worm does not die, and the fire is not quenched.[103]

By the witness of our lives and as images of Christ crucified, we
must send a clear and strong message to this culture that there is a
God who saves and His name is Jesus Christ! "Blessed be the LORD,
my rock, who trains my arms for battle, who prepares my hands for
war. He is my love, my fortress; he is my stronghold, my savior, my
shield, my place of refuge. He brings peoples under my rule."[104] We
must remember that we are not alone in this fight—that the battle
belongs to the Lord, and He has already won the war through His
victory over death on the Cross. To fight and win, we must pick up
our Crosses and lead our families, the Church, and the culture to
deeper union with Christ through uniting ourselves completely to
His holy will. "For it was not in my bow that I trusted nor yet was
I saved by my sword: it was you who saved us from our foes, it was
you who put our foes to shame. All day long our boast was in God
and we praised your name without ceasing."[105]

Men of God, let us gird our loins and be resolved that what happened to Adam will not happen to us. When Satan tries to hand
us the poisoned fruit of sin in the form of sexual temptation, take
the sword of the Spirit and cut off his arm! When Satan tries to
destroy our hearts by making pleasure the god of our life, put on
the breastplate of righteousness, grab your rosary, and head to the
Adoration chapel. When you want to make excuses for not attending Mass on Sunday or a Holy Day, pull the helmet of salvation
tighter around your head, grab you Bible, and read John 6. When
you wake up every morning, start your day by praying in the Spirit
and thanking God for allowing you to see the light of another day.
When you begin to doubt, and your adversary the devil begins to
prowl around like a roaring lion, seeking to devour you,[106] resist

[103] Mk 9:43–48. Cf. Mt 5:29–30 and Mt 18:7–9.
[104] Ps 144:1–2.
[105] Ps 44:7–9.
[106] See 1 Pet 5:8.

and block him with the shield of firm faith, and start praying: "I love you, Lord, my strength, my rock, my fortress, my savior. My God is the rock where I take refuge; my shield, my mighty help, my stronghold. The Lord is worthy of all praise, when I call I am saved from my foes",[107] and head to the nearest Catholic men's group. In short, "Put on the whole armor of God, that you may be able to stand against the wiles of the devil. For we are not contending against flesh and blood, but against the principalities, against the powers, against the world rulers of this present darkness, against the spiritual hosts of wickedness in the heavenly places. Therefore take the whole armor of God, that you may be able to withstand in the evil day, and having done all, to stand."[108]

[107] Ps 18:2–4.
[108] Eph 6:11–13.

# EPILOGUE

[I]f a wicked man turns away from all his sins which he has committed and keeps all my statutes and does what is lawful and right, he
shall surely live; he shall not die. None of the transgressions which
he has committed shall be remembered against him; for the righteousness which he has done he shall live.... Cast away from you
all the transgressions which you have committed against me, and get
yourselves a new heart and a new spirit!... For I have no pleasure in
the death of any one, says the LORD God; so turn, and live.

—Ezekiel 18:21–22; 31–32

Where do we go from here? What changes are you going to make
today, next week, next month? Men of God, the Catholic man is not
an endangered species! Let us clean out the caverns and dark places
of our lives so that Jesus may come and make His home with us. Let
us get past our preoccupation with the materiality of the world and
allow God's power and peace, God's love and life, to draw us into
a place where there is nothing standing between us and Him. Let
us give ourselves over to God's will and have the courage to prefer
absolutely nothing to the love of Christ.

Open your hearts to Jesus! Just as a mother nourishes her child
with her own body and blood, Jesus feeds and gives life to His Bride,
the Church, with His own Body and Blood in the Most Blessed Sacrament. In response to receiving our Precious Lord in the Eucharist,
we are called to lay down our lives in our families, parishes, work-
places, or wherever we find ourselves as men. We must sacrifice our
minds, our hearts, our souls, our bodies—everything we have and
everything we are in total, self-giving love. "I rejoice in my sufferings
for your sake, and in my flesh I complete what is lacking in Christ's
afflictions for the sake of his body, that is, the Church".[1]

[1] Col 1:24.

The Eucharistic Jesus is our true model of holiness, for it is in the crucified Christ that we recognize what it means to be a real man. Being a real man means embracing the Cross we have been given with love, because it is in the Cross that we discover why we exist at all. In the Eucharist, we receive answers to the most difficult questions in our minds, and find true meaning in the deepest longings and desires of our hearts. Through the Eucharist, we can say with confidence and joy, "This is my body, broken and given for you. This is my blood, the blood of the covenant, poured out for you." It is the Cross that leads us to the Eucharist, for the Cross is the meaning of sacrifice; the Cross is the meaning of love.

# SUGGESTIONS FOR FURTHER READING

**CDs and DVDs:**

Abramowicz, Danny, et al., *Crossing the Goal*. Eternal Word Television Network, 2013. DVDs.

Bollman, Steve. *That Man is You!* Paradisus Dei, 2004. DVDs.

Burke-Sivers, Deacon Harold. *God's Life in Us: The Eucharistic Heart of Male Spirituality*. Servant Enterprises, Inc., 2011. CD.

————. *Sword of the Spirit: Reclaiming Manhood*. Servant Enterprises, Inc., 2014. DVD and CD.

————. *Christian Fatherhood*. Servant Enterprises, Inc., 2011. CD.

————. *Naked and Not Ashamed: Seeing Women through the Father's Eyes*. Third Millennium Media, Inc., and Servant Enterprises, Inc., 2015. DVD and CD.

————. *Behold the Man: Spirituality for Men*. Eternal Word Television Network, 2005. DVDs.

Burke-Sivers, Deacon Harold, Gloria Purvis, Damon Owens. *Authentically Free at Last*. Eternal Word Television Network, 2011. DVDs.

Cavins, Jeff. *The Great Adventure Catholic Bible Study*. Ascension Press, 2014. DVDs.

Molina, Hector. *Evangelization: Making Jesus' Last Command Our First Priority*. Catholic Answers, 2014. DVD.

Richards, Father Larry. *Be a Man: Becoming the Man God Created You to Be*. Eternal Word Television Network, 2014. DVDs.

Romero, Jesse, et al., *Joseph, the Man Closest to Christ*. Ignatius Press, 2007. DVD.

West, Christopher. *An Introduction to the Theology of the Body*. Ascension Press, 2014. DVDs.

**Books and E-Books:**

Calloway, Donald H., MIC. *No Turning Back: A Witness to Mercy*. Stockbridge, Mass.: Marian Press, 2010.

Barbeau, Clayton C. *The Father of the Family: A Christian Perspective.* Manchester: Sophia Institute Press, 2013.

Calvillo, David N. *Real Men Pray the Rosary: A Practical Guide to a Powerful Prayer.* Notre Dame: Ave Maria Press, 2013.

Caulfield, Brian, ed. *Man to Man, Dad to Dad: Catholic Faith and Fatherhood.* Boston: Pauline Books and Media, 2013.

Fradd, Matt. *Delivered: True Stories of Men and Women Who Turned from Porn to Purity.* San Diego: Catholic Answers, 2013.

McClane, Joe. *Muscle Memory: Beating the Porn Temptation.* Lulu.com, April 23, 2014. Kindle e-book.

Richards, Father Larry. *Be a Man! Becoming the Man God Created You to Be.* San Francisco: Ignatius Press, 2009.

Sarkisian, Rick. *Not Your Average Joe: The Real St. Joseph and the Tools for Real Manhood in the Home, the Church and the World.* Fresno, Calif.: LifeWork Press, 2004.

Zimmerer, Jared, ed. *Man Up! Becoming the New Catholic Renaissance Man.* Waterford, Mich.: Bezalel Books, 2014.

Apostolates:

National Fellowship of Catholic Men (http://www.nfcmusa.org)
Real Men Pray the Rosary (http://www.realmenpraytherosary.org)
Catholic Answers (http://www.catholic.com)
Parousia Media (http://www.parousiamedia.com)
The Greatest Commandments (http://www.greatestcommandments.com)
Saint Joseph Center for the Domestic Church (http://www.domesticchurch.us)
The King's Men (http://thekingsmen.org)
The Catholic Hack (http://www.joemcclane.com)
The Motivangelist (http://www.hectormolina.net)
e5men (http://e5men.org)
The Pope Paul VI Institute (http://www.popepaulvi.com)
The Alexander House (http://thealexanderhouse.org)
The John Paul II Foundation for Life and Family (http://www.forlifeandfamily.org)
The New Emangelization (http://www.newemangelization.com)
Knights of the Holy Eucharist (http://www.knightsoftheholyeucharist.com)

Vocation Boom! (http://www.vocationboom.com)
Fathers for Good (http://www.fathersforgood.org)
Reclaim Sexual Health (http://www.reclaimsexualhealth.com)
Pure Intimacy (http://www.pureintimacy.org)
Courage (http://couragerc.org)

# BIBLIOGRAPHY

Listed below are the titles of all the secondary literature quoted in the above text, as well as other titles that are not directly quoted but whose contents have been incorporated into the text, as well as a selection of important titles, the contents of which could not be discussed.

*The Abbey Psalter.* New York: Missionary Society of Saint Paul the Apostle, 1981.

Abbott, Walter M., S.J., ed. *The Documents of Vatican II.* New York: Corpus Books, 1966.

Aumann, Jordan, O.P. *Spiritual Theology.* 7th ed. London: Sheed and Ward, 1993.

Balmes, Dr. Jaime Luciano. *El Protestantismo Comparado Con El Catolicismo.* Barcelona, Spain: Brusi, 1849. Translated into English by C.J. Hanford and Robert Kershaw. *European Civilization: Protestantism and Catholicity Compared.* Baltimore: Murphy, 1850.

Barbeau, Clayton C. *The Father of the Family: A Christian Perspective.* Manchester: Sophia Institute Press, 2013.

————. *The Head of the Family.* Collegeville, Minn.: Liturgical Press, 1970.

Benedict XVI. *Encyclical Letter of the Supreme Pontiff Benedict XVI, Charity in Truth* (Caritas in Veritate) [June 29, 2009]. Vatican translation. Boston: Pauline Books and Media, 2009.

————. *Encyclical Letter of the Supreme Pontiff Benedict XVI, God Is Love* (Deus Caritas Est) [December 25, 2005]. Vatican translation. Boston: Pauline Books and Media, 2006.

————. *Encyclical Letter of Benedict XVI, Saved in Hope* (Spe Salvi) [November 30, 2007]. Vatican translation. Boston: Pauline Books and Media, 2007.

Bouyer, Louis. *Introduction to Spirituality.* Translated by Mary Perkins Ryan. Belgium: Desclee, 1961.

Brown, Raymond E., S.S., Joseph A. Fitzmyer, S.J., and Roland E. Murphy, O.Carm., eds. *The New Jerome Biblical Commentary.* Upper Saddle River, N.J.: Prentice Hall, 1990.

Burke-Sivers, Deacon Harold. *The Mass in Sacred Scripture.* Portland, Ore.: Aurem Cordis Publications, 2012.

Calvillo, David N. *Real Men Pray the Rosary: A Practical Guide to a Powerful Prayer.* Notre Dame: Ave Maria Press, 2013.

Carmody, John. *Toward a Male Spirituality.* Mystic, Conn.: Twenty-Third Publications, 1989.

*Catechism of the Catholic Church.* 2nd ed. Washington, D.C.: Libreria Editrice Vaticana—United States Conference of Catholic Bishops, 2000.

Cathcart, Kevin, Michael Maher, and Martin McNamara, eds. *The Aramaic Bible: The Targums.* Vol. 1B, *Targum Pseudo-Jonathan: Genesis.* Translated by Michael Maher. Collegeville, Minn.: Liturgical Press, 1992.

Caulfield, Brian, ed. *Man to Man, Dad to Dad: Catholic Faith and Fatherhood.* Boston: Pauline Books and Media, 2013.

Charles, Rodger, S.J., with Drostan MacLaren, O.P. *The Social Teaching of Vatican II: Its Origin and Development.* 2nd ed. San Francisco: Ignatius Press, 1988.

Charpentier, Etienne. *How to Read the Old Testament.* Translated by John Bowden. New York: Crossroads, 1984.

Cirrincione, Msgr. Joseph A., with Thomas A. Nelson. *St. Joseph, Fatima and Fatherhood: Reflections on the Miracle of the Sun.* Rockford, Ill.: Tan Books and Publishing, 1989.

Clines, David J. A., and Philip R. Davies, eds. *Journal for the Study of the Old Testament.* Supplement Series 91, *The Ideology of Ritual: Space, Time and Status in the Priestly Theology,* by Frank H. Gorman. England: JSOT Press, 1990.

*Codex Iuris Canonici.* Translated by the Canon Law Society of America. Latin-English ed. Washington, D.C.: Canon Law Society of America, 1983. Reprint, Washington, D.C.: Canon Law Society of America, 1995.

*Compendium of the Catechism of the Catholic Church.* Official English translation. 3rd printing. Washington, D.C.: USCCB, 2006.

Congregation for the Clergy et al. *Instruction on Certain Questions Regarding the Collaboration of the Non-Ordained Faithful in the Sacred*

*Ministry of Priest*, August 15, 1997. www.vatican.va/roman_curia /pontifical_councils/laity/documents/rc_con_interdic_doc _15081997_en.html.

Congregation for the Doctrine of the Faith. *Considerations regarding Proposals to Give Legal Recognition to Unions between Homosexual Persons*, June 3, 2003. http://www.vatican.va/roman_curia/congregations /cfaith/documents/rc_con_cfaith_doc_20030731_homosexual -unions_en.html.

——. *Instruction on Certain Aspects of the "Theology of Liberation"*, August 6, 1984. www.vatican.va/roman_curia/congregations/cfaith /documents/rc_con_cfaith_doc_19840806_theology-liberation_en .html.

——. *Letter to the Bishops of the Catholic Church on the Collaboration of Men and Women in the Church and in the World*, May 31, 2004. http://www.vatican.va/roman_curia/congregations/cfaith /documents/rc_con_cfaith_doc_20040731_collaboration_en.html.

Copleston, F. C. *Aquinas*. Baltimore: Penguin Books, 1965.

Coriden, James A., Thomas J. Green, and Donald E. Heintschel, eds. *The Code of Canon Law: A Text and Commentary*. New York: Paulist Press, 1985.

Cross, F. L., and E. A. Livingstone, eds. *The Oxford Dictionary of the Christian Church*. 2nd ed. Oxford: Oxford University Press, 1974. Reprint, New York: Oxford University Press, 1989.

Dawson, Christopher. *Christianity and the New Order*. London: Sheed and Ward, 1931.

De Cervinara, Fr. Tarcisio. *The Devil in the Life of Padre Pio*. 3rd ed. 2008. Reprint, San Giovanni Rotondo, Italy: Edizioni Padre Pio da Pietrelcina, 2012.

De Haro, Ramón García. *Marriage and the Family in the Documents of the Magisterium: A Course in the Theology of Marriage*. 2nd ed. Revised with the help of Carla Rossi Espagnet. Translated by William E. May. San Francisco: Ignatius Press, 1993.

DeLambo, David. *Lay Parish Ministers: A Study of Emerging Leadership*. New York: National Pastoral Life Center, 2005.

De Monfort, Louis. *True Devotion to Mary*. Translated by Fr. Frederick Faber. Rockford, Ill.: Tan Books, 1985.

De Sales, Francis. *Introduction to the Devout Life*. 2nd ed. Translated and edited by John K. Ryan. New York: Doubleday, 1989.

Elliott, Fr. Peter J. *What God Has Joined: The Sacramentality of Marriage.* New York: Alba House, 1990.

Evert, Jason. *Pure Manhood.* San Diego: Catholic Answers, 2007.

Farmer, William R., Sean McEvenue, Amando J. Levoratti, and David L. Dungan, eds. *The International Bible Commentary: A Catholic and Ecumenical Commentary for the Twenty-First Century.* Collegeville, Minn.: Liturgical Press, 1998.

Finn, Bishop Robert W. "Blessed Are the Pure in Heart: A Pastoral Letter on the Dignity of the Human Person and the Dangers of Pornography", February 21, 2007. http://www.diocese-kcsj.org/_docs/Pastoral-02–07.pdf.

Francis. *Encyclical Letter of the Supreme Pontiff Francis, The Light of Faith* (Lumen Fidei) [June 29, 2013]. Vatican translation. Boston: Pauline Books and Media, 2013.

Fry, Timothy, O.S.B., Imogene Baker, O.S.B., Timothy Horner, O.S.B., Augusta Raabe, O.S.B., and Mark Sheridan, O.S.B., eds. *The Rule of St. Benedict 1980: In Latin and English with Notes.* Collegeville, Minn.: Liturgical Press, 1980.

Girgis, Sherif, Ryan T. Anderson, and Robert P. George. *What Is Marriage? Man and Woman: A Defense.* New York: Encounter Books, 2012.

Gray, Tim, and Curtis Martin. *Boys to Men: The Transforming Power of Virtue.* Steubenville, Ohio: Emmaus Road Publishing, 2001.

Hahn, Scott. "Going on Vacation: Why Fathers Are Priests and Priests Are Fathers". In *Scripture Matters: Essays on Reading the Bible from the Heart of the Church.* Steubenville, Ohio: Emmaus Road, 2003.

Hardon, John A., S.J. *Modern Catholic Dictionary.* New York: Doubleday, 1979.

Hauf, John, ed. *The Message of Fatima: Lucia Speaks.* Washington, N.J.: AMI Press, 1997.

Hauke, Manfred. *Women in the Priesthood?* San Francisco: Ignatius Press, 1988.

Heid, Stefan. *Celibacy in the Early Church: The Beginnings of a Disciple of Obligatory Continence for Clerics in East and West.* San Francisco: Ignatius Press, 2000.

Hogan, Richard M., and John M. LeVoir. *Covenant of Love: Pope John Paul II on Sexuality, Marriage, and the Family in the Modern World.* 2nd ed. San Francisco: Ignatius Press, 1992.

*The Holy Bible.* Revised Standard Version, Catholic Edition. Prepared by the Catholic Biblical Association of Great Britain. With a Foreword by Richard Cardinal Cushing. San Francisco: Ignatius Press, 1966.

*Ignatius Catholic Study Bible: The New Testament.* Revised Standard Version, Second Catholic Edition. San Francisco: Ignatius Press, 2010.

Jamart, François, O.C.D. *Complete Spiritual Doctrine of St. Thérèse of Lisieux.* Translated by Walter van de Putte, C.S.Sp. New York: Alba House, 2001.

John Paul II. *Post-Synodal Apostolic Exhortation of John Paul II, The Lay Members of Christ's Faithful People* (Christifideles Laici) [December 30, 1988]. Vatican translation. Boston: Pauline Books and Media, 1988.

———. *Crossing the Threshold of Hope.* New York: Alfred A. Knopf, 1994. PDF e-book.

———. *Encyclical Letter of John Paul II, On the Eucharist in Its Relationship to the Church* (Ecclesia de Eucharistia) [April 17, 2003]. Vatican translation. Boston: Pauline Books and Media, 2003.

———. Encyclical Letter *Evangelium Vitae* (The Gospel of Life), March 25, 1995. http://www.vatican.va/holy_father/john_paul_ii/encyclicals/documents/hf_jp-ii_enc_25031995_evangelium-vitae_en.html.

———. Apostolic Exhortation *Familiaris Consortio,* On the Role of the Christian Family in the Modern World, November 22, 1981. http://www.vatican.va/holy_father/john_paul_ii/apost_exhortations/documents/hf_jp-ii_exh_19811122_familiaris-consortio_en.html.

———. *Encyclical Letter Fides et Ratio, On the Relationship between Faith and Reason* [September 14, 1998]. Vatican translation. Boston: Pauline Books and Media, 1998.

———. *Encyclical Letter of John Paul II, On the Human Work* (Laborem Exercens) [September 14, 1981]. Vatican translation. Boston: Pauline Books and Media, 1981.

———. *Letter to Families from Pope John Paul II, 1994, the Year of the Family* [February 2, 1994]. Vatican translation. Boston: Pauline Books and Media, 1994.

———. *Apostolic Letter of Pope John Paul II, On the Dignity and Vocation of Women* (Mulieris Dignitatem) [August 15, 1988]. Vatican translation. Boston: Pauline Books and Media, 1988.

————. *Original Unity of Man and Woman: Catechesis on the Book of Genesis*. Boston: Daughters of St. Paul, 1981.

————. *Pastores Dabo Vobis* [*I Will Give You Shepherds*], *Encyclical Letter of Pope John Paul II* [March 25, 1992]. Vatican translation. Boston: St. Paul Books, 1992.

————. *Post-Synodal Apostolic Exhortation Reconciliation and Penance* (Reconciliatio et Paenitentia) [December 2, 1984]. Vatican translation. Boston: Pauline Books and Media, 1984.

————. *Apostolic Exhortation, Guardian of the Redeemer* (Redemptoris Custos) [August 15, 1989]. Vatican translation. Boston: Pauline Books and Media, 1989.

————. Encyclical Letter *Redemptor Hominis* (The Redeemer of Man), March 4, 1979. http://www.vatican.va/holy_father/john _paul_ii/encyclicals/documents/hf_jp-ii_enc_04031979 _redemptor-hominis_en.html.

————. Encyclical Letter, *Mother of the Redeemer* (Redemptoris Mater) [March 25, 1987]. Vatican translation. Boston: Pauline Books and Media, 1987.

————. Apostolic Letter *Salvifici Doloris*, On the Christian Meaning of Human Suffering, February 11, 1984. www.vatican.va/holy _father/john_paul_ii/apost_letters/documents/hf_jp-ii_apl _11021984_salvifici-doloris_en.html.

————. *The Theology of the Body: Human Love in the Divine Plan*. Boston: Pauline Books and Media, 1997.

————. *Encyclical Letter of John Paul II, The Splendor of Truth* (Veritatis Splendor) [August 6, 1993]. Vatican translation. Boston: Pauline Books and Media, 1993.

Latourelle, Rene, S.J. *Théologie De La Révélation* [Theology of Revelation]. New York: Alba House, 1966. Reprint, New York: Alba House, 1967.

Lawler, Fr. Ronald, Joseph Boyle Jr., and William E. May. *Catholic Sexual Ethics: A Summary, Explanation, and Defense*. Updated. Huntington, Ind.: Our Sunday Visitor, 1985. Reprint, Huntington, Ind.: Our Sunday Visitor, 1996.

Leo XIII. Encyclical Letter *Quamquam Pluries*, April 15, 1889. http:// www.vatican.va/holy_father/leo_xiii/encyclicals/documents /hf_l-xiii_enc_15081889_quamquam-pluries_en.html.

*Liturgy of the Hours*. Vols. 1 and 4. New York: Catholic Book Publishing, 1975.

Livingston, G. Herbert. *The Pentateuch in Its Cultural Environment.* 2nd ed. Grand Rapids: Baker Book House, 1987. 5th printing, Grand Rapids: Baker Book House, 1991.

Loverde, Bishop Paul S. "Bought with a Price: Every Man's Duty to Protect Himself and His Family from a Pornographic Culture". Arlingtondiocese.org, December 2006. http://www.arlington diocese.org/documents/bp_boughtwithaprice.pdf.

Marmion, Abbot D. Columba, O.S.B. *Christ, the Life of the Soul: Spiritual Conferences.* 11th ed. Translated by a nun of Tyburn Convent. London: Sands, 1925.

Martin, Curtis. *Made for More.* Denver: Epic Publishing, 2008.

May, William E. *Marriage: The Rock on Which the Family Is Built.* San Francisco: Ignatius Press, 1995.

McAuliffe, Clarence, S.J. *Sacramental Theology.* St. Louis: B. Herder, 1958.

McClane, Joe. *Muscle Memory: Beating the Porn Temptation.* Lulu.com, April 23, 2014. Kindle e-book.

McKenna, Kevin E. *The Ministry of Law in the Church Today.* Notre Dame, Ind.: University of Notre Dame Press, 1998.

McKim, Donald K. *Westminster Dictionary of Theological Terms.* Louisville, Ky.: Westminster John Knox Press, 1996.

Merton, Thomas, O.C.S.O. *Praying the Psalms.* Collegeville, Minn.: Liturgical Press, 1956.

————. *Spiritual Direction and Meditation.* Collegeville, Minn.: Liturgical Press, 1960.

Miravalle, Mark. *Introduction to Mary: The Heart of Marian Doctrine and Devotion.* 3rd ed. Santa Barbara, Calif.: Queenship Publishing, 2006.

Moore, Robert, and Douglass Gillette. *King, Warrior, Magician, Lover: Rediscovering the Archetypes of the Mature Masculine.* San Francisco: HarperCollins, 1991.

National Pastoral Life Center. *Lay and Religious Parish Ministry: A Study Conducted for the National Conference of Catholic Bishops,* 1991. http://www.resourcingchristianity.org/grant-product/lay-and -religious-parish-ministry-a-study-conducted-for-the-national -conference-of-catholic-bishops-1991 and http://www.usccb.org /about/laity-marriage-family-life-and-youth/lay-ecclesial-ministry /lay-ecclesial-ministry-faqs.cfm#q7.

Neuner, Josef, S.J., and Jacques Dupuis, S.J., eds. *The Christian Faith in the Doctrinal Documents of the Catholic Church.* 6th revised and enlarged ed. New York: Alba House, 1996.

Orchard, Dom Bernard, Edmund F. Sutcliffe, S.J., Reginald C. Fuller, and Dom Ralph Russell, eds. *A Catholic Commentary on Holy Scripture*. New York: Thomas Nelson and Sons, 1953.

Ott, Ludwig. *Grundriss der Katholischen Dogmatik* [Fundamentals of Catholic Dogma]. Eichstätt: Verlag Herder, 1952. Reprint, 4th ed., translated by Patrick Lynch. Edited in English by James Canon Bastible. Rockford, Ill.: Tan Books and Publishers, 1974.

Pable, Martin W., O.F.M.Cap. *A Man and His God*. Notre Dame: Ave Maria Press, 1988.

Panzer, Fr. Joel S. *The Popes and Slavery*. New York: Alba House, 1996.

Paul VI. *Humanae Vitae* [*Of Human Life*]: *Encyclical Letter of His Holiness Pope Paul VI* [July 25, 1968]. Rev. ed. Translated by Marc Calegari, S.J. San Francisco: Ignatius Press, 1978.

Pieper, Josef. *About Love*. Chicago: Franciscan Herald Press, 1974.

————. *Guide to Thomas Aquinas*. Translated by Richard Winston and Clara Winston. New York: Pantheon Books, 1962.

————. *Living the Truth: The Truth of All Things* and *Reality and the Good*. Translated by Lothar Krauth and Stella Lange. San Francisco: Ignatius Press, 1989.

Pontifical Council for Culture and Pontifical Council for Inter-religious Dialogue. *Jesus Christ, the Bearer of the Water of Life: A Christian Reflection on the "New Age"*. June 2003. www.vatican.va/roman_curia/pontifical_councils/interelg/documents/rc_pc_interelg_doc_20030203_new-age_en.html.

Pontifical Council for the Family. *Family, Marriage and "De Facto" Unions*, July 26, 2000. http://www.vatican.va/roman_curia/pontifical_councils/family/documents/rc_pc_family_doc_20001109_de-facto-unions_en.html.

————. *The Truth and Meaning of Human Sexuality: Guidelines for Education within the Family*, December 8, 1995. http://www.vatican.va/roman_curia/pontifical_councils/family/documents/rc_pc_family_doc_08121995_human-sexuality_en.html.

Pritchard, James B., ed. *Ancient Near Eastern Texts: Relating to the Old Testament*. 3rd ed., with supplement. Princeton, N.J.: Princeton University Press, 1969.

Richards, Fr. Larry. *Be a Man! Becoming the Man God Created You to Be*. San Francisco: Ignatius Press, 2009.

Sarkisian, Rick. *The Mission of the Catholic Family: On the Pathway to Heaven*. San Diego: Basilica Press, 1999.

————. *Not Your Average Joe: The Real St. Joseph and the Tools for Real Manhood in the Home, the Church and the World*. Fresno, Calif.: LifeWork Press, 2004.

Scheeben, Matthias Joseph. *Mariology: Volume One*. 2nd ed. New York: B. Herder, 1946.

Sheed, Frank. *Theology and Sanity*. Rev. ed. San Francisco: Ignatius Press, 1978.

Smith, Janet E. *Humanae Vitae: A Generation Later*. Washington, D.C: Catholic University of America Press, 1991.

————. "Paul VI as Prophet". In *Why Humanae Vitae Was Right: A Reader*. San Francisco: Ignatius Press, 1993.

Tresmontant, Claude. *Saint Paul and the Mystery of Christ*. Men of Wisdom Series. Translated by Donald Attwater. New York: Harper Torchbooks, 1957.

United States Conference of Catholic Bishops. *Hearing Christ's Call: A Resource for the Formation and Spirituality of Catholic Men*. Washington, D.C: USCCB, 2002.

Vatican Council II, Decree on the Ministry and Life of Priests, *Presbyterorum ordinis*, December 7, 1965. http://www.vatican.va/archive/hist_councils/ii_vatican_council/documents/vat-ii_decree_19651207_presbyterorum-ordinis_en.html.

Von Balthasar, Hans Urs. *Light of the Word: Brief Reflections on the Sunday Readings*. San Francisco: Ignatius Press, 1993.

————. *You Crown the Year with Your Goodness: Sermons through the Liturgical Year*. San Francisco: Ignatius Press, 1989.

Whiston, William, trans. *The Works of Josephus: Complete and Unabridged*. New updated edition. Peabody, Mass.: Hendrickson Publishers, 1987.

Wojtyla, Karol. *Love and Responsibility*. Translated by H. T. Willetts. Rev. ed. New York: Farrar, Straus and Giroux, 1981. Reprint, San Francisco: Ignatius Press, 1993.

Wood, Stephen. *Christian Fatherhood: The Eight Commitments of St. Joseph's Covenant Keepers*. Greenville, S.C.: Family Life Center Publications, 1997.

Zimmerer, Jared, ed. *Man Up! Becoming the New Catholic Renaissance Man*. Waterford, Mich.: Bezalel Books, 2014.

# INDEX